The Myth of China's No Strings Attached Development Assistance

The Myth of China's No Strings Attached Development Assistance

A Caribbean Case Study

Theodor Tudoroiu
with
Amanda R. Ramlogan

LEXINGTON BOOKS
Lanham • Boulder • New York • London

Published by Lexington Books
An imprint of The Rowman & Littlefield Publishing Group, Inc.
4501 Forbes Boulevard, Suite 200, Lanham, Maryland 20706
www.rowman.com

6 Tinworth Street, London SE11 5AL, United Kingdom

British Library Cataloguing in Publication Information Available

Library of Congress Control Number:2019952873

ISBN 978-1-7936-0322-7 (cloth : alk. paper)
ISBN 978-1-7936-0323-4 (electronic)

Contents

Acknowledgments

I would like to thank Lexington Books and the Senior Acquisitions Editor for Economics, International Relations, and Political Science, Joseph C. Parry, for supporting this project.

I would also like to thank Amanda R. Ramlogan for her valuable contribution to this book, and an anonymous reviewer for their useful suggestions.

I am grateful for the moral support provided by my colleagues in the Department of Political Science at the University of the West Indies, St. Augustine campus.

Finally, I want to acknowledge the financial support of the Campus Research and Publication Fund Committee of the University of the West Indies, St. Augustine campus, under Grant CRP.3.NOV16.10.

Chapter One

Introduction

The goal of this book is to put an end to what can be called the "myth" of China's "no strings" assistance to its partners in the developing world. Almost all scholars exploring the increasingly visible involvement of China in the Global South feel obliged to mention the lack of conditionality. Beijing-friendly ones confidently state that "the idea that China gives aid 'without strings' or conditions has become one of the key 'facts' about Chinese aid" (Brautigam 2009: 148). At times, this is used as an argument demonstrating the sincerity of China's win-win, disinterested South-South cooperation discourse. Yet, even such authors note the obvious exception represented by the required support for the "One China" principle. Moreover, elsewhere in the same text, they might acknowledge the fact that "[Chinese] economic engagement usually *does* come with conditions, some of it even (indirectly) governance-related" (Brautigam 2009: 21; emphasis in the original). A popular example is "tied aid," i.e., the compulsory use of exclusively or mainly Chinese contractors, labor, and materials in Chinese-financed infrastructure projects (see Chapter 5). In fact, closer scrutiny reveals a picture that has very little in common with the aforementioned "myth."

I will start by presenting an example that is brief and easy to understand for any reader. The conditionalities I analyze include the social one, i.e., the fact that China does not allow states that receive its development assistance to regulate the inflow and the economic activities of Chinese entrepreneurial migrants. In many developing countries, these newcomers are active and highly successful in retail trade, groceries, Chinese restaurants, and casinos. Critically, they displace similar locally owned small businesses. Frequently, this has led to frustration, protests, and even riots. Yet, few governments that receive consistent development assistance from Beijing dare to act against the Chinese migrants because

> in Zambia, Fred Mutesa, a former finance minister, told me that whenever his government sent delegations to Beijing for talks, in at least one session they would be leaned upon to maintain relaxed immigration policies toward Chinese. The language, he said, wasn't particularly subtle either; something along the lines of: We are making so many friendly gestures to your country, building roads and stadiums, etc. We would consider it a friendly gesture if you did not enforce such strict immigration controls on our citizens (French 2014: 83).

Yet, in one case measures were taken by a genuinely pro-Chinese government against a group of illegal Chinese immigrants who were mining gold illegally. This happened in Ghana, and the government only acted under considerable public pressure (for details see the section *Government Compliance vs. Popular Discontent* of Chapter 6). The Chinese were finally expelled, but in response their government stalled a US $3 billion payment from a China Development Bank loan that funded twelve development projects and tried to renegotiate the terms of the loan. Moreover, it also changed visa requirements for Ghanaian citizens, making it more difficult for merchants from Ghana to conduct their trade activities in China (Hess and Richard Aidoo 2015: 52). I think that anyone who reads this cannot reasonably claim that there is no Chinese conditionality whatsoever.

The question, then, is how—or, rather, why—the "myth" has come into being. This has much to do with the peculiarity of the field of study related to China's involvement in the Global South. Today, it probably represents one of the most polarized branches of International Relations. As explained in detail in the section *China in Africa* of Chapter 3, there is heated debate between China-optimists and China-pessimists. The first group basically mirrors Beijing's official discourse, which presents China's interactions with the developing world as a purely win-win form of South-South cooperation. Many in the opposing camp are obsessed with China's predatory policies, which sometimes are presented using almost journalistic terms and approaches. Needless to say, Beijing-friendly authors have no reason to speak about conditionality. At times, they even use a rather strange argument to show that conditionality *cannot* exist in the case of China. They explain that the "no-string-attached" policy has its origin in the famous five principles of peaceful co-existence, which I present in the section *China's Engagement with the Developing World* of Chapter 3. The essence of these principles is the respect for other countries' sovereignty and the non-interference into their internal affairs; accordingly, the government in Beijing *could never* impose conditionalities. It is not difficult to note that taking a regime's political discourse for reality is hardly a sound research strategy.

Even more strangely, scholars who do not necessarily share pro-Chinese biases nevertheless support the idea that there is no China-imposed conditionality. They acknowledge the fact that Beijing imposes the non-recognition of Taiwan and "tied aid" in exchange for its development assistance; but they insist on the fact that in the literature these conditions "are not considered" to represent conditionality. It should be mentioned that Chinese foreign aid is very different from the Western one. China's conditionality is also very different from that of Western donors, and this—in conjunction with Beijing's vocal claims—might create the impression that, indeed, there is no [Western-type] conditionality to talk about. This is hardly the only case when scholars prefer to be blind to novel interpretations of "facts" that have uncritically been assimilated from the literature and to stubbornly reject any re-reading of a well-know "reality." Yet, I strongly believe that this is in no way what scholars should do. This book does bring in previously little-known empirical evidence as well as new concepts, such as the aforementioned social conditionality. But fundamentally, it proposes a critical re-reading of a reality usually perceived through the reassuring but distorting lens of academic routine.

The following chapters show that China's actions in a Global South region, namely the Caribbean, actually involve the use of political, economic, and social conditionalities supported by Chinese economic incentives. Critically, these conditionalities are not and should not be studied as separate phenomena. They are parts of a complex process of international socialization allowing China to construct a cognitive and normative space conducive to a new regional order which should be politically friendly, economically profitable, and socially open to its government, firms, and citizens.

Unless otherwise stated, I use "the Caribbean" to refer to the English-speaking Commonwealth Caribbean, which is inclusive of Guyana and Belize but not of non-sovereign English-speaking territories in the region. Unlike Africa or Latin America, it has not been the target of extensive China-related research. The existing literature is undertheorized and centered on the first-order analysis of empirical facts, based on which it frequently formulates policy recommendations to the region's governments. The absence of sustained academic interest simply mirrors the lack of reasons for major Chinese involvement other than the diplomatic duel with Taiwan and, more recently, growing geopolitical rivalry with the United States. Paradoxically, this is a situation that facilitates this book's task. China's "scramble for African resources" or its deindustrialization of Latin America (see Chapter 3) are issues that dominate public debates and scholarly analyses in and about those regions, leaving little room for the study of other aspects such as conditionality. In the Caribbean, Chinese trade and investment are many times inferior to American ones (see the section *China's Economic Presence in Trinidad and the Caribbean* of Chapter 5). The bilateral agenda is therefore dominated by China's development assistance, which in many cases takes the form of prestige infrastructure projects financed by loans provided by Chinese state-owned banks. The resulting leverage allows Beijing to impose its conditionalities, which can be studied here in their purest form. Some of the instruments and approaches used by Beijing in the framework of its Caribbean conditionalities have first been experimented in other regions. Yet, this does not automatically imply that the same conditionalities are used elsewhere in the Global South. This may or may not be the case; even if they do exist, their features and consequences might be different. The Caribbean is a small, relatively homogenous, and geopolitically relevant region. Unless field research proves otherwise, it cannot be taken for granted that China is able and willing to treat similarly much larger and more complex regions such as Africa. Moreover, conditionality can be used as a means to obtain immediate economic benefits (such as access to markets or raw materials), and not necessarily as part of a Caribbean-type process of international socialization. I leave it to specialists of other areas to identify and analyze such issues. I can only formulate a common sense hypothesis: it is more probable to find conditionality employed in the case of less developed countries that depend in large measure on China's development assistance; and international socialization is more likely to be experimented—or, at least, to be successful—in smaller and homogenous sub-regions such as, say, Central America than on the scale of entire continents. This book is opening a window that future research could take advantage of.

The rejection of an almost generally accepted idea is normally met with a fair amount of hostility. In this case, a predictable line of action of unsympathetic critics is likely to be related to the very definition of the concept of conditionality. Indeed, the latter's narrow definition proposed by Tony Killick mentions "a mutual arrangement by which a government takes, or promises to take, certain policy actions, in support of which an IFI (International Financial Institution) or other agency will provide specified amounts of financial assistance" (Killick 1998: 5–6). In other words, conditionality is present only if the donor's actions are intended to impact directly on the recipient's policies. The government in Beijing and some academics claim that this is not the case when Chinese development assistance is considered. In their view, Beijing's conditions do exist but pertain to China's "normal" interactions with other states. They do not qualify as conditionality because they were not purposely conceived to shape the domestic policies and development of target countries.

First, I do not agree with this narrow definition of conditionality. I prefer the more general one proposed by Olav Stokke, who believes that conditionality simply means

> the use of pressure, by the donor, in terms of threatening to terminate aid, or actually terminating or reducing it, if conditions are not met by the recipient. Foreign aid is used as a lever to promote objectives set by the donor which the recipient government would not otherwise have agreed to (Stokke 1995/2006: 11–12).

This author distinguishes between six levels of conditionality that range from the systemic one to mere "administrative conditions" that involve procedures for the transfer of resources, accounting, reporting, evaluation, privileges enjoyed by technical co-operation personnel, and so on (Stokke 1995/2006: 13–15). Accounting or reporting on aid-related issues are not intended to influence the domestic policies of the target country; and yet, they are considered as pertaining to conditionality, be it at a very basic level.

Second, I argue that even if the narrow definition of conditionality is preferred, the conditions imposed by China on its less developed partners in the Caribbean do qualify as conditionality because, on purpose, they effectively and visibly shape those countries' domestic policies in ways that favor Chinese interests. This is not about indirect impacts or about consequences that may or may not materialize. It is about inevitable and well-known-in-advance effects that the government of a small developing country does not reject only because their acceptance is a key precondition for receiving China's much-needed development assistance. As such, they are undoubtedly part of a Chinese conditionality. Incidentally, this gives me the opportunity to briefly present here the content of Beijing's three conditionalities. The first one is political. It was well summarized by one of the Trinidadian respondents as "no Taiwan; no Tibet; no Tiananmen Square." As I explain in Chapter 4, it compels the partner state to reject Taipei and its development aid, no matter how useful the latter might have been—ideally, in conjunction with the Chinese one—for that country's socio-economic development. China thus limits the choices of a sovereign state concerning its own developmental path, a situation that should be acknowledged as genuine conditionality even based on Killick's definition.

Beijing's political conditionality also dictates the behavior of democratic partners with regard to China's non-respect of democracy and human rights. This should not be taken as an insignificant detail. The states of the Caribbean Community (CARICOM) "have had a consistent record of democracy and respect for the rule of law and for human rights norms" which, despite their size, allowed them to be elected to a wide range of United Nations key positions (Braveboy-Wagner 2010: 422). Their genuine repulsion for brutal antidemocratic practices and their interest in China's situation is illustrated by Grenada's and Belize's recognition of Taiwan in response to the 1989 Tiananmen massacre (Hu 2015: 11). Forcing such states not to express any human rights-related concern when, as revealed by a 2018 report of the United Nations Committee on the Elimination of Racial Discrimination, China abusively detains up to one million Uyghurs in "reeducation camps" (The United Nations Office of the High Commissioner for Human Rights 2018) does impact directly and unequivocally their domestic and foreign policies of support for democracy and human rights. The democratic conditionality of Western donors is universally described—and frequently condemned—as genuine conditionality. It would be difficult to understand why the much narrower and considerably downscaled but nevertheless related imposition of the opposite trend by China does not fall into the same category.

The second conditionality is economic. On the one hand, it relates to the aforementioned "tied aid," which compels partner states to use exclusively or mainly Chinese contractors, labor, and materials for Chinese-financed large infrastructure projects. It is important to note that in many countries such projects represent by far the largest part of China's development assistance, a trend further enhanced by the infrastructure-centered nature of the Belt and Road Initiative. In small and less developed Caribbean states, a huge infrastructure project represents a considerable part of the local construction market. The fact that national contractors and laborers are excluded affects severely the business sector and the level of employment. This is not a side effect. This is a structural component of Beijing's view of Chinese-financed infrastructure projects as lucrative activities whose profit has to go to Chinese firms and not to the local economy. To use the words of a respondent, China is "giving with one hand and taking with the other." In doing this, it compels the recipient state to accept a policy which shapes its economy in ways that serve Chinese economic interests instead of national ones.

On the other hand, part of the Chinese economic conditionality is the constraint that these infrastructure projects be typically agreed on in non-transparent, secretive government-to-government negotiations between China and the Caribbean partner state that result in undisclosed agreements. This prevents, on purpose, the public scrutiny of their content and the criticism of questionable aspects. In Trinidad there have been many examples of large infrastructure projects eventually affected by major failures that have frequently been attributed to the non-transparent agreements (see the section *China's "Tied Aid" and Its Reception in Trinidad and the Caribbean* of Chapter 5). This has been severely criticized by the civil society and by the general public as it affects negatively previously existing policies and practices of transparency and public accountability. This is to say that the conditions associated with Chinese development assistance modify the target state's governance in ways that tend to bring it closer to China's own opaque and corruption-prone domestic system.

The third conditionality is social. The very concept represents an original contribution of this book; unlike the political and economic ones, this type of conditionality is not mentioned in the theoretical literature. As briefly explained at the beginning of this Introduction, I use it with respect to the huge flow of Chinese entrepreneurial migrants who set up retail stores, groceries, and Chinese restaurants all over the world. In the Caribbean—as well as in other small and less developed Global South countries—their impact on local small business is dramatic and has resulted in various forms of public discontent. Yet, due to Beijing's explicit and implicit pressure, the governments of concerned countries are prevented from adopting policies limiting the inflow of Chinese nationals or their economic activities. This is clearly a specific type of conditionality as China—which benefits economically and politically from the activities of its citizens abroad—effectively shapes the immigration-related policies of aid-recipient states in ways that serve its own interests. In Chapter 6, I supplement my Caribbean observations with the analysis of the already mentioned and particularly relevant example of Ghana. This case of actual Chinese retaliation is unambiguously illustrative of a type of relationship based on "a mutual arrangement by which a government takes (. . .) certain policy actions, in support of which an (. . .) agency will provide specified amounts of financial assistance" (Killick 1998: 5–6), which represents Tony Killick's narrow definition of conditionality. This book shows that Trinidad and the rest of the Caribbean have experienced exactly this type of constraint.

All these elements suggest that Chinese conditionality does exist no matter how narrow that concept is defined. Furthermore, as already mentioned, China's Caribbean strategy goes beyond the separate use of the three conditionalities. The starting point is represented by generous development assistance consisting mainly of prestige infrastructure projects financed by the state-owned China Export-Import Bank and China Development Bank. The ensuing leverage on the region's states is used to impose the three conditionalities that, in turn, become part of a complex process of international socialization. Its ultimate goal is to instill pro-Chinese convictions ("China is good"; "China helps us") and norms ("we should not criticize China"; "we should cooperate with China"), i.e., to construct a cognitive and normative space conducive, in the long term, to the creation of a new regional order which should be politically friendly, economically profitable, and socially open to China's government, companies, and citizens. I argue that it is too early to speak of a fourth, geopolitical conditionality (see Chapter 7); but the very process of socialization sketched here is geopolitical *par excellence* and as such represents a constitutive part of China's transformation into a global power.

In theoretical terms, I analyze this process by adapting the rich Constructivist literature on the European Union's socialization of its post-communist neighbors before the 2004–2007 Eastern enlargement to the process of great power socialization of client states first explored by John Ikenberry and Charles Kupchan in their 1990 seminal article on hegemonic socialization (Ikenberry and Kupchan 1990) and equally analyzed in my study of the USSR/Russia-Syrian process of reciprocal socialization (Tudoroiu 2015). Using Jeffrey Checkel's approach (Checkel 2005), I argue that the stage of Type I socialization, based on role playing, has already been reached by China and—in response to its conditionalities—by its Caribbean partners such as Trinidad and Tobago. They have all learned and play well their respective roles within an apparently "win-win" South-South cooperative relationship. However, I also claim that Beijing's ultimate objective is the more advanced Type II socialization: a fundamental identity shift making the region's actors perceive the creation and further development of close multidimensional strategic partnerships with China as "the right thing to do."

It is useful to mention the fact that, during the Cold War, Cuba, Syria, Vietnam, Mongolia, and other similar states experienced Type II Soviet socialization which turned them into Moscow's client states. This had obvious geopolitical consequences as shown, in the Caribbean, by the Cuban case. This is to say that what might seem an abstract, purely theoretical analysis has in fact very much to do with actual international politics. At present, China is socializing a large number of Caribbean small states. If it succeeds in reaching the Type II stage of this process, Beijing will become a major actor in America's backyard. Of course, the present level of Sino-American antagonism cannot be compared to that of the Cold War. However, the challenge to US regional hegemony could not be ignored and would trigger major regional and global developments.

Returning to theory, I argue that the analysis of this process of international socialization imposes the adoption of Alexander Wendt's state-society complex as the book's unit of analysis. On the one hand, there is the state, controlled by the government and, more generally, by the political elites. In the case of Trinidad and Tobago and similar Caribbean countries, these elites use the prestige infrastructure projects offered by the Chinese to their own electoral interests. In addition, secret diplomacy between state leaders associated with the secretive government-to-government negotiation of the agreements on these infrastructure projects has been employed by Beijing as a tool of socialization (see the section *The Socialization of Caribbean Elites* of Chapter 5). As a result, the political elites have fully accepted China's political, economic, and social conditionalities, which have resulted in their (and their state's) successful socialization.

On the other hand, I claim that a country's society cannot be perceived as unrelated to the process of international socialization. The complete success of the Chinese Type II socialization through conditionality depends on the latter's acceptance by both the political elites (and, implicitly, the state) and the society at large. My research shows that, unlike the elites, the society has internalized only the cognitive and normative content of China's political conditionality. The negative consequences of the economic and social conditionalities have translated into their rejection by the society; few citizens are happy with the use of Chinese contractors and labor, with the non-transparent government-to-government agreements, or with the inflow of Chinese entrepreneurial migrants. Consequently, a clear gap exists between the degrees of socialization of top-level political decision makers and of the society. This limits the depth of China's process of socialization of the state-society complex, which is unlikely to reach Checkel's Type II, more advanced stage associated with a radical pro-Chinese identity change.

In turn, this will limit the growth of China's regional and, ultimately, global influence despite its use of a sophisticated soft power strategy. It can be concluded that Beijing's main problem in the Caribbean is the discrepancy between the generosity and disinterest of its cooperative, "win-win" discourse and the undeniably selfish features of much of its actual interactions with the region's states. Furthermore, as shown in the book's last chapter, the balance between these two approaches is likely to influence considerably China's identity as a global actor and, implicitly, the very future of the international system.

Turning to methodological aspects, I have already mentioned the fact that, quantitatively and qualitatively, the secondary literature on the Chinese presence in the Caribbean can in no way be compared to that concerning other regions of the Global South. In particular, the number of peer-reviewed publications is extremely limited. This will probably change in the near future due to the growing interest in China's increasing involvement in the region. For the time being, however, the scarcity of academic sources has compelled me to extract much of the empirical information from newspaper and magazine articles as well as from various internet sources such as briefs and reports. The key issue scrutinized in this book is of course the very different perception of China's actions by the political elites and the society at large, respectively. Its analysis is based on discourses, policy documents, and interviews with various members of the two groups made available by the mass media. In addition, 30 interviews made in Trinidad between 2017 and 2018 were also used.[1] The respondents included members of the public, businessmen, journalists, scholars, public servants, and politicians directly involved or highly interested in China-related issues. Interviews lasted between 40 and 90 minutes and were based on a structured questionnaire containing 40 questions divided into eight categories ranging from the personal attitude toward China to the latter's position in the international system. Thirty-five questions were multiple choice closed-ended; five were open-ended. The respondents were strongly encouraged to make extensive written or oral comments and many of these revealed beliefs and attitudes previously unmentioned by the scholarly literature. In certain cases, the analytical depth of the comments was impressive. This compensates for the relatively limited number of interviewees. Trinidad is a small country and there are not many individuals able to discuss competently China-related issues. Moreover, key aspects analyzed in this book—such as the secretive government-to-government negotiations related to infrastructure projects—may be taken by some directly involved individuals as too sensitive to be discussed freely. Nevertheless, the combination of interviews and mass media has provided a clear, detailed, and convincing picture of the topic under scrutiny.

I am aware of the fact that criticism might be formulated targeting the solely Trinidadian origin of the respondents and, more generally, the centering of the analysis mainly on Trinidad and Tobago. As shown in the section *China in the Caribbean* of Chapter 3, a number of factors make Chinese conditionalities more visible and therefore easier to study in the Caribbean than in other Global South regions. Within the Caribbean, the same thing can be said about Trinidad, which has "the highest connectivity with China in the region" (Khan 2017). This concerns all types of exchanges and in particular the abundant Chinese-financed and built prestige infrastructure projects provided by Beijing as development assistance. Trinidad is also one of the most developed and, at 1.4 million inhabitants, one of the largest Caribbean states. Its natural resources already are exported to China and there is room for significant expansion. It even has a non-negligible industrial sector that in part has negatively been affected by Chinese competition. As these elements are seldom reunited within the borders of one Caribbean state, Trinidad represents an excellent case study for China's multidimensional involvement in the region. Moreover, I use numerous examples taken from the literature and mass media showing that the same elements can be found elsewhere in the Caribbean, which supports the idea that Trinidad and Tobago is representative for the entire region. Furthermore, the goal of this book is to put an end to the "myth" of China's "no strings" development assistance. If conditionalities are shown to exist in just one specific case—and they obviously do in Trinidad—the health of that "myth" is certainly in very poor shape.

Returning to the interviews, I have to mention the fact that they were made by Mrs. Amanda R. Ramlogan, a Ph.D. student at the Institute of International Relations of the University of the West Indies at St. Augustine who works toward the completion of a doctoral dissertation on the China-Trinidad and Tobago relationship. In addition to interviews, Mrs. Ramlogan has brought a valuable contribution to various parts of this book for which I am very grateful indeed. However, it should be emphasized that her work diverges significantly from this book in terms of theoretical approach, research priorities, and assessment of the overall consequences of the Chinese-Trinidadian interactions. Consequently, the conclusions of the following chapters should be taken as exclusively reflecting my point of view. I am looking forward to the new and interesting alternative perspective that Mrs. Ramlogan's dissertation will certainly provide.

The book is structured as follows. The next chapter constructs the appropriate theoretical framework, which addresses international socialization, development assistance and conditionality, and the specificities of small states. Chapter 3 analyzes China's expansion in the Global South, with an emphasis on Africa and Latin America. The goal is to identify the genesis and features of the main strategies and instruments used by Beijing in the developing world and to explain why the study of Chinese conditionalities is significantly more difficult in regions other than the Caribbean. Chapters 4 to 6 scrutinize the political, economic, and social conditionalities employed by China in the Caribbean. The particularly important issue of the socialization of political elites and bureaucrats is addressed in the section *The Socialization of Caribbean Elites* of Chapter 5. Chapter 7 assesses Beijing's regional enterprise in the context of the China-Caribbean-United States geopolitical triangle. The final chapter provides an in-depth analysis of the socialization mechanisms employed by Beijing, of the state-society gap created in the Caribbean by the Chinese conditionalities, of their power-related dimension, and of the consequences of the Caribbean enterprise for China's new identity as a global power.

To conclude, it is perhaps useful to remind that this book is the first scholarly work that studies the following elements:

- China's use of conditionality and international socialization in its interaction with at least one region of the Global South;
- China's three conditionalities;
- the concept of social conditionality; and

- the Caribbean as a particularly useful example of Chinese socialization in the developing world.

NOTE

1. I received oral permission from the respondents to use their words, provided that names and all other identifying elements are removed. This is why the interviewees are identified as "Respondent 1" to "Respondent 30" and no mention is made of their social or professional profile.

Chapter Two

Conditionality and Socialization

THE STATE-SOCIETY COMPLEX

This being a book about socialization through conditionality, it is important to begin the theoretical chapter by identifying its unit of analysis. Much of the literature focuses on attitude and belief changes in individuals; but there are also studies emphasizing the "transformation of state-level rules rather than individual beliefs" (Schimmelfennig et al. 2006: 2). Indeed, an approach focusing on the state was notably used by Frank Schimmelfennig and his colleagues in their analysis of international socialization in Europe (Schimmelfennig et al. 2006: 2). Outside the field of socialization, the same level of analysis is present in much of the existing research on Global South development assistance. The state does play a key role in the interactions of the Caribbean and of the rest of the developing world with China, which include a strong intergovernmental dimension. However, I believe that the state level of analysis cannot help elucidate in full the nature and features of the complex phenomenon under scrutiny. In order to be entirely successful, socialization also needs to reach all or at least most of that state's citizens. If this is not the case, major tensions can occur within the target country between the pro-Chinese government and the anti-Chinese population, with highly detrimental consequences for both that country's stability and Beijing's ability to shape the local environment in ways fully beneficial to its interests (for examples see Chapter 8). The conclusion is that both the state and the individual levels need to be addressed, which makes me follow Alexander Wendt in choosing the state-society complex as a unit of analysis (Wendt 1999/2003: 197).

It was Robert Cox's neo-Gramscian perspective that introduced this concept in the realm of the International Political Economy and International Relations (IR) (Van Apeldoorn 2004: 143). In the present interdependent world, "state and civil society are so interpenetrated that the concepts have become almost purely analytical (. . .) and are only very vaguely and imprecisely indicative of distinct spheres of activity" (Cox 1986: 205). Turning them into components of a unitary state-society complex allows for an understanding of the International Relations that goes far beyond the Realist billiard ball model: using the new concept, IR researchers can give "proper attention to social forces and processes and see how they relate to the development of states and world orders" (Cox 1986: 205). In fact, in this view, states represent expressions of particular configurations of social forces rather than international actors in their own right (Overbeek 2004: 127). More generally, in his rejection of "the static, timelessness of Neorealism, in which motivations are assumed to be fixed" (Sinclair 2016: 512), Cox used the state-society complex and its various configurations to reinforce the sense of ontological complexity associated with his examination of a plurality of forms of state and with his call for the study of "world order 'in the whole' but without 'reifying a world system'" (Sinclair 2016: 511).

An interesting development of the concept of state-society complex that illustrates its versatility was due to the work of the "Amsterdam Project" in International Political Economy, which expanded Cox's historical materialism (see Cox 1986: 214–217) into "transnational historical materialism" (Van Apeldoorn 2004: 142). Kees van der Pijl created the concept of "Lockean heartland," which originated in the development of the English Lockean state-society complex after the Glorious Revolution of 1688. The initial one-country complex was transnationalized mainly due to the pattern of self-government taken by British settlers to North America and Australia. In turn, this resulted in the development of a transnational "Lockean heartland" of the global political economy. Bringing together the present-day English-speaking countries, this atypical, transnational state-society complex is characterized by its industrial and commercial centrality and predominance (Fichtner 2016: 6) that historically has been contested by the so-called Hobbesian contender states (see Van der Pijl 1998; Van Apeldoorn 2004: 156–158; Overbeek 2004: 126–127). Incidentally, certain Caribbean states have been analyzed as belonging to and playing a key role in the "Lockean heartland" due to their activity as offshore financial centers (see Fichtner 2014: 37).

International Political Economy is hardly the only sub-field of International Relations that showed a marked interest in Cox's concept. The state-society complex was used in order to create a critical perspective for the study of global governance and global civil society (Massicotte 1999: 139–140).

In the realm of security studies, the way in which a state-society complex organizes for and conducts war is considered to represent a key aspect in the analysis of the social, economic, and deep technological forces that shape the current "revolutionary military transformation" (Latham and Sethi 2012: 175). Within the Weberian historical sociology, John Hobson's call for the development of a "second wave" approach that "breaks with neorealism, and adopts a *non*-realist conception of both the state and the international" (Hobson 2002a: 21; emphasis in the original) is based on the idea that state-society complexes both constitute and are constituted by socio-domestic and international/global structures. This "thick" conception of the state-society complex implies that domestic and international structures "are co-constituted and are fundamentally embedded within a series of social relationships" (Hobson 2002a: 21; see also Hobson 2002b: 66, 75; Bhambra 2010: 132).

This is very close to the use of Cox's concept made by Constructivists and, in particular, by Alexander Wendt. He similarly argued that "not only is the state constituted by its relationship to society, but so is society constituted by the state" (Wendt 1999/2003: 210). Wendt identifies five properties of the state: (1) an institutional-legal order; (2) an organization claiming a monopoly on the legitimate use of organized violence; (3) an organization with sovereignty; (4) a society; and (5) territory. In order to refer to all five properties at once, he employs the term of state-society complex (Wendt 1999/2003: 202): when states interact on the international arena, "they do so as parts of state-society complexes which affect their behavior" (Wendt 1999/2003: 197). A critical aspect of such interactions is represented by the process of international socialization presented in the following section.

INTERNATIONAL SOCIALIZATION

Some literature on China-related international socialization already exists. However, it does not analyze the rising global power as playing the role of a socializer. Its focus is on China itself being socialized into adopting the norms and values of various international organizations or international regimes (see for example Kent 2002; Tao 2015; Hao 2015). At the same time, in theoretical terms socialization is hardly limited to Constructivism. To give an unexpected example, Kenneth Waltz presented it as a mechanism that brings members of a group into conformity with its norms. Yet, to him IR socialization meant a process that makes international actors conform to the norms dictated by the [anarchical] structure of the international system (Waltz 1979: 74–76; Ikenberry and Kupchan 1990: 290). This is obviously much narrower than and, with respect to empirical analyses, hardly as useful as the socializer-socializee relationship analyzed by Constructivists.

The latter's understanding of international socialization has much to do with the concept of identity, which is defined as relatively stable, role-specific understandings and expectations about self that represent "a property of international actors that generates motivational and behavioral dispositions" (Wendt 1999/2003: 224; for a discussion of the "identity literature of IR" see Flockhart 2006: 94–97). State-society complexes are considered to be permanently involved in socialization processes that modify their interests and identities. In turn, the new identities lead to changes in the international environment, sometimes modifying the very "culture" of international anarchy (Wendt 1999/2003).

International socialization was defined as the "process by which principled ideas held by individuals [or agents] become norms in the sense of collective understandings about appropriate behaviour which then lead to changes in identities, interests and behaviour" (Park 2014: 337; see Risse et al. 1999: 11; Checkel 1999: 548; Johnston 2001: 494) or, if the state level of analysis is preferred, as "a process in which states are induced to adopt the constitutive rules of an international community" (Schimmelfennig et al. 2006: 2). My use of the state-society complex makes me refer to a process that affects both the state and the society dimensions of the complex and whose outcome is sustained compliance based on the internalization of new norms. This is to say that an international actor adheres to shared understandings of appropriate behavior by switching from following a logic of consequences to a logic of appropriateness (Checkel 2005: 804; Park 2014: 337).

If this line of reasoning is applied to Beijing's strategy toward the Caribbean, China's socialization can be defined as the process of inducing both states and societies in concerned countries to adopt collective understandings about the desirable and beneficial nature of a special relationship with China, to internalize such beliefs as norms, and ultimately to develop a new international identity as a Chinese-friendly state-society complex. Both cognitive and normative levels are involved, leading to attitudes and actions favorable to China's government, companies, and citizens.

The Chinese inducement is based on material incentives offered in the framework of the three conditionalities. This material aspect is related to a key theoretical issue. There are different degrees of norm internalization resulting in different degrees of identity change. At one extreme there is the purely instrumental modification of behavior in a new normative environment. At the other, the complete internalization of norms associated with a fundamental identity shift (Park 2014: 339). This topic was first explored by

Jeffrey Checkel, who introduced the terms of Type I and Type II socialization. In the former, in exchange for material rewards, actors simply learn a role and act in accordance with expectations even if they do not agree with that role. In the latter, they go beyond role playing; instrumental calculation is replaced with the "taken for granted" logic of appropriateness. Material incentives become irrelevant; the new norms are accepted as the right thing to do (Checkel 2005: 804). Other authors developed similar views. In each of his three cultures of anarchy, Wendt identified three degrees of cultural interiorization respectively based on force, price (*i.e.* interest), and legitimacy (Wendt 1999/2003). Thomas Risse and his colleagues described four parts of the socialization process (denial; strategic bargaining and tactical concessions; adherence; and habitualization of norms); Lewis analyzed thick, thin, and deep socialization (Park 2014: 340). This book uses Checkel's two types mainly because they also correspond to two very different approaches of the international socialization. Indeed, not all authors in this field accept the Constructivist idea that a fundamental identity shift is possible. Rationalist ones claim that international socialization is characterized by strategic action and extrinsic learning. Actors only adopt international rules due to incentives or coercion and never change their interests and identity (Schimmelfennig et al. 2006: 16–17). Some "institutionalist" rationalists such as Frank Schimmelfennig and his colleagues do accept the Constructivist assumptions of an institutional and cultural international environment, of the normative content of international socialization, and of strong international organizations as socialization agencies; but they claim that actors act strategically to maximize their utility ('strategic socialization') and never change their identity (Schimmelfennig et al. 2006: 6, 9).

It is not difficult to note that, for Rationalists, socialization cannot go beyond Checkel's Type I. I argue that, on the contrary, it is the shift from Type I to Type II that is critical for the complete success of China's strategy in the Caribbean. The present, rationalist Type I stage ultimately means little more than buying the compliance of the target state-society complex. This is already happening, but it does not leave room for qualitative progress in the bilateral relationship that will most likely preserve its present nature and intensity. I claim that China's goal is much more ambitious: to upgrade the socialization process to Type II, thus changing the very identity of its partners in the Caribbean in ways favoring its own regional and global interests. The details and importance of such a development are discussed in the section *Socialization and Power* of this chapter. Critically, it would represent a major exercise of power that cannot be fully understood outside the theoretical framework of a Constructivist perspective.

MECHANISMS OF SOCIALIZATION

Before addressing the key aspect of the relationship between socialization and power, the mechanisms of international socialization that are essential for the empirical analysis of China's three conditionalities need to be examined. It is particularly important to show how both the state and the society levels of the target complex can be impacted by external inducements provided by Beijing in the framework of mainly state to state interactions and to identify the consequences of their possible uneven degrees of socialization.

In their 1990 pioneer study, John Ikenberry and Charles Kupchan noted that socialization can work in two ways. In cases such as that of normative persuasion (see below), there are "beliefs before acts": elites in the target state first internalize the socializer's norms and only then modify national policies. There is a *normative persuasion—norm change—policy change* sequence. In the case of external inducement, however, there are "acts before beliefs": everything starts with economic and perhaps military incentives provided by the socializer in order to manipulate the preferences of elites and secure compliance. It is only later that normative principles promoted by the socializer are gradually embraced as rightful by the local elites. The causal chain is therefore *external inducement—policy change (cooperation through interest)—norm change (cooperation through legitimacy)* (adapted from Ikenberry and Kupchan 1990: 290). It is clear that in the case of China the latter pattern applies. Initially agnostic Caribbean elites are tempted by Beijing's inducements, adapt their policies for purely instrumental reasons, and only later start to internalize pro-Chinese norms that they eventually diffuse in the local society. This, of course, can stop at the level of role playing or further advance toward Type II socialization.

The literature presents a wide range of socialization mechanisms ranging from bargaining and coercion to persuasion and imitation (Schimmelfennig et al. 2006: 2–3). Fundamentally, two categories of actors can enact them: on the one hand, states and elites; on the other, non-state actors such as citizens, non-governmental organizations, and transnational advocacy networks. Societal mobilization associated with the latter category is a bottom-up diffusion pathway consisting in a change in attitudes coming from individuals, citizens, and civil society (Park 2014: 337). Yet, in cases that include the tremendously successful process of Europeanization of former communist countries in Eastern Europe, societal mobilization proved ineffective. Scholars such as Frank Schimmelfennig, Stefan Engert, and Heiko Knobel argued that EU norms were not transmitted to the target state via domestic societal actors. This is explained as a consequence of a prevailing domestic structure of weak societies—too fragmented and unable to force governments to comply—and of electoral volatility (Schimmelfennig et al. 2006: 9–10).

Most frequently, it is the first category—that of elites—that is able to contribute effectively to successful socialization. Political elites include people in government, the opposition and, more generally, the political parties. As they are in control of the state, the norms they internalize are rapidly institutionalized through the legal and bureaucratic apparatus and lead to the adoption of corresponding national discourses, policies, and practices that result in the socialization of the state. Social learning by elite decision makers—and the political elites in general—is the main form of manifestation of normative persuasion that frequently takes place within the context of regularized inter-state interactions (Park 2014: 337). The framework might be that of an international organization, but forms of sustained bilateral contact such as visits and negotiations, cultural exchanges, and foreign studies are equally effective (Ikenberry and Kupchan 1990: 290). This is the first part of a two-stage process: "norms are internalised within a supranational context and then transferred into domestic contexts" (Wiener 2004: 196; Park 2014: 337). In the second part, elites turn themselves into "norm entrepreneurs" that try to similarly shape the normative beliefs of citizens through domestic micro-processes that include persuasion (changing attitudes through ongoing, iterative interactions) and various forms of social influence such as shaming (shunning, excluding, and demeaning those who do not behave in accordance with their role and identity), rewards for conforming to role expectations, and coercion (which is part of the socialization process if material power is used for normative purposes) (Park 2014: 338).

The following chapters show that, in the case of China's socialization of the Caribbean in general and of Trinidad and Tobago in particular, elite social learning has been extremely effective. This is due to the inducement represented by Chinese development assistance consisting mainly in large prestige infrastructure projects that have been used by local leaders for political self-legitimation, especially in an electoral context. This assistance came with conditionalities that, as explained in the Introduction, included non-transparent practices related to the negotiation and conclusion of secretive government-to-government agreements. As shown in more detail in the section *The Socialization of Caribbean Elites* of Chapter 5, this type of secret diplomacy has been used as a tool of reciprocal socialization between Chinese and Trinidadian elites. Top-level "personalized interactions" are seldom publicly discussed, but are believed to help strengthening trust through personal relationships and to create much needed "back channels" of communication (Terhalle 2011: 353). In addition to numerous less opaque, "normal" bilateral contacts, these channels allow for the regularized interactions that are a precondition of the elite social learning presented in the previous paragraph.

What has not worked well in the case of the Caribbean is the elites' "norm entrepreneurship," which failed to transfer to the local society the norms associated with China's economic and social conditionalities. Details are analyzed in Chapters 5 and 6. What needs to be discussed here is the relevance of such hybrid situations where huge gaps exist between the degrees of socialization of the elites/the state and of the society, respectively. Scholars such as Ikenberry and Kupchan argue that the only relevant role in international socialization is that played by elites. In fact, they even define socialization as "a process through which the value orientations of a leading state are transmitted to *elites* in other nations" (Ikenberry and Kupchan 1990: 290; emphasis added). They claim that, in order to have a long-term and consequential impact on the behavior of the state, new norms need to be internalized by elites, not by the society: "it is through the dynamics of elite politics and coalition-building that socialization takes place." Nothing relevant happens if only "the public at large" internalizes the norms (Ikenberry and Kupchan 1990: 293). This is true in a certain measure, but also illustrates a Rationalist approach incompatible with the in-depth understanding of the dynamic and consequences of the process of socialization. The two authors study the socialization of the state, not of the state-society complex, and limit it to rationalist, Type I role playing. My point is precisely that, short of reaching the Type II phase—which needs to involve the society—socialization is incomplete and this deprives the socializer of considerable benefits, including geopolitical ones. This latter issue is detailed in the following section.

SOCIALIZATION AND POWER

International Socialization as Exercise of Power

Rationalist scholars understand socialization as the use of soft power in order to change the behavior of weaker states (Park 2014: 338). For Ikenberry and Kupchan, "power is exercised through a process of socialization" (Ikenberry and Kupchan 1990: 286). They stated that both the manipulation of material incentives and the ensuing projection by the socializer of a set of norms that leaders of socialized states embrace are parts of this exercise of power (Ikenberry and Kupchan 1990: 283). At the same time, the development assistance conditionality associated with socialization that I examine later in this chapter is unanimously considered to "operate in an environment of power asymmetry between dominant and subordinate actor(s)"; its use inevitably involves "power flows" (Hughes et al. 2005: 3, 14). For their part, Constructivists take a different stand. They believe that "interaction is not so much about power-based bargaining, but rather, about 'common knowledge' as to how to 'share basic assumptions about the deep structure of their interaction'" (Terhalle 2011: 349). Yet, even in their case international socialization is not dissociated from power. It's just that their understanding of this concept is different: "power is the production, in and through social relations, of effects that shape the capacities of actors to determine their circumstances and fate" (Barnett and Duvall 2005: 42). This is to say that power does not need to be causal (A compels B to take a certain action). It can be constitutive, i.e. it can lead to the constitution of rules, knowledge, positions, and identities that in turn influence "the capacities of actors to determine their circumstances and fate" (Skovgaard 2011: 446). Accordingly, for Constructivists the process of socialization is influenced by power in a different way but as strongly as in the case of Rationalists. To give an example, in the case of the European Union's enlargement-related conditionality that led to the successful Europeanization of East European countries, three categories of power were identified by certain Constructivist authors: economic, bureaucratic, and normative (Hughes et al. 2005: 12). Rationalist scholars might acknowledge only the first one as relational and therefore genuine power; but to both groups there is no doubt that power played a major role in that socialization process.

A critical aspect is represented by the fact that socialization has been studied as a process related to the reproduction and diffusion of a social order (Schimmelfennig 2000: 112; Park 2014: 341). This is an idea supported not only by Constructivist authors but also by Rationalist ones. Indeed, in their study of hegemonic socialization, Ikenberry and Kupchan showed that socialization is part of "the efforts of the hegemon to propagate its conception of international order" (Ikenberry and Kupchan 1990: 313). Robert Cox's neo-Gramscian view of legitimacy as one of the main dimensions of hegemony as well as Robert Keohane's use of this idea in *After Hegemony* immediately come to mind (see Ikenberry and Kupchan 1990: 286, 288–289). At least for the time being, China is not trying to turn itself into a hegemon of the Caribbean and therefore the concept of hegemonic socialization cannot be used in this book. However, the related concept of great power socialization of weaker partners is most helpful in understanding Beijing's strategy in this region.

International Socialization as Source of Power

At system level, socialization "can function effectively as a source of power" simply because the ability to generate shared beliefs in the legitimacy and in the ensuing acceptability of a particular international order is "an important if elusive dimension of hegemonic power" (Ikenberry and Kupchan 1990: 284, 289). The same line of reasoning can be applied at the regional level, for example in the case of the construction of a sphere of influence by a regional power. This can be further expanded to any relationship between a great power and its partners that, through a process of socialization, are turned into client states. In the case of hegemony, socialization is used as an instrument of power during critical historical periods—such as the aftermath of war or of imperial penetration—when international change overlaps with domestic crisis in the target countries. Internationally, the new hegemon takes advantage of a new constellation of power and tries to recast the international order in a way favorable to its own interests. An important element is the production of a clear set of normative claims about the international order, which is followed by the effort to accordingly alter the normative orientation of secondary states. Chances of success are higher if domestic conditions in those states are favorable to the importation of new ideas and normative claims about international behavior (Ikenberry and Kupchan 1990: 292). A similar situation can be identified in the case of the relationships between a great power and its weaker partners. During the Cold War, such partners were typically medium or relatively small states located in turbulent regions and having recently experienced regime change or ideological reorientations. The support of an external great power would have increased considerably the resources and legitimacy of the new regimes, thus significantly contributing to their stability and consolidation. It was to such potential partners that the Soviet Union proposed its set of norms. Their acceptance led to processes of socialization resulting in the creation of special patron-client relationships that considerably expanded Moscow's world influence. I have studied elsewhere the specific situation of Syria (Tudoroiu 2015); Cuba, Vietnam, Mongolia, and other similar countries that also experienced Soviet socialization that started with role playing but evolved in time toward full Type II socialization. It should be noted that not all of them were communist, as shown by the Syrian example. Yet, despite the huge differences that existed between the two partner's ideologies and political systems,

> during the last two decades of the Cold War [the Soviet-Syrian partnership] represented an almost ideal-type example of a relationship between a superpower and its regional ally that, through its complex consequences, shaped significantly the two partners themselves, the Middle Eastern political and security environment, and the international system as a whole (Tudoroiu 2015: 143).

It goes without saying that for the USSR this was a significant source of power. Highly relevant for this book, the similar case of the Soviet-Cuban relationship shows how successful Type II socialization became an undeniable source of power for the Soviet Union and allowed it to actually and effectively project power in the Caribbean.

This means that China's socialization efforts in the region cannot be dissociated from the use and production of power. Chinese development assistance inducements offered to countries like Trinidad and Tobago are expressions of the asymmetry between the two states and, ultimately, of Beijing's power. Associated Type I socialization of Caribbean state-society complexes can be considered an effect of the use of Chinese soft power and also represents a source of power for China, be it a non-spectacular one. Fully successful Type II socialization, however, could result in the creation of a large number of fully-fledged, Cuban-style client states that would turn Beijing into a key regional actor. As this would happen in America's Caribbean backyard, this power dimension would have considerable geopolitical implications that are analyzed in Chapter 7.

Reciprocal Socialization

Previous paragraphs have presented the socialization process—and the associated use and production of power—as a socializer-centered phenomenon. Indeed, in the literature "we witness the notion of a one-way socialization prevailing" (Terhalle 2011: 349). The socialized state-society complex typically plays a purely passive role. This is due to the fact that the huge majority of socialization studies examine how states join groups such as the European Union, other international organizations, or various international regimes (Park 2014: 334). In situations of this kind, already socialized members adopt newcomers into their club and unilaterally transmit to them the predominant norms of the structure (Terhalle 2011: 349). In the case of EU accession, for example, the candidate can either accept the EU norms as part of Brussels' conditionality or reject them and remain outside the Union. Given the huge asymmetry between the EU and the candidate state, the latter cannot realistically hope to renegotiate the "club's norms." Different situations, however, do exist. Maximilian Terhalle examined the case of major rising powers that are socialized into the international order while renegotiating the latter's existing settlement and trying to change its configuration (Terhalle 2011: 341, 351). The term "reciprocal socialization" was coined to describe situations where new members try to renegotiate the order of the community that receives them (Terhalle 2011: 342, 349). Ultimately, this mirrors Wendt's image of states changing their identity under the influence of the international environment but at the same time modifying that environment.

Ikenberry and Kupchan have noted that hegemonic socialization is also a two-way process which does affect the normative orientation of elites in the hegemonic state. These elites might need to rework the set of principles that should support the new international order to make it more easily acceptable; or might even engage in a process of compromise with elites from secondary states in order to reach the same result (Ikenberry and Kupchan 1990: 293). Something similar happens in the case of great power socialization of partner states. Of course, the great power plays the major role as it has largely superior material resources and a favorable position in cognitive terms resulting from its experience with other regional allies. Critically, this is an asymmetrical process within which the great power establishes the socializing norms. However, the great power is only a state and therefore its identity—defined as relatively stable, role-specific understandings and expectations about self (Wendt 1999/2003: 224; see the section *International Socialization* of this chapter)—is much more vulnerable to external influence than the European Union or other large and complex communities. Returning to Jeffrey Checkel's two-stage model, Type I socialization has the two self-interested partners learning to take advantage of the opportunities offered by the new relationship while assuming their respective roles. In exchange for material incentives, the regional ally conforms to the norms of international behavior proposed by the great power. In turn, the latter uses its partner as a regional proxy; moreover, this extension of its international reach allows it to enhance its global status (Tudoroiu 2015: 144). However, in order to preserve and further develop this advantageous relationship, the great power has to take into consideration and accommodate its partner's specific needs and interests. This involves modifying in a certain measure its own discourse, actions, policies, and normative views, and is not limited to one partner: all the great power's clients have a similar impact. The cumulative effect on the great power's very identity cannot be ignored (Tudoroiu 2015: 150).

In the case of the China-Trinidad relationship, the Caribbean state has learned and plays its role of special regional partner. It takes advantage of Chinese developing assistance mainly consisting of large infrastructure projects and, in exchange, responds positively to Beijing's three conditionalities. China has also learned and plays its role of generous Global South provider of development assistance. In the process, it needs to respond favorably to at least some of Trinidad's unexpected demands. A case in point is the issue of the long-range maritime patrol vessel presented in Chapter 7. China's cooperation with various Caribbean states includes security aspects, but their scale has been modest and they clearly are not part of Chinese conditionalities. Yet, in February 2014 the then Prime Minister of Trinidad and Tobago visited Beijing and secured an agreement to purchase a patrol vessel, which represented a major breakthrough for China's arms sales to the region (Southerland 2017; Badri-Maharaj 2016). This was not a Chinese-originated plan (see the section *The Chinese-Caribbean Security Cooperation and Its Prospects* of Chapter 7), and it advanced very slowly. It was only in 2017 that a framework agreement for the provision of the associated concessional loan was signed with Trinidad's next government; the actual delivery has not yet taken place. All this looks very much like a Trinidadian initiative on which Beijing had its doubts, as it threatened to uselessly antagonize the United States. China seriously engaged in the project only after President Trump's actions considerably tensioned the transpacific relationship. And yet, back in 2014, the Chinese did not coldly reject Trinidad's demand. At least in principle, they accepted it, thus starting to add a new dimension to the already close and complex bilateral relationship. This extension of the repertoire of their Caribbean actions is not part of China's socialization *of* Trinidad. It is an example of China's socialization *by* Trinidad, which opened a window toward Beijing's enhanced involvement in the region's security affairs. It is of course very modest; but China is not interacting only with Trinidad. It plays the same role with respect to many similar partners in the Caribbean and elsewhere in the Global South, all of which contribute to shaping Chinese actions, policies, normative views, and identity. It should not be forgotten that China's ongoing rise as a global power presupposes a major change of its role-specific understandings about self. Its identity is still very fluid and as such vulnerable to the influence of its partners. Their interests and actions therefore help shape the China of tomorrow, a process that will further intensify if Type II socialization is reached. Paradoxically, the giant socializer is itself socialized by the Lilliputians.

DEVELOPMENT ASSISTANCE AND CONDITIONALITY

Development Assistance

Official development assistance has been defined by the Development Assistance Committee of the Organization for Economic Cooperation and Development as "grants or loans undertaken by the official sector, with the promotion of economic development and welfare as main objectives (. . .), at concessional financial terms" (Copper 2016: 1). This definition has been criticized as too narrow and restrictive, and definitely does not cover the full extent of China's assistance to developing countries, an issue I discuss in Chapter 5. But at this point it is more important to note that development assistance, no matter how it is defined, is always associated with "an extremely asymmetric power relationship" (Stokke 1995/2006: 33). "Aid giving clearly has political purposes and indeed may be regarded in large measure as a political act" (Copper 2016: 1). Development assistance adds to trade and investment as an important component of economic diplomacy (Trinidad 2013: 22) and, despite its altruistic claims, represents "an instrument to pursue foreign policy objectives" (Stokke 1995/2006: 2). In particular, "economic assistance is the principal means of influence employed by China in its foreign policy in the Caribbean" (Bernal 2016: 5623–5625). At the same time, development assistance represents an intervention in the recipient country: the way it is channeled, the form it takes, and its target groups decisively influence who the domestic beneficiaries and losers are and therefore significantly affect their resources and power position (Stokke 1995/2006: 34). It is not a coincidence that political decision-makers in Trinidad welcome Chinese-built prestige infrastructure projects which they eventually use for electoral purposes. Critically, "conditions set by the donor are part of everyday life in aid relations—they are the 'normal' pattern" (Stokke 1995/2006: 34). This brings the discussion to the key issue of conditionality.

Development Assistance Conditionality

In the Introduction I have already presented Tony Killick's narrow definition of conditionality as "a mutual arrangement by which a government takes, or promises to take, certain policy actions, in support of which an IFI (International Financial Institution) or other agency will provide specified amounts of financial assistance" (Killick 1998: 5–6), and explained that I prefer to use the more general definition proposed by Olav Stokke, to whom conditionality represents

> the use of pressure, by the donor, in terms of threatening to terminate aid, or actually terminating or reducing it, if conditions are not met by the recipient. Foreign aid is used as a lever to promote objectives set by the donor which the recipient government would not otherwise have agreed to (Stokke 1995/2006: 11–12).

There is *ex ante* conditionality, when the actual pursuit of such objectives is a precondition for entering into an assistance relationship, and *ex post* conditionality, when expectations are formulated beforehand and followed up afterwards (Stokke 1995/2006: 12). Negative conditionality refers to adopting sanctions to secure compliance while positive conditionality rewards compliance with increased assistance (Hughes et al. 2005: 14; Dipama and Dal 2015: 114). There is also formal conditionality, based on publicly stated preconditions, and informal conditionality, which includes operational pressures and recommendations (Hughes et al. 2005: 26). As mentioned in the

Introduction, Olav Stokke identified six levels of conditionality associated with different degrees of intervention: (1) the systemic level, which involves the system of government and governing institutions; (2) attempts to change the national policies and priorities of the government in the target country; (3) attempts to change specific policies within an area or sector; (4) the program/project level (concerning institutional reform, official regulations, and financial or personnel contributions of the recipient state); (5) financial conditions; and (6) administrative conditions that involve procedures for the transfer of resources, accounting, reporting, evaluation, privileges enjoyed by technical co-operation personnel, etc. (Stokke 1995/2006: 13–15). Hardly all of these levels are compatible with Tony Killick's narrow definition of conditionality, which suggests that his approach does not provide the best theoretical instrument for the study of this topic.

Few authors fail to mention the asymmetry and the "power flows" implicitly associated with development assistance conditionality. A clear divide is emphasized in the literature between donors in pursuit of their own interests and recipients subject to donor conditionality and therefore finding themselves in a position of dependency (Hughes et al. 2005: 3, 14). Historically, since the end of World War II there has been a steady expansion of development assistance conditionality. There has been an increasing linkage between aid disbursement and donors-imposed conditions while the nature of the conditionality grew more complex (Hughes et al. 2005: 14). The literature identifies first generation conditionality, associated with IMF and World Bank structural adjustment programs imposing economic and administrative reforms in recipient countries; and second generation conditionality, which developed after the end of the Cold War and imposed political and administrative reforms promoting democracy, human rights, and good governance. Because of their different emphasis, the two generations are associated with economic and political conditionality, respectively (Stokke 1995/2006: 1; Dipama and Dal 2015: 112). Many authors have deemed conditionality "inefficient in attaining its desired objectives and favourably changing economic and political developments" (Zimelis 2011: 395; for a brief literature review on the effectiveness of political conditionality see Dipama and Dal 2015: 114–116). Indeed, the empirical evidence seems to be mixed, regardless of the donors' "enthusiastic support for aid conditionality" (Li 2017b: 203). Yet, "despite its well-documented failures, conditionality remains ubiquitous"; imagining the IMF or the World Bank giving up conditionality is "nearly impossible," as "conditionalizing states, societies, and individuals is essential to their operation" (Shelton 2015: 180). It is nevertheless on the European Union that the most interesting practical and theoretical developments of conditionality have been centered.

EU Enlargement Conditionality and Constructivism

EU conditionality evolved significantly and has been studied by large numbers of scholars in the context of the Eastern enlargement and of the ensuing European Neighborhood Policy and Eastern Partnership. It was the enlargement that considerably "stimulated and shaped the debates on the scope and effectiveness of conditionality" (Gateva 2015: 22). Enlargement conditionality should be "seen as part of a broad pattern of 'Western' international conditionality" and represents an extension of the EU external developmental strategy targeting ACP (Africa-Caribbean-Pacific) countries; but it is a "gargantuan extension" (Hughes et al. 2005: 12, 13; for a brief history of European Union conditionality see Shelton 2015: 4–10). It was the successful attempt to simultaneously operationalize the totality of economic and political elements across a whole region that made the European Union's conditionality "exceptional in its scope and intent" (Hughes et al. 2004: 18). Critically, by exploring the mechanisms for inducing compliance and by assessing their impact on the domestic politics of the target states, the enlargement-related literature revealed the "transformative power" of the European Union (Gateva 2015: 2) and created a new approach that studies conditionality as an integral part and a key element of a larger process of international socialization. After enlargement, the post-accession sustainability of conditionality as well as its impact on non-candidate neighboring countries have also been analyzed. According to the context, the details of enlargement conditionality, membership conditionality, accession conditionality, *acquis* conditionality, democratic conditionality, and political conditionality were examined by various authors (Gateva 2015: 2–3). Trying to systemize this abundance of perspectives, Joel Shelton identified four established approaches to thinking about conditionality: (1) conditionality as rational incentive; (2) conditionality as state normalization; (3) conditionality as geopolitics; and (4) conditionality as class domination (Shelton 2015: 35).

I do not present the last two as they are not relevant to the topic of this book. For the third, it is true that conditionality can be construed as geopolitical (Duke 2017: 79); it is also true that China's socialization of the Caribbean has major geopolitical implications. However, as argued in Chapter 7, it is simply too early to speak about Chinese geopolitical conditionality in this region. For the class domination approach, I do not reject the idea that neo-Marxist approaches could be helpful in the exploration of the external projection of China's capitalism. Still, such an analysis would bring this book into the realm of International Political Economy; I prefer to keep it within the borders of the field of International Relations. Accordingly, I will only detail the features of Shelton's first two approaches. The first one, conditionality as rational incentive, is closely related to the rationalist view of international socialization described in the section *International Socialization* of this chapter. It defines conditionality as a set of material incentives offered to candidate states to make them adopt EU rules. The adoption is successful if material benefits outweigh material costs. Conditionality acts mainly at the macro-political level; state-level rules, not individual beliefs, are transformed (Shelton 2015: 35, 37). For its part, the normative democratic conditionality of the European Union is perceived as a reinforcement strategy and not as a strong causal mechanism (Hughes et al. 2005: 11). Frank Schimmelfennig's institutionalist approach falls into the same category, even if it admits that the adoption of rules and norms might alter the interest calculations of mainly rational states. In this case, it is the institutionalization of particular rules that is emphasized; conditionality becomes a set of rules or norms that are adopted by the state and its institutions. Yet, norms are only "instrumental weapons" (Shelton 2015: 38, 39).

The second approach is very different, as it proposes an understanding of conditionality as state normalization, thus emphasizing the social, normative, and ideational context. This is of course related to the Constructivist analysis of international socialization championed by authors such as Heather Grabbe. It starts from the idea that mechanisms of conditionality modify the candidate states' very logic of political behavior. State actors are "normalized," which leads to bargaining outcomes that do not strictly reflect material interests. The key role is played by the political institutions inside candidate states that become Europeanized at a micro-level as their staff is increasingly socialized by the EU (Shelton 2015: 40–41; Grabbe 2006: 198–199). Conditionality is defined as a series of mechanisms that extends beyond material incentives. They are targeted toward socialization, i.e. at transforming the social and subjective dimensions of persons—who are asked to act as particular kinds of political, economic, and social beings—in line with a particular vision of the political-economic life (Shelton 2015: 41–42). James Hughes, Gwendolyn Sasse, and Claire Gordon have argued convincingly that "conditionality is insufficiently understood within a narrowly positivist framework" (Hughes et al. 2005: 3). As an ideal type, conditionality is characterized by essential features such as a consensus on its substance between actors applying it and actors fulfilling it; clear criteria that should be verifiable; testable benchmarks to assess its fulfillment; power flows readily transmitted and understood by all concerned; and explicitly predetermined outcomes (whether rewards or sanctions). But its actual working is a much more complex process affected by "interaction between multi-level actors, perceptions, interests, different rewards and sanctions, temporal factors, institutional and policy compliance" (Hughes et al. 2005: 3). All these involve and are significantly impacted by cognitive and normative factors that the analysis cannot afford to ignore. This does not mean that the Rationalist view of conditionality is completely ineffective. The study of conditionality as exclusively based on material incentives is quite relevant as long as only Type I socialization is scrutinized, which is the case of China's present interaction with the Caribbean. It cannot, however, provide instruments for the study of Type II socialization. Moreover, it prevents the scholar from even realizing that a more advanced stage might exist. That is a serious analytical issue because China's status in those parts of the Global South it is trying to socialize depends precisely on its ability to reach the Type II stage. This is why this book uses the Constructivist approach to analyze both international socialization and conditionality.

CHINA'S THREE CONDITIONALITIES

For analytical reasons, I prefer to split China's conditionality toward the Caribbean into "conditionalities" that, in terms of impact, cover specific domains. All of them are supported by the same material incentives, which are economic in nature. By Chinese political conditionality I understand Beijing's use of those incentives in order to shape the recipient state's China-related foreign policy preferences as well as its attitude toward democracy and human rights in China. As already shown in the Introduction, these actions impact Caribbean states' foreign and domestic policies by preventing them from taking advantage of Taiwanese development assistance which, ideally in conjunction with the Chinese one, could be highly beneficial to their socio-economic development; and by compelling them to hide their concerns for the situation of human rights in China despite their constant criticism of antidemocratic practices abroad. This definition of political conditionality is not very different from that used by most of the literature on development assistance, which refers to "a situation in which the validity of an international agreement is made dependent upon the partner's mutual respect for certain principles" (Dipama and Dal 2015: 112). It is only that the principles promoted by Western donors relate to the respect of democracy and human rights; China's political conditionality rejects these very principles, even if only in a narrow and limited way.

China's economic conditionality is based on the imposition of "tied aid" and of the non-transparent, secretive negotiation of associated government-to-government agreements. Beijing gives with one hand and takes with the other as it demands that most or all of the contractors, labor, and materials used in Chinese-financed large infrastructure projects come from China. In the Caribbean, these projects represent by far the majority of the Chinese development assistance. As most of the region's economies are small and less developed, the fact that local companies and workers are left aside has considerable negative socio-economic consequences. At the same time, the way these agreements are negotiated threatens local policies and practices of transparency and public accountability. Typically, most of them are never made public and, rightly or wrongly, are believed by many citizens to be at the origin of the numerous failures that plague the completed projects (see the section *China's "Tied Aid" and Its Reception in Trinidad and the Caribbean* of Chapter 5). This is to say that, in order to promote its own interests, China uses development assistance to prevent partner governments from adopting economic policies that would protect their own companies and labor force; and to actually damage good governance in their countries. Once more, common elements can be identified if the economic conditionality of Western donors is taken as a term of comparison. It also uses "tied aid"—which represents 18 percent of all Western bilateral aid, against 100 percent in the case of China (Clay et al. 2009: 12; Mattlin and Nojonen 2011: 18)—and tries to shape the recipient state in terms of good governance. Of course, it is the direction of this shaping that differs considerably.

Finally, I define China's social conditionality in a donor-related perspective that is distinct from the social consequences for the recipient country of the Chinese political and economic conditionalities. Social conditionality represents the use of incentives and sanctions to prevent the adoption by recipient states of policies that would regulate the inflow and the activities of entrepreneurial migrants coming from the donor country despite the negative impact of their economic actions on local businesses and workers. In this case the Chinese go beyond positive conditionality, i.e. rewarding compliance with increased development assistance. The example of Ghana presented in Chapter 6 shows that, in response to legitimate, small scale, and ultimately irrelevant non-compliance with its conditions, Beijing made use of negative conditionality, i.e. adopted sanctions against its African partner. Moreover, penalties within the framework of development assistance offered to Ghana were supplemented with further retaliatory measures. China did stall a US$3 billion payment from a China Development Bank loan that funded twelve development projects and tried to renegotiate the terms of the loan; but it also changed visa requirements for Ghanaian citizens, thus making it more difficult for merchants from Ghana to conduct their trade activities in China (Hess and Aidoo 2015: 52). The likely reasons for this harsh approach are discussed in Chapter 6. Anyway, some of the most radical negative reactions to the Chinese presence among the citizens of developing states are precisely those against the newly arrived entrepreneurial migrants. In many occasions, large scale public discontent has resulted in protests and even riots. If this inflow is supported by China's social conditionality, which is the case in the

Caribbean, it is hardly surprising that within the host society there is a high degree of rejection of this conditionality.

It should be noted that, unlike the political and economic ones, social conditionality is not mentioned in the literature on development assistance; its study represents an original contribution of this book. The absence can be explained by the fact that Western conditionality has developed during an historical period which, unlike older ones, was not marked by massive inflows of entrepreneurial migrants from the West into the developing world. Accordingly, conditionality "as we know it"—that is, Western conditionality—did not need to develop a donor-related social dimension even if, of course, it did indirectly affect social conditions locally.

An example of failure to note this important dimension is represented by the only previous attempt to analyze China's conditionality of which I am aware. In 2011, the Institute for Economies in Transition of the Bank of Finland published a discussion paper prepared by Mikael Mattlin and Matti Nojonen about "Conditionality in Chinese Bilateral Lending" (Mattlin and Nojonen 2011). Four years later, the same text was published by the *Journal of Contemporary China* (Mattlin and Nojonen 2015). In January 2012, the Carnegie Endowment for International Peace even organized a roundtable at the Tsinghua University in Beijing attended by the two authors (see Xuefeng et al. 2012). However, the only significant use of their ideas is that made by Hao Tian in his chapter of a 2018 edited book about the impact of the Belt and Road Initiative on Central Asia (Tian 2018). This dramatic lack of audience is due to the serious flaws of the paper. Its authors take into consideration only parts of China's political and economic conditionalities; ignore social conditionality; uselessly add two supplementary forms—"cross-conditionality" and "emergent conditionality'—whose actual existence they cannot confirm; claim that economic conditionality is imposed by "Chinese state-linked lenders and enterprises," not by the Chinese state; and do not use any theoretical framework whatsoever, preferring a purely factual analysis to the elaboration of a more abstract construct. In more detail, their political conditionality is exclusively associated with the diplomatic non-recognition of Taiwan. The critical dimension of forcing vocal democracies to restrain themselves from criticizing human rights infringement in China is completely ignored. Similarly, economic ('embedded') conditionality is exclusively about "tied aid." It does not mention the Chinese imposition of secretive negotiations and agreements that damage good governance practices in the partner country. "Cross-conditionality" is introduced which describes the use by China of its financing for a large project as a lever to get concessions on other, unrelated deals. For its part, "emergent conditionality"—"merely hypothetical as we have yet to see solid empirical validation" (Mattlin and Nojonen 2011:

22)—is about the possible future instrumentalization by Chinese state-owned banks and enterprises of the influence acquired through massive investments in strategic sectors. The authors admit that these two forms of conditionality "are constructs arising mainly from scattered case-evidence"; "further empirical research obviously is required to validate their prevalence" (Mattlin and Nojonen 2011: 7). Critically, they also claim that "in all likelihood" economic ("embedded") conditionality, like the "cross-" and "emergent" ones, is "not imposed by a unitary state actor." Rather, it is "an indirect consequence of the voluminous business activities of Chinese state-linked lenders and enterprises in developing countries" (Mattlin and Nojonen 2011: 3). At least in the case of the Caribbean, such a statement can in no way be seriously taken into consideration: the non-transparent negotiations that set the flow of Chinese "tied aid" are government-to-government. In fact, all China's conditionalities are part of a coherent strategy characterized by clear goals and effective implementation. Preferring to see only parts of it, adding speculative dimensions of which "we have yet to see solid empirical validation," and claiming that the only involvement of the Chinese state is related to the "One China" principle is hardly the best way to address such an important topic. Accordingly, the work of Mattlin and Nojonen failed to effectively question the "no strings attached" "myth."

However, the two authors were right in associating the creation of this "myth" with "a limited view of conditionality encompassing only the kinds of conditions attached by the IMF and World Bank" (Mattlin and Nojonen 2011: 6). Indeed, the denial by many scholars of the existence of conditionality in the case of China's development assistance is due to their implicit understanding of conditionality as Western conditionality. A somewhat different approach therefore seems to them as necessarily falling outside this category. Roughly speaking, Western conditionality normally concerns democratization and promotion of human rights on the political side; the adoption of mainly neoliberal policies on the economic one; and good governance, which is related to and affects both fields. It is clear that this is a strong form of conditionality that is intended to shape deeply many of the recipient state's policies. As shown in the previous paragraphs, the Chinese conditionality does not go that far. It concerns a smaller number of national policies and it is less ambitious. It could be said that Western donors target an in-depth transformation of which they could take advantage in the long term. China's actions are more short-term oriented and closer to its immediate economic interests. However, this does not mean that there is no conditionality at all. As already mentioned, Chinese development assistance is very different from the Western one and much of it does not even qualify as such if assessed by Western criteria; yet, it is development assistance. The same can be said about Chinese conditionality. It differs from the one we are accustomed to, but this does not mean that it does not exist. Moreover, even a more limited and narrower set of conditionalities can lead to successful international socialization and therefore to an overall transformative effect in no way inferior to that of the West.

SMALL STATES

Many of China's partners in the developing world are small states. This is not a coincidence. In the Global South, such states are more likely to lack resources, be less developed, and rely more on foreign aid than many of their larger neighbors; hence their interest in as well as their opening to any new provider of development assistance. Moreover, due to their dimensions they do not require large amounts of aid. Cynically speaking, their vote at the United Nations is much cheaper than that of larger states that share similar conditions of development. There is, of course, the ongoing dispute on how small a state needs to be in order to qualify as small. It seems reasonable to admit that less than 10–15 million citizens form a small state and less than one million a very small state, ministate, or microstate (Cooper and Shaw 2009: 4; Braveboy-Wagner 2008: 11). Many of China's partners in regions such as the Caribbean, Central America, the Pacific, and, in a lesser measure, Africa fall into these two categories. Critically, it is over such states that most of the "diplomatic duel" between Beijing and Taipei has been fought (see the section *China vs. Taiwan* of Chapter 3), which explains China's special interest in turning them into its development partners. Accordingly, this section analyzes the consequences of their particular features with respect to Beijing's expansion in the Caribbean.

It has been noted that "domestic factors rarely predict the foreign policy of small states" (Jesse and Dreyer 2016: 177). Indeed, their international actions are heavily constrained by systemic factors. Global and regional dynamics dictate their agendas and associated behavior. There is always the specter of marginalization (Braveboy-Wagner 2008: 2, 10), and this permanent threat makes small states behave in a different manner than "normal" ones. It was even argued that they "are worthy of being studied as a completely separate, and different, unit of analysis" (Jesse and Dreyer 2016: 178). A key feature is their vulnerability, which can be defined as "a naturally imposed and predictable condition in which the room for maneuver is severely constrained" (Cooper and Shaw 2009: 4). Small states are vulnerable to pressure from or even intervention by larger states and international financial institutions as well as to new transnational threats. Economically, they are weak due to undiversified economic structures, high infrastructural costs, remoteness, high dependence on external trade, vulnerability to the forces of nature, and limited access to external financing (Braveboy-Wagner 2008: 12; Commonwealth Consultative Group 1985).

Yet, in an effort to overcome their vulnerability, small states have developed resilience—the ability to recover from or adjust to change—that does allow structural factors to be resisted and reshaped (Cooper and Shaw 2009: 1, 4). In order to escape marginalization, they have become "particularly clever, efficient, and economical in devising appropriate strategies to meet their foreign policy goals" (Braveboy-Wagner 2008: 2). In particular, they have taken advantages of the "myriad opportunities" provided by globalization (Cooper and Shaw 2009: 4; Briguglio 2007: 105). While there obviously are commonalities of responses among all small states, "a considerable emphasis is placed on individual actorness" (Cooper and Shaw 2009: 4). Some succeeded in building up economic niches through the use of well-planned strategies while others have adapted in a more opportunistic manner. The first category includes the "developmental island states" exemplified by Singapore, Iceland, and Ireland but also by Mauritius and Trinidad and Tobago (Cooper and Shaw 2009: 4, 6–7). The second, which in part does overlap with the first, comprises the many Global South small states that benefit from China's development assistance. As already mentioned, in many cases this assistance has been related to the Chinese-Taiwanese dispute (see the section *China vs. Taiwan* of Chapter 3). Other factors—such as, in the case of the Caribbean, the development of the Sino-American geopolitical rivalry—have eventually enhanced it. The Belt and Road Initiative provides new opportunities. Overall, it can be concluded that small states' vulnerability and resilience create the conditions for a genuine complementarity of interests with China and therefore predispose them to accept its development assistance. However, the same vulnerability makes them unable to resist the imposition of Beijing's conditionalities. This is why small states are likely to provide useful case studies to students of China's socialization efforts in the Global South.

To conclude, this chapter provides the theoretical instruments needed to study China's interactions with the Caribbean, which is analyzed as a group of Global South small states. These interactions are characterized by the use of the three conditionalities as part of a complex process of international socialization that is implicitly associated with the use and production of power. The following chapters provide empirical evidence supporting this line of reasoning and allowing for a detailed understanding of the working of involved mechanisms.

Chapter Three

China's Mixed Record in the Global South

THE "PANDA COMETH" AND "GLOBALIZATION WITH CHINESE CHARACTERISTICS"

The "Panda Cometh," as Kevin Gallagher appropriately called the rising global power, stands at the intersection of two developmental paths. The domestic one was launched four decades ago by Deng Xiaoping's economic reforms; the external one is due to American-led globalization. They are, of course, interconnected. Domestic reforms were stimulated and turned into a spectacular success by the opportunities created by globalization. In turn, the speed and magnitude of globalization were significantly enhanced by China's impressive integration into the capitalist world economy. Politically, Chinese totalitarianism was replaced by what I called elsewhere neo-communism. Well illustrated in Eastern Europe by the regimes of Zhan Videnov in Bulgaria (1995–1996), of Ion Iliescu in Romania (1990–1996), and of Alyaksandr Lukashenka in Belarus (since 1994), this is a post-communist authoritarian construct preserving (or restoring) communist structures and personnel. Key features include (1) the link with the communist past; (2) the regime's authoritarian character; (3) a specific ideology; (4) a false discourse about redistributive social and economic policies; and (5) the systematic harassment and control of the nascent civil society (Tudoroiu 2011: 420). Unknown to many, the discourse mentioned at point 4 does exist in China despite the "wild" capitalism that allowed Chun Lin to rightly claim that "if Marx could see Guangdong today he would die of anger" (Lin 2006: 9). Indeed, promoting "social equity and justice" represents one of the key elements of the concept of "Harmonious Socialist Society" introduced by former President Hu Jintao (2002–2012) as part of an "agile, responsive, and creative party effort to relegitimate the postrevolutionary regime" (Holbig and Gilley 2010: 406). This new harmonious Chinese society was first mentioned officially at the very beginning of Hu's presidential tenure, in November 2002. It received a formal definition in 2004 and one year later it was proclaimed as China's driving ideology. In 2006, specific objectives and tasks as well as the year 2020 as a target date were announced (Taylor and Calvillo 2010: 140–142; for more details see Han 2008: 148–150). By then, "the emergence of a reasonable and orderly income distribution pattern" and the establishment of a social security system covering both urban and rural residents would have been turned into reality (Xinhua News Agency 2006; Tudoroiu 2011: 423). All this might have very little in common with the social reality of present China, but serves as proof of ideological continuity with the Maoist communist past and as such helps legitimate the present neo-communist regime.

A more genuine form of continuity concerns the involvement of the state in the economy and is illustrated by what has been called "China's state-orchestrated market capitalism" (Ampiah and Naidu 2008: 330; Mohan et al. 2014: 13). Economic reforms did not put an end to the key role played by state actors. In fact, they "remain central to the functioning of an economic system that has dysfunctionally emerged to suit their interests" (Breslin 2007: 40; Ziso 2018: 3). As shown in Chapter 5, it is the *sui generis* collaboration among the Chinese state, Chinese state-owned banks, and Chinese state-owned enterprises that represents a considerable competitive advantage at the origin of much of China's success in the Global South (Ellis 2013: 2). There as well as in the rest of the world, China's "athletic trade growth, massive market size, huge appetite for raw materials, and aggressive development strategy" (le Pere 2015: 379) have turned it into a major economic actor whose geopolitical influence and ambitions are increasingly visible. It is true that in recent years much literature has been produced about the "pivot strategy" launched in 2013 and leading to the reorientation of the Chinese economy from export-led growth toward raising consumption levels, as per capita income is lower in China than in Brazil or Mexico and represents only 13 percent of that of the US (Menéndez, 2014: 1; Cypher and Wilson 2015: 15). However, this shift from investment and manufacturing toward consumption and services (Lahtinen 2018: xiv) is not likely to limit China's global expansion. In fact, since his coming to power in November 2012 as General Secretary of the Communist Party of China, which was followed by his nomination as President of China in March 2013, Xi Jinping has promoted both this domestic change and the globally relevant Belt and Road Initiative (see the section *The Belt and Road Initiative* of this chapter).

The latter magnifies China's contribution to the present "significant spatial reorganization of global capitalism" (Ayers 2013: 13; Mohan et al. 2014: 13).

The accommodation of the new economic power into a global order largely defined by Western actors and interests has posed significant challenges (Tull 2008: 7; Ziso 2018: 2) as "China has gone from being a vessel to becoming an increasingly transformative actor in its own right" that "reinvent[s] globalization in its own image" (French 2014: 3–4). "Globalization with Chinese characteristics" has become a fashionable term, based on the idea that globalization "needs to be understood, in part, as the externalization of particular national forms of capitalism in particular historical periods" (Henderson et al. 2013: 1221). Today, China is "increasingly writing its own rules, and reinventing globalization in its own image"; gradually, it jettisons norms and conventions created and used by the United States, Europe, and Japan, thus threatening, among others, their "hitherto largely unchallenged tutelage of the Third World" (French 2014: 4). In addition to this process of structural change, President Xi Jinping has abandoned Deng Xiaoping's principle of "peaceful rise with a low profile" in favor of a foreign policy far more active than that of his predecessors (Lahtinen 2018: 19). Some authors claim that, after having acquired absolute authority inside the Communist Party, President Xi "is aiming for a new regional order alternative to the Pax Americana" (Li 2017a: 24) in Asia: a "community of shared destiny" taking the form of a Sino-centric network of economic, political, cultural, and security relations (Callahan 2016: 226; Li 2017a: 24). At the same time, it is claimed that Chinese activities in Africa and other regions of the Global South described in the following chapters are "part of an attempt to enlarge [China's] global influence sphere more generally both from above and from below" (Röschenthaler and Socpa 2017: 183). The evolution and features of Beijing's relationship with the developing world are analyzed in the next section.

CHINA'S ENGAGEMENT WITH THE DEVELOPING WORLD

From Bandung to Present

It is generally admitted that communist China's relations with what was then called the Third World began with Prime Minister Zhou Enlai's participation in the 1955 Bandung conference. During the following decades, various anti-colonial political movements and guerilla groups were supported, armed, and trained by Beijing, which shared their aspirations for independence and for being able to choose freely their own economic and political path (Freeman 2015: 1). Chairman Mao Zedong believed that, due to similar historical experiences, China and developing countries "found it easier to understand each other and long had deep sympathy and concern for one another." Furthermore, as he adopted proletarian internationalism as a foreign policy principle, he saw the support for the struggle of oppressed nations as "a duty and an obligation" (Zhang 2015: 52). This engagement was rewarded by the political support of newly independent states that allowed mainland China to replace the government in Taipei as a member of the United Nations and of the UN Security Council in 1971 (Freeman 2015: 2). Eventually, this led to the recognition of the government in Beijing by numerous developing states. When "reform and opening up" were launched in 1978 by Deng Xiaoping, the emphasis of bilateral relations started to shift from anti-imperialism toward the shared objective of economic development. Prime Minister Zhao Ziyang's extensive visits to Global South states in the early 1980s were accompanied by the adoption and implementation of specific sets of principles on developing economic cooperation with African and Latin American countries, respectively (Zhang 2015: 57; see the sections *China in Africa* and *China in Latin America* of this chapter). They were conceived as the economic extension of China's famous Five Principles of Peaceful Coexistence which, even today, continue to represent a major pillar of Beijing's foreign policy. In fact, these principles were included by Jawaharlal Nehru, India's Prime Minister, and his Chinese counterpart, Zhou Enlai, in a 1954 bilateral treaty. One year later they were made famous by the Bandung Conference, which placed them among the ten principles of the newly created Non-Aligned Movement. They include (1) mutual respect for each other's territorial integrity and sovereignty; (2) mutual non-aggression; (3) mutual non-interference in each other's internal affairs; (4) equality and cooperation for mutual benefit; and (5) peaceful co-existence. The present Chinese official discourse promotes them as "peace principles" and presents them as an illustration of Beijing's positive contributions to international affairs (Panda 2014).

Yet, China's enthusiastic embrace of globalization made it increasingly dependent on Western technology, investment capital, and markets for its goods. For a time, this "magnetic force" pulled Beijing away from the developing countries; consequences included the reduction of the Chinese development assistance (Zhang 2015: 57–58). The problems associated with this trend became visible in an unexpected way. The 1989 Tiananmen massacre significantly damaged China's international prestige precisely at the time of Taiwan's successful democratization. In the Caribbean, Grenada and Belize switched their diplomatic recognition to Taipei (Li 2005: 81–82). However, most developing countries did not follow the West in condemning the repression. On the contrary, in the words of a Beijing University scholar, "they showed sympathy with China and expressed understanding of and voiced support for" its actions. They also "criticiz[ed] Western interference in

China's internal affairs" (Zhang 2015: 59). In fact, during the next 12 years, the draft resolutions of the UN Human Rights Council condemning China's non-respect of human rights were constantly rejected due to the opposition of Global South states. For Beijing, the lesson was clear: the developing world continued to represent a very useful political partner. On the economic side, the increasing need for raw materials and export markets also created conditions for a mutually beneficial renewed relationship. Once more, China started to perceive itself as a genuine developing country and to see the cooperation with similar states as central to its national priorities (Zhang 2015: 59). Accordingly, besides the intensification of relations at the bilateral level, various platforms were progressively created to enhance interactions with developing regions. They include, among others, the Forum on China-Africa Cooperation, the China-Caribbean Economic and Trade Cooperation Forum, the China-Pacific Island Countries Economic Development and Cooperation Forum, and the China-Community of Latin American and Caribbean States Forum. Moreover, under president Xi Jinping, the increasingly visible rivalry with the United States analyzed in Chapter 7 has further stimulated the Chinese interest and presence in geopolitically relevant Global South regions and states. To summarize, the historical evolution of China's relations with the developing world started during the 1950s with a strong emphasis on political objectives, moved toward an interest in mainly economic ties after 1978, and involves today both dimensions (Freeman 2015: 2, 6). Key features of this latter stage are analyzed in the following section.

China's South-South Solidarity Discourse and the "Beijing Consensus"

China's political messages to Global South partners are constantly marked by its self-identification as a developing country and by the emphasis on the promotion of peace and development throughout the developing world (Cypher and Wilson 2015: 16). A key dimension is the support for South-South cooperation, which the United Nations Office for South-South Cooperation defines as a broad framework for collaboration among developing countries in the political, economic, social, cultural, environmental, and technical domains. By sharing knowledge, skills, expertise, and resources, this manifestation of solidarity is intended to contribute to national well-being, national and collective self-reliance, and the attainment of internationally agreed development goals. Its guiding principles are the respect for national sovereignty, national ownership and independence, equality, non-conditionality, non-interference in domestic affairs, and mutual benefit (United Nations Office for South-South Cooperation 2017). As shown in the following sections, there is a heated debate between scholars and journalists who accept the Chinese win-win discourse as accurately reflecting Beijing's intentions and actions and those who, on the contrary, see behind it a darker neo-colonial reality. However, it is important to note that even if the first view is preferred, China's specific understanding and practice of South-South cooperation is in fact based on a pattern that was anathema to its traditional *tiersmondiste* promoters. Indeed, this is an approach driven by capitalism, global value chains, highly asymmetrical economic relations, and interdependence. In the case of the China-Africa relationship, for example, "South-South co-operation (. . .) has proven to be as challenging for African countries as relations with the North" (Wissenbach 2011: 22; see below the section *China in Africa*).

Beijing's emphasis on South-South cooperation is particularly relevant in the discussion of a key issue: China's ability to provide a valid model of development for Global South countries that would represent a true alternative to the Western one. It was noted that China itself developed through reforms and policies centered on economic relations with Western countries and on joining international institutions dominated by the West. This is fundamentally different from the South-South cooperation it promotes today in the developing world. Moreover, China is less active than India or Brazil as a leader of developing states. Many of its relations with such states are economic in nature and simply represent one of the many dimensions of its integration into the global economy. China is interested in Africa and Latin America for certain resources or market segments, but most of its imports—in terms of resources, components, and machinery—as well as exports focus on large industrialized economies and on the Asian region (Wissenbach 2011: 22). Critically, as explained later in this chapter, in practical terms China is responsible for the deindustrialization and reprimarization of certain developing states, mainly but not exclusively in Latin America (see the sections *China in Africa* and *China in Latin America* of this chapter); at times, it also adopts predatory practices such as debt traps (see the section *The Belt and Road Initiative* of this chapter). One might wonder if affected countries will prefer to take their inspiration from such a partner. Overall, China proposes to the South a path different from its own while its efforts to make it successful cannot be dissociated from a certain amount of ambiguity.

Still, the fact is that China does provide a developmental model for the Global South. Within the larger framework of "globalization with Chinese characteristics," its features are defined by the so-called "Beijing consensus" (Paladini 2011: 83). Despite its rejection by Chinese officials and scholars, this concept is representative of China's philosophy of development that is very different from that of the neoliberal "Washington Consensus."

Described as "a symbiotic or mutually reinforcing dynamic of state-led pragmatic nationalism" (le Pere 2015: 376), it is based on five principles: (1) an emphasis on incremental reform; (2) innovation and experimentation in promoting productivity and competitiveness; (3) export-led growth and promotion of high global demand for the country's manufactured goods; (4) state-driven regulation of market forces and a leading role for state-owned enterprises; and (5) an authoritarian approach to governance based on concentrated and centralized power (Williamson 2012: 6–7; le Pere 2015: 376). Their effective implementation is responsible for much of China's economic success. Yet, consequences also include a number of less fortunate aspects: depressed wages; heavy environmental degradation and pollution; sacrificing public welfare and social safety nets, especially for the rural population; "unrestrained and corrupt business practices that have little regard for social responsibility, labor, and environmental standards"; increasing social stratification; and reinforced authoritarianism (le Pere 2015: 376). Accordingly, some scholars claim that this developmental path actually leads to "naked greed, ruthless competition, hysterical consumerism and the commodification of human values" (Lin 2007: 12; le Pere 2015: 376).

In both cognitive and political terms, the South-South cooperation discourse and the creation of the "Beijing consensus" as a developmental model are important components of China's interaction with the Global South. At a factual level, this interaction obviously comprises many other dimensions. They are detailed later in this chapter with respect to Africa, Latin America, and the Caribbean, while the following chapters emphasize the issue of development assistance and its instrumentalization through conditionality. At this point, I will only mention the fact that a number of major contradictions were identified with respect to China's actions in the developing world. Mel Gurtov's list includes (1) "political impotence if not outright indifference": despite economic prowess, China's voice is weak or silent as it lacks political and strategic influence; (2) problems with leadership capacity and lack of alliances; (3) the incompatibility between China's economic security and some of its political interests; (4) the contradiction between the self-proclaimed principles of non-aggression and respect for other states' territorial integrity and Chinese belligerent actions related to territorial disputes with neighboring countries; and (5) the contrast between the idea of win-win cooperation and actual economic practices that led to "accusations of self-interested aggrandizement and unfairness" (Gurtov 2015: 80–83). Importantly, there is a major tension arising from China's strange position as a self-proclaimed developing country and, at the same time, as a highly industrialized global power in the process of becoming the world's largest economy. No matter the official discourse, the structural features and key interests of such a global power are not and cannot be completely different from those of similar Western actors. In turn, this is likely to prevent a genuinely harmonious relationship with the Global South.

Chinese Popular Perceptions of Global South Regions

It is hardly a secret that China is a dictatorship where foreign policy making is monopolized by the leadership of the Communist Party and, in recent years, by President Xi Jinping personally. However, it would be a mistake to believe that dictators can completely ignore the foreign policy preferences of their subjects. They are necessarily interested in preserving and enhancing the legitimacy of their regime, and as such they do not tend to uselessly antagonize the population by promoting unpopular external actions. Ultimately, the international actor is always the state-society complex, even if authoritarian regimes give a much more prominent role to the state dimension than democratic ones. Consequently, it is useful to explore the Chinese popular perception of various Global South regions in order to compare it with the official enthusiasm for South-South cooperation.

Simon Shen has published a very interesting analysis of this perception based on the scrutiny of Chinese online blogs and forums. His surprising findings "have disquieting implications for Beijing's approach to Africa and Latin America" (Freeman 2015: 7). The two regions are very differently perceived; more importantly, in both cases there are major "discrepancies from the images promoted by official propaganda" (Shen 2015: 115). Shockingly, the dominant opinion is that Africans are both economically and *spiritually* poor. While the Chinese workers are "industrious," their African counterparts are "lazy and inefficient at their workplaces." This idea is supported even by Chinese claiming that they have actually visited African countries. Strange arguments are used to explain the laziness: it is due "to the hot weather in Africa." Illegal African immigrants come to China because they want to stay in a "paradise forever." Racist and offensive statements are made in relation to various aspects, including sexual ones. Chinese women are warned to "beware of the Africans." During the 2008 Beijing Olympics, there were many comments such as "it seems that the darkest among [African competitors] are the most powerful" (Shen 2015: 115–116).

The perception of Latin Americans is even more negative, but of a different nature. It originates in Mao era anti-US propaganda that presented Latin American regimes as American protégés trying to contain China internationally on behalf of their imperialist masters (Shen 2015: 112). Other historical arguments are added: a probably apocryphal story is widely circulated about thousands of former Taiping rebels (1850–1863) being sold to Peru, badly mistreated, and finally joining the Chilean military to fight "Peruvian colonialists" in the War of the Pacific (1879–1884). Another one relates to the 300 Chinese immigrants killed ("massacred") in 1911 in Torreon, Mexico, and to a Chinese "gunboat" sent in response by the Qing court to the Mexican coastal area to put pressure on the authorities. In fact, Latin America is not always regarded as a Third World region. Rather, its situation is seen as closer to that of Europeans and North Americans, who perceived themselves as being superior and discriminated against the Chinese. At times, even official media in China presents Latin America as part of the West (Shen 2015: 116–117). Yet, "Latin Americanization" is a pejorative term harsher than "Africanization." The point is that in the past pro-imperialist and anti-Chinese Latin Americans performed relatively well in economic terms; but now their economic situation is disastrous, they experience high levels of corruption and social polarization, no security (Rio de Janeiro is the "most terrible city in the world"), and poor hygiene (thus the "Mexican flu"). Things are further worsened by "incapable dictatorships like that of Hugo Chavez." All this is due to the fact that, unlike China, Latin America has not found a way to develop and therefore cannot resist American capitalist exploitation (Shen 2015: 119–120). However, it is precisely the US influence in Latin America that makes the latter interesting to Chinese netizens. Present rivalry and possible future Cold War compel China to "unite" with the "strategic zones" of Latin America and the Middle East in order to isolate Washington and to secure energy resources. Therefore, Latin Americans have to be engaged to "light a fire in the US's backyard" (Shen 2015: 124). As shown in Chapter 7, this might well be the long-term plan of President Xi Jinping at least for the Caribbean, if not for all of Latin America. Yet, for the time being, he remains firmly committed to the win-win cooperation discourse and is far from openly embracing any of his countrymen's radical ideas.

While I am not aware of any study of the Chinese perception of the Caribbean, a Trinidadian respondent complained that the Chinese take "a lengthy amount of time to make a decision" on investments. More specifically, one needs to "have their viewpoint changed about what Trinidad and Tobago is about, they assume it is a little backward island" (Respondent 1). Chinese IR scholars also do not seem to have a high opinion of the region, even if this is related to its political and diplomatic potential: "the Caribbean countries are small and have little influence and a limited role in the international pattern [*sic*]" (Hongbo 2017: 307). However, this is hardly enough for any generalization.

What can be turned into a general conclusion is that Chinese netizens and, by extension, Chinese citizens do not tend to share convictions compatible with Beijing's official discourse on solidarity and harmony between their country and developing states in Africa and Latin America.

CHINA VS. TAIWAN

Long before reforms and globalization brought Chinese firms and migrants to the most remote places on Earth, the government in Beijing assiduously sought the interested friendship of Global South states, including that of tiny Caribbean or South Pacific islands. The reason is simple: the "diplomatic duel" for international recognition with the anti-communist government in Taiwan. This is a well-known topic that I analyzed elsewhere (Tudoroiu 2017). I nevertheless have to briefly present it here because it continues to represent one of the reasons for Beijing's interest in the Caribbean.

In 1949, the communists won the civil war and took control of China. The defeated Kuomintang and its leader Chiang Kai-shek as well as two million mainlanders took refuge in the island of Taiwan. Ever since, the governments in Beijing and Taipei have been perceived as rivals engaged in an intra-state struggle for the control of all China. Today, this is pure political fiction. Nobody seriously believes that Taiwan represents the government-in-waiting of all China (Tudoroiu 2017: 194). Moreover, a decades-long process has been at work that led to the development of a genuinely Taiwanese national identity: a "New Taiwan" has emerged "as a state separate from that controlled by the government in Beijing" (Atkinson 2010: 410). "Mainlanders" represent only 13 percent of the population, as opposed the local Hoklo (73 percent) and Hakka (12 percent) groups (Brown 2010: 461). Chiang Kai-shek's Chinese-based ideology was increasingly challenged by political opposition, a process accelerated by the democratization initiated in 1986. After the 1992 election an "irresistible trend toward a Taiwanese Renaissance emerged" (Chen 2012: 845). When the 2000 presidential election brought to power Chen Shui-bian, the leader of the opposition Democratic Progressive Party (a first in China's entire history), a series of "de-Sinification" processes in education, culture, and other fields were launched as parts of a "self-conscious nation-building project" (Li 2014: 132–133). There were also a number of attempts to promote *de jure* independence (Chen 2012: 870). This trend was modified during the 2008–2016 tenure of Ma Ying-jeou of the Kuomintang, but widespread dissatisfaction with his pro-Beijing policies led to the election of Tsai Ing-wen of the pro-independence Democratic Progressive Party in January 2016. Critically, there is an identity shift illustrated by the fact that in 1992 17.6 percent of the island's inhabitants described themselves as Taiwanese and 25.5 as Chinese. In 2011, the figures were 54.2 and 4.1, respectively (Li 2014: 119, 133). This is mainly due to the different social experiences of the Taiwanese—who, for more than one generation, have lived under democracy—and of the authoritarian-ruled mainlanders. The former fear that unification would endanger their political liberties (Chen 2012:

850–851), a scenario that seems to be confirmed by recent developments in Hong Kong. Logically, the formal proclamation of independence should be Taiwan's natural choice. Yet, China believes otherwise and is ready to go to great lengths to impose its views. To Beijing, the island is a rebel province that should return under its control as Hong Kong and Macao did. Military intimidation was used, most recently during the 1995 and 1996 Taiwan missile crises. As this proved ineffective among the Taiwanese (Li 2014: 128; Chen 2012: 853), softer economic means have been employed. But China insists on the respect of the "1992 consensus" on the existence of "one China," even if the two sides understand it differently. If the "hallucination of independence" is turned into reality, Beijing clearly stated that it would respond militarily (*The Economist*, January 23, 2016). Moreover, this was turned into law: the use of "non-peaceful means" if independence is proclaimed is mentioned in the Chinese 2005 Anti-Secession Law (Esteban 2007: 26). All Taiwanese take these threats very seriously, which makes most of them adopt a "maintain status quo, decide at later date" approach with regard to independence (Li 2014: 134, 142).

This prevents both Taiwan and China from escaping the trap of the "duel" for international recognition. In 1963, 66 states recognized the former—that is, recognized its regime as the legitimate representative of all China—as opposed to 50 that sided with the latter. In 1975 the numbers had shifted to 26 versus 112 (Hu 2015: 5), with consequences that included Beijing replacing Taipei as a permanent member of the UN Security Council. Today, only 15 "diplomatic allies" continue to recognize Taiwan. However, this was hardly a linear process. There were new Global South states that, upon independence, recognized Taiwan, such as St. Vincent and the Grenadines in 1981 or St. Kitts and Nevis in 1983. As already mentioned, after the Tiananmen massacre Grenada, Belize, and—one year later—Nicaragua shifted allegiance from Beijing to Taiwan. The term "flip-flop allegiance" was coined to describe "swing states" such as Saint Lucia that changed sides twice (from Taiwan to China in 1997 and back to Taiwan in 2007) or, in the remarkable case of the Central African Republic, no less than six times (Mendelson Forman and Moreira 2008: 4; Li 2005: 88; Hu 2015: 18). There was even a 2008–2016 "diplomatic truce" during the tenure of the pro-Beijing Taiwanese President Ma Ying-jeou (Tudoroiu 2017: 206). Most of the "swing states" and of Taiwan's remaining supporters are underdeveloped, poor, heavily indebted, and frequently small Global South states in need of foreign aid (Li 2005: 88) located mainly in the Caribbean Basin and in the South Pacific. Accordingly, generous packages of development assistance were instrumental in directing their diplomatic recognition to Taipei or Beijing. Before the "diplomatic truce," Taiwan's aid programs included technical assistance, human resource development, banking and finance, overseas volunteers, and mobile medical services for a total of approximately $500 million annually, which turned it into one of the most important donors among the newly industrialized states and the emerging economies (Chien et al. 2010: 1184, 1190). It also provided humanitarian assistance in case of natural disasters and refugee crises and created a $250 million fund to facilitate Taiwanese investment in "allied" countries (Mendelson Forman and Moreira 2008: 2; Hu 2015: 12). For Caribbean states such as St. Kitts and Nevis or St. Vincent and the Grenadines it became the largest single aid donor (Li 2005: 88). Symmetrically, most of China's $1.5–2 billion annual foreign aid served the objective of diplomatic recognition (Atkinson 2010: 408).

This phenomenon had two important consequences for Beijing's interactions with the Global South. On the one hand, it helped China understand the effectiveness of "chequebook diplomacy." To quote a Beijing author, "China should soften and break those links which hinder the realization of its national interests through different methods of assistance" (Hongbo 2017: 323). This is an excellent depiction of the line of reasoning that led to the setting up of conditionalities analyzed in this book. It started many decades ago as a relatively modest "duel" with Taipei. Even in 1992, the ratio between the GDP of China and that of Taiwan was only 1.9, which did not allow for very many recognition-unrelated Chinese actions in the developing world. But in 2014, the same ratio had increased to almost 20 (*The Economist*, March 26, 2016). This allowed Beijing to considerably expand its development assistance (see Chapter 5) as well as the range of its objectives. The know-how acquired in Taipei-hostile deals with micro-states like Saint Lucia was successfully used on a large scale to secure access to raw materials and energy resources all over the Global South.

On the other hand, however, actual or potential "swing states" also learned how to take advantage of China's prosperity and of the fact that, despite the huge diversification of its external interests and activities, it continues to be trapped in the "diplomatic duel." "Rather than being passive victims of the China-Taiwan rivalry, [these countries] are active participants in the process" (Atkinson 2010: 408). They have adopted smart tactics in exploiting the two rivals that illustrate the opportunistic behavior which, as explained in the section *Small States* of Chapter 2, represents a component of small state resilience. Selling (or, in fact, renting) very expensively their diplomatic recognition to the most generous of the two donors (Atkinson 2010: 411) ultimately became very frustrating for both China and Taipei, which in part explains their 2006–2016 "diplomatic truce" (Hu 2015: 9; Atkinson 2010: 407). Yet, after the election of a Beijing-unfriendly President in Taiwan, China preferred to renew the costly competition. One of the possible reasons might be that, in regions relevant to the "duel" such as the Caribbean, the Chinese have been using their recognition-related development assistance as a starting point for the much more ambitious project of international socialization analyzed in this book.

THE BELT AND ROAD INITIATIVE

The Belt and Road Initiative represents the most visible element of President Xi Jinping's assertive foreign policy in the developing world. The "Silk Road Economic Belt" was first mentioned by the then new President at the September 2013 summit of the Shanghai Cooperation Organization in Kazakhstan. In October, he added the "twenty-first century maritime Silk Road." After discussions through 2014, the "Vision and Actions on Jointly Building Silk Road Economic Belt and Twenty-First Century Maritime Silk Road" was released in March 2015 (Summers 2018: 25) by the National Development and Reform Commission, the Ministry of Foreign Affairs, and the Ministry of Commerce, with State Council authorization. Predictably, the new initiative was described as "a win-win cooperation that promotes common development and prosperity, peace, and friendship by enhancing mutual understanding and trust, and strengthening all-round exchanges" (Lahtinen 2018: 24). At a more practical level, it consists mainly in the "construction of a system of roads, railways, oil and natural gas pipelines, fiber-optic and communication systems, ports, and airports" (Lairson 2018: 40). Its goals are (1) to create new forms of connectedness in concerned regions, resulting in (2) greater interdependence and enhanced growth for involved states; (3) to greatly enhance the stature of the Chinese economic model; (4) to increase China's soft power; (5) to reignite Chinese economic growth by using the present surplus of capital and overcapacity in construction-related heavy industries; and (6) to develop Chinese regions (Lairson 2018: 40–41; Summers 2018: 24). Implementation is based on already existing mechanisms associated with multilateral institutions but also with bilateral cooperation (for more details see Summers 2018: 32). It is clear that connectedness is at the center of the Chinese initiative (Lairson 2018: 40). In terms of spatial structures, it is through the nodes of a network of major urban clusters that capital flows will be directed. This network is so important in the architecture of BRI that the latter has actually been described as "a state-led infrastructure-heavy spatial fix to facilitate the development of networks of capital across the Eurasian continent" and beyond (Summers 2018: 28–29, 34). This might push the present shifts in the power relations of global political economy "further or faster in the direction of China, while incorporating more rapidly into the global economy areas which had previously been peripheral" (Summers 2018: 34). Countries located in such areas will certainly profit, but Beijing's ultimate goal is "to develop alternative and countervailing institutions and systems that create *structural power* linked to Chinese resources and capabilities" (Lairson 2018: 41; emphasis added).

This latter aspect has led to the emergence of a debate between two groups of scholars and practitioners. Those interested in business and investment argue that BRI is mainly a response to Chinese domestic economic challenges (especially in terms of industrial overcapacity) and a way to help Chinese companies access new markets. International Relations and International Security authors and analysts do not deny the importance of such economic objectives, but nevertheless see the initiative as mainly a geopolitical and diplomatic offensive (see Summers 2018: 24). Frequently, the comparison is made with the Marshall Plan, whose economic nature did not diminish its key role in the construction of the post–WWII US-centered global order (Lairson 2018: 43). Numerous Chinese scholars and officials reject this comparison as they define China not as a challenger but as "a participant in and contributor to the existing order" (Summers 2018: 33). Yet, BRI promotes the *status quo* only in terms of perpetuating the existing structures of global political economy. In terms of the power relations within these structures, its objective is clearly related to change (Summers 2018: 34). The ability to develop large-scale systems of economic interdependence and growth is indeed synonymous with structural power as it creates major public goods-like resources that influence the choices of actors in concerned regions. There already are large numbers of states and firms that have expressed their strong interest in becoming recipients of BRI projects. Furthermore, companies from outside the regions targeted by the Chinese initiative adapt their capabilities and products to win construction contracts. This shows that "there is a wellspring of structural power to be created and tapped by China" (Lairson 2018: 40, 43). BRI-related efforts to supply capital, to define and implement a system providing mutual growth, and to potentially set up the rules, norms, and institutions of such a system suggest that China is simply copying the arrangements used in the past by the United States to promote their structural power (Lairson 2018: 40–41). Accordingly, "should the BRI system achieve even some degree of success, China's regional and global position will be vastly enhanced" (Lairson 2018: 42; Wong 2016).

However, success is not certain despite the huge financial means made available by Beijing. On the one hand, some authors question China's capacity for achieving such a vast project. Many partner states have significant capability deficits that prevent them from adequately contributing to its implementation. China itself has a record of poor projects choices coupled with loan defaults in its similar African and Asian efforts. In particular, as shown in the following chapters, there has been "considerable hostility due to the inability to organize sufficient mutual gains" (Lairson 2018: 45). On the other hand and no less importantly, there is an expanding soft balancing arrangement of resistance to Chinese expansion orchestrated over the past decade by the United States and, more recently, by India. As shown in Chapter 7, President Obama's "pivot to Asia" and President Trump's trade wars pertain to this line of action that Vietnam, Japan, Australia, and other states in the region tend to support. BRI might face the coordinated and systematic opposition of a powerful coalition, and "it is far from clear that China can manage such a large and difficult task" (Lairson 2018: 49).

BRI and the Debt Trap

A good example of developments that BRI might stimulate with highly detrimental consequences for both the partners' socio-economic situation and China's image is represented by the issue of indebtedness. Loans—and especially loans related to large infrastructure projects—are one of the most frequently used Chinese instruments in much of the Global South. BRI's emphasis on such projects will considerably increase the number and value of Beijing's loans to developing countries. For economies already suffering from crippling debt burdens, this brings in the danger of serious financial troubles. IMF head Christine Lagarde explicitly warned the Chinese government on this issue, noting that the careful management of financing terms would protect both China and its partners from serious difficulties (Oosterveld et al. 2018: 23). The problem is that certain actions of the government in Beijing suggest that it might not always perceive its partners' indebtedness as negative, a situation—or, rather, a strategy—that has been labeled the "debt trap." China's disinterest in promoting good governance is hardly a secret (see Chapter 5). But in certain cases, basic common sense should prevent it from disbursing money that is absurdly spent. To give a recent example, during the 16 months that followed China's June 2017 diplomatic recognition by Panama, the latter initiated "an array of projects that defy economic rationale" (Ellis 2018). They include a $5.5 billion railway to be built by Chinese companies and paid for by the local government that makes no economic sense; and a port for cruise ships on the Pacific side of the canal (to be built by China Harbor and paid for by the same Panamanian government) whose economic rationale is very questionable as there are no significant cruise ship destinations on the Pacific side of the continent. These "mystery projects" will end up by pushing the country into a desperate financial situation (Ellis 2018).

The similar example of Sri Lanka—a key participant in BRI—provides a grim explanation. Equally irresponsible financial policies of former President Mahinda Rajapaksa were complemented by identical Chinese largesse. The bilateral relationship started in 2007, led to numerous high-profile construction projects financed by Chinese loans, and ultimately resulted in the Sri Lanka government's debt reaching 77.6 percent of the GDP in 2017, with an annual budget deficit of 5.5 percent. The same China Harbor Engineering Company that is now constructing the useless port in Panama built the Hambantota Port Development Project in Sri Lanka for $1.5 billion (Mourdoukoutas 2018). Upon completion, the port drew only 34 ships in 2012 (Abi-Habib 2018). Unable to service the debt, the government in Colombo had to hand over economic control of the Hambantota port and of 15,000 acres of land around it for 99 years to China Merchants Port Holdings in exchange for $1.12 billion used to reduce its debt to China (Mourdoukoutas 2018). This gave Beijing a strategic foothold along a critical commercial and military waterway, and a few hundred miles off the shores of India; not a bad return for an apparently counterproductive approach. Concerns related to the geopolitical instrumentalization of the Chinese debt trap were complemented by those associated with fueling corruption and autocratic behavior in a struggling democracy. It was revealed that during the 2015 Sri Lankan elections, which President Rajapaksa lost, his associates and campaign aides received at least two payments of $7.6 and $3.7 million from China Harbor, which hoped to preserve the fruitful relationship with Sri Lanka's executive (Abi-Habib 2018). Yet, not everybody in Colombo takes such things negatively. In February 2018, Dr. Palitha Kohona, a former Ambassador and Permanent Representative of Sri Lanka to the United Nations, stated emphatically that BRI "provides Sri Lanka with a unique opportunity to fast track its economy along the path to development." An "investment bonanza" is made available by China, and the Maritime Silk Road "could revive the glory days of the ancient Silk Route for Sri Lanka" (Kohona 2018). This suggests that, despite recent scandals and the still important level of foreign debt, in Sri Lanka—as in Panama—new loans from the Chinese benefactors might be on their way. In turn, this illustrates the perfect fit between Beijing's expansionist interests in the Global South and the responsiveness of self-interested, cynical, and short-sighted local political elites. While, in the long term, this might seriously endanger the success of the BRI initiative, it certainly provides a strong basis for China's socialization of such elites and, as long as debt traps are not used too outrageously, of their entire state-society complexes.

BRI in Latin America and the Caribbean

The aforementioned prospect of US negative reactions initially made Beijing reluctant to invite Latin American and Caribbean states to join BRI (*The*

Economist, February 1, 2018). Yet, by 2017, against a background of growing Sino-American tensions, Chinese diplomats started to refer to the region as a "natural extension" and an "indispensable participant" in the initiative (Barrios 2018). The enthusiasm created locally by this opening is well illustrated by Jamaica's Prime Minister, Andrew Holness, who called BRI a "noble expression" that promoted cooperation and inclusiveness across the developing world and expressed his country's vivid interest in formally joining it (Ward 2017: 14). The January 2018 "Special Declaration on the Belt and Road" signed during the Second China-CELAC Ministerial Forum provided an open invitation to the entire region to join the initiative. Individual states started to be formally incorporated into BRI through bilateral "Belt and Road Cooperation Agreements" (Barrios 2018). The first to sign was Panama, followed by Trinidad and Tobago, Antigua and Barbuda, and Bolivia. It is true that, for the time being, there are no visible consequences other than the retroactive BRI rebranding of older Chinese projects. But Beijing's opening "confirms China's desire to gradually incorporate the region into its colossal enterprise" (Barrios 2018), a situation that cannot fail to trigger major economic and, in the longer term, geopolitical consequences. In the Caribbean, this will certainly translate into the further enhancement of the process of international socialization presented in this book. At the same time, however, it might also lead to American concern and, perhaps, counteractions as explained in Chapter 7.

China's relationships with Latin America and the Caribbean are presented in more detail later in this chapter. First, however, the involvement in Africa is scrutinized as it represents the most important, the most innovative, and the most criticized of China's Global South actions.

CHINA IN AFRICA

Some scholars go as far as claiming that China in Africa—and, more specifically, the impact of its investments there—"has become one of the most central questions in international relations and international political economy" (Ziso 2018: 1). It is, in any case, one of "the most fashionable topics for researchers of many nationalities" (Shen 2015: 109); and, very probably, it will indeed "determine Africa's future for the next fifty years" (French 2014: 8). China has been successful in Africa due to an approach first experimented there and eventually used in other regions. Its features include (1) stretching commerce and investments by adding aid and finance; (2) the willingness to work with any state, including brutal dictatorships; (3) the adoption of a lowest-cost bidding strategy; (4) lavishing diplomatic attention toward its partners; (4) involvement in prestige projects that local political elites use for electoral and broader legitimating purposes; and (5) development assistance (Lahtinen 2018: 84). Opinion polls in 36 African countries show that, on average, the most important factors that give China a positive image are its infrastructure/development actions (32 percent), the low cost of its products (23 percent), and its business investments (16 percent) (Lahtinen 2018: 47; Lekorwe et al. 2016). It should also be mentioned that, at least in the opinion of many Chinese scholars, forging strategic partnerships with the Africans is part of "a diplomatic battle with status quo powers, notably the US" (Shen 2015: 110). In other words, there is a certain degree of continuity with Beijing's Cold War anti-imperialist actions on the continent (Shen 2015: 113).

The Evolution of Chinese-African Relations

Communist China's relations with Africa started, as those with the rest of the developing world, at the 1955 Bandung conference. That event was followed by the progressive establishment of diplomatic relations (Li 2017a: 76) and placed the continent "prominently and strategically" on Beijing's Third World-related agenda (le Pere 2015: 361). During the Cold War, China supported the anti-colonial struggle but also tried to deprive the Soviet Union of its leadership of the international communist movement. Accordingly, it criticized both Washington's and Moscow's relationships with African leaders (Mohan et al. 2014: 56). Under Chairman Mao, thousands of Chinese engineers, doctors, and technicians were sent to the newly independent African states and a number of infrastructure projects were financed and built there (Lahtinen 2018: 37–38) such as the famous TanZam railway between Zambia and the Tanzanian port of Dar es Salaam. After 1976, bilateral relations were visibly scaled down, as "most of the political and economic investments made by China in Africa proved to be of doubtful value" (Shen 2015: 8, 113). This "retreat from Africa" (Stahl 2018: 8) was due to and accompanied by a clear orientation toward purely economic objectives. During his December 1982–January 1983 visit to 11 African countries, Prime Minister Zhao Ziyang made public Beijing's four principles on developing economic cooperation with the continent: (1) equality and mutual benefit; (2) a stress on practical results; (3) diversity in form; and (4) the attainment of common progress (Zhang 2015: 57). A new and increasingly strong relationship emerged after the adoption in the late 1990s of China's "Go out" or "Going Global" strategy intended to provide new international market and investment opportunities (Stahl 2018: 8–9). The "re-entry into Africa" was symbolically represented by President Jiang Zemin May's 1996 visit, during which he presented a Five-Point Proposal for Sino-African relations based on reliable friendship, sovereign equality, non-intervention, mutually beneficial development, and international cooperation (Shen 2015: 113). The economic exchanges soon reached impressive levels. China proclaimed 2006 the "Year of Africa" (Stahl 2018: 8). In 2012 it became Africa's largest trading partner, surpassing the United States and Europe. Shortly after his inauguration as president, Xi Jinping made his first overseas visit to Africa in March 2013 (Lahtinen 2018: 1, 37). It is claimed that no less than one million Chinese currently live and work on the continent (French 2014; Mohan et al. 2014: 2).

The "main institutional platform and operational vehicle for shaping and managing China's cooperation framework" is represented by the Forum on China-Africa Cooperation (FOCAC) established in 2000 (le Pere 2015: 369). Its promotion of multilevel cooperation is based on the mechanism of ministerial conferences held every three years that bring together ministers of foreign affairs, international cooperation, and financial and economic affairs. However, major developments are normally announced at the summits of heads of state and government (Stahl 2018: 11). The first such summit took place in Beijing in November 2006 and led to the establishment of a Chinese-African "strategic partnership (. . .) featuring political equality and mutual trust, economic win-win cooperation and cultural exchanges" (Lahtinen 2018: 20). In January 2006 the first Policy Paper on China's Africa Policy was published to promote increased transparency in response to international criticism of China's engagement in Africa (Stahl 2018: 12). The document laid out the fundamental principles of sincerity, friendship, and equality; mutual benefit, reciprocity, and common prosperity; mutual support and close coordination; and mutual learning and common paths of development (Dent 2011: 7). A second Policy Paper on Africa was released in 2015 at the second FOCAC summit held in Johannesburg under the theme "Africa-China Progressing Together: Win-Win Cooperation for Common Development" (Lahtinen 2018: 21). This updated document was primarily directed toward African stakeholders and drew on the lessons learned over the previous 15 years (Stahl 2018: 12). In particular, it promised to help Africa overcome the bottlenecks of infrastructure and human resource development (Lahtinen 2018: 20). It also shifted the emphasis of the cooperation on security issues to non-traditional security threats such as piracy and terrorism (Stahl 2018: 12; see below).

Africans' very positive response to these manifestations of Chinese interest was significantly stimulated by the associated financial dimension. At successive FOCAC meetings, Beijing's pledges reached $5 billion in 2006, $10 billion in 2009, $20 billion in 2012, and $60 billion in 2015, which included $5 billion for grants and zero-interest loans as well as $35 billion for concessional loans and buyer's credit. Also in 2015, ten cooperation plans were announced for the following three years covering industrialization, agricultural modernization, infrastructure, financial services, green development, trade and investment facilitation, poverty reduction and public welfare, public health, people-to-people exchanges, and peace and security (Lahtinen 2018: 21). Of course, there are good reasons for this generosity: it stems from and ensures the further development of the highly successful Chinese economic activities on the continent presented in the next section.

Chinese Interests, Actors, and Patterns of Action in Africa

China's multifaceted involvement in Africa includes trade, aid, debt cancellation, development financing, investment, and other activities (Ziso 2018: 7). Its impressive dynamic is due to (1) the Chinese drive for natural resources, new markets, investment opportunities, and security; (2) symbolic diplomacy and development cooperation, which makes frequent use of high-profile infrastructure projects; and (3) forging strategic partnerships intended to deprive Taiwan of diplomatic recognition, to counter American hegemony, and to turn African states into "vital partners in China's global ambitions" (which, in practical terms, includes voting at the United Nations and other international organizations) (Mohan et al. 2014: 54–55). On the Chinese side, various actors are involved: diplomats and political officials, bureaucratic agencies, state-owned enterprises, individual workers, and private entrepreneurs. While the development of Chinese-African relations has been based on a country-by-country approach, there is a clear common pattern of action. First, officials of the government in Beijing conclude a deal with their local counterparts for, mainly, access to natural resources and consumer markets in exchange for China's diplomatic support, aid, assistance, favorable trade deals, and high-prestige infrastructure projects. Then, Chinese state-owned enterprises enter the scene. They complete the infrastructure projects using Chinese equipment and material as well as Chinese and local laborers. Both high and low skill Chinese workers are brought as they are paid lower wages than those demanded by local employees. This makes Chinese firms afford extremely low bids and outmaneuver foreign rivals. If needed, they even offer unprofitably low bids subsidized with Chinese state funds and for a time operate at a loss in order to eliminate competition (Hess and Aidoo 2015: 8–9, 137). In 2014, there were major Chinese infrastructure projects in 35 African states. Most of them were funded by loans provided by China's state-owned ExIm Bank at "marginally concessional" rates (Mohan et al. 2014: 58), which represents a further—and, frequently, decisive—advantage over Western competitors. Finally, when the Chinese political and economic presence is established, a new and very visible wave of independent actors—entrepreneurs, farmers, and laborers—arrive, either through informal personal networks or as contracted workers who do not return to China at the end of their contracts (Hess and Aidoo 2015: 137). Two thousand Chinese companies are investing in Africa and as many as one million Chinese nationals live there. Many of the latter have set up small firms that are ignored by official statistics but are representative for China's role in what has been called "globalization from below" or "low-end globalization" (Mohan et al. 2014: 2).

In this context, development assistance plays a central role. Beijing claims that more than half of its foreign aid is directed to 51 African countries. The 2014 White Paper on China's Foreign Aid mentions no less than eight forms of development assistance: turnkey projects, goods and materials, technical cooperation, human resource development cooperation, medical teams, emergency humanitarian aid, overseas volunteer programs, and debt relief. Financially, three categories of aid are identified: grants, interest-free loans, and concessional loans. The Chinese are very secretive and release few details about the amounts related to their development assistance. However, AidData calculated that between 2000 and 2013 China provided $31.5 billion of aid to Africa, in comparison to $92.7 billion disbursed by the US. Like Western donors, Beijing has a vast portfolio of aid investments in agriculture, education, and health. Yet, its focus is clearly on infrastructure projects (roads, ports, railways, refineries, and electrical grids) financed by preferential loans (Lahtinen 2018: 38).

Perhaps surprisingly, Chinese Foreign Direct Investment to Africa is quite limited. Between 2003 and 2012 it increased by only 47.8 percent, reaching no more than $3.5 billion in 2013. Most of it is related to oil, minerals, and large infrastructure projects in construction, mining, and chemicals. On the contrary, trade has experienced an impressive boost. Bilateral exchanges rose from $8 billion at the end of the 1990s to $86 billion in 2008, to $210 billion in 2013, and to $300 billion in 2015 (Lahtinen 2018: 40–41). China exports mainly cheap manufactured goods and imports natural resources. Overall, many of its interactions with Africa are associated with the so-called "infrastructure-for-resources deals." The main Chinese objective within this business-oriented cooperation is to secure a growing inflow of Sub-Saharan Africa's natural resources in exchange for is generous development assistance (Stahl 2018: 14).

However, the complexity and dimensions of these economic interactions made the Chinese-African cooperation spill over to other, sometimes unexpected fields. Perhaps the most interesting case is that of security.

China's African Security Involvement

Initially, the Chinese involvement in Africa was "decidedly non-interventionist in its pursuit of economic interests" (Alden and Barber 2018: 2). Yet, some of its inbuilt features made the development of political and security dimensions inevitable. Unlike the West, China chose to exploit economic opportunities in conflict-ridden, post-conflict, and fragile African states while providing support for dictators such as Omar al-Bashir in Sudan or Robert Mugabe in Zimbabwe. Its numerous citizens who settled in African countries became exposed to violence and crime. In recent years, President Xi Jinping's assertive foreign policy added "pressures to demonstrate greater global activism" to the already growing exposure to "the vagaries of African politics" (Alden and Barber 2018: 1). Three types of risk have to be faced: reputational ones, related to the association with disreputable African governments; risks to business interests due to mercurial local leaders and weak regulatory regimes; and risks faced by its citizens located in politically unstable environments. This resulted in the gradual Chinese involvement in African security (Alden and Barber 2018: 1–2) illustrated by the introduction of security cooperation in the 2006 first Policy Paper on Africa and by its development in the updated 2015 document (Stahl 2018: 12). In 2012, the China-Africa Cooperative Partnership for Peace and Security was announced while the integration of security into the FOCAC process was promised. Beijing contributed to the setting up of peace support missions both within the UN Security Council and by enhancing its cooperation with the African Union (Alden and Barber 2018: 2). To facilitate this task, a specific Chinese diplomatic mission to the African Union has been recently established in Addis Ababa. In 2016, when Ambassador Xu Jinghu replaced Ambassador Zhong Jianhua as Special Representative of the Chinese Government on African Affairs, she insisted on Beijing's commitment to fostering peace on the continent (Stahl 2018: 12). Indeed, by 2017 more than 2,500 Chinese troops, police, and military experts had taken part in six UN peacekeeping missions in Africa (in Darfur, the Democratic Republic of the Congo, Mali, South Sudan, and, in smaller numbers, in the Ivory Coast and Western Sahara) (Lahtinen 2018: 27). China has also increased its financial assistance for such missions (Alden and Barber 2018: 1).

However, it is not certain that the Chinese government is willing to fully incorporate its participation into an institutionalized multilateral form of involvement. On the one hand, it is not clear what the consequences might be for its established interests in Africa. On the other, there is "an underlying ambivalence towards some of the normative dimensions integrated into the African Peace and Security Architecture" (Alden and Barber 2018: 2). This is why Beijing is also acting unilaterally. Most notably, it established its first overseas military base in Djibouti (close to the French, American, and Japanese ones) (Stahl 2018: 12; Lahtinen 2018: 28). Its involvement in Sudan is even more relevant. Chinese oil companies took over the southern petroleum fields and supplied oil to China during the civil war. The oil revenue was used by the government in Khartoum to buy more than $55 million worth of small arms from China between 2003 and 2006. When South Sudan became independent, Beijing hurried to establish diplomatic relations in order to protect its oil-related interests. The beginning of the South Sudanese civil war in December 2013 threatened investments and the lives of Chinese citizens. In response, China took a more proactive role. It joined Western diplomats and African mediators and participated actively in the peace negotiations that began in January 2014. Overall, while officially Beijing continues to insist on its non-interference policy, it can be concluded that the Chinese non-intervention approach has come to an end (Lahtinen 2018: 27, 29). At a rhetorical level, South-South cooperation continues to be promoted; but in practical terms, China has become a more "normal" great power engaged in protecting its multiple interests in Africa. This can only intensify the heated debate concerning the actual consequences of the Chinese-African relationship.

China in Africa: The Optimistic View

An impressive volume of literature is associated with the "China good vs. China bad" debate in relation to Beijing's African enterprise. This is illustrative of the prominence of China's involvement in this continent as part of its wider Global South expansion. Two schools have emerged that do share two convictions: that the Chinese presence is a decisive factor for the future of Africa; and that there is an asymmetrical power dynamic, which has made the continent's states unable to manage or, at best, allowed them to respond only passively to China's impressive engagement (Lam 2017: 1). However, skeptics emphasize exploitative aspects; optimists highlight opportunities provided by China (Hess and Aidoo 2015: xvi). This is to say that the dispute opposes views of neocolonialism versus South-South cooperation, of detrimental importation of Chinese labor versus skills transfer, and of promoting poor governance versus non-interference in the domestic affairs of sovereign states (Mohan et al. 2014: 1). China is depicted as either a predatory dragon or a friendly panda.

To start with the pro-panda optimists, they "celebrate" China's re-entry into Africa that promotes a "new-type strategic partnership" featuring cooperation in multiple fields, from which "Africa stands to gain much" (Ziso 2018: 10): "China is the hope for Africa's development" (Lam 2017: 1). Indeed, Chinese development assistance, investment, and demand for African exports "will stimulate further growth and development" (Hess and Aidoo 2015: 133). China is already helping the continent's economies "to boost their capacity and capability after years of redundancy" (Ziso 2018: 11; Wenping 2007).

Socio-economic development is on its way: the cost of living has diminished and Africans' purchasing power has increased due to cheaper Chinese manufactured goods. Respondents all over the continent note proudly that there are almost no more children going barefoot to school. Middle-class consumers have been even bigger winners. The continent benefits from Chinese-built low-cost infrastructure projects. Moreover, all this shows "the potential of a China model in African states" (Hess and Aidoo 2015: 12, 13, 133). The associated "Beijing Consensus" does not impose onerous conditions and can ensure the industrialization of the Global South more effectively than its Western counterpart (Sautman and Hairong 2007: 81; Ziso 2018: 11). This alternative development paradigm based on a more assertive role for the state and on the rejection of neoliberal policies promoted by multilateral institutions is "more suited to African needs and dreams" (Ziso 2018: 1, 198). Critically, China helps Africa to achieve freedom from Western hegemony (Konings 2007: 341; Ziso 2018: 198). The narrative of Chinese neo-colonialism in Africa is rejected as inaccurate and ideologically biased. Chinese economic actions are fully legitimate due to the "consent between Chinese agencies and national and regional bureaucracies and local populations in Africa" (Li 2017a: 32–33). Through its cooperation with various states, including pariah regimes, "the Chinese government has demonstrated that it can quite happily work with any political and social environment it finds itself in" (Alden 2008: 355–356; le Pere 2015: 361). Its business-is-business, noninterference approach to development assistance involves no conditionality (Hess and Aidoo 2015: 133); furthermore, it has the merit of allowing African states to choose from different offers, to reject alternatives that are too intrusive, to avoid the bureaucracy of Western donors, and to finance large infrastructure investments even if they are short of capital or affected by political and economic instability. Last but not least, paying for African imports with packages that include finance, infrastructure investment, and turn-key aid projects prevents corruption as such packages cannot "easily be transferred to Swiss bank accounts" (Wissenbach 2011: 24). Overall, China's win-win, South-South cooperation with Africa is fundamentally different from Western self-interested practices and is already in the process of bringing development and prosperity to the entire continent.

China in Africa: The Pessimistic View

The rival school provides the very different picture of China-the-predatory-dragon, whose new form of imperialism—based on resource expansionism—only reinforces Africa's exploitation and underdevelopment. The interests behind the Chinese presence are related to extractive resource diplomacy, political and soft power, the internationalization of the Chinese state abroad, and the "Going global" strategy (Ziso 2018: 1, 11, 198). Ultimately, this is "naked imperialism" (Lee 2006: 325; Ziso 2018: 198), a new "Scramble for Africa," or "New Neo-colonialism." Neocolonialism is indeed a very frequently used term. Beijing's infrastructure-for-resources approach is criticized as identical with older colonial powers' competition for African resources (Lahtinen 2018: 6, 84). Mozambique, to take an example, is described as "the Chinese takeaway" and "at risk of being recolonized" (Lahtinen 2018: 6; Lemos and Ribeiro 2007). Various scholars at universities in South Africa, Kenya, and Senegal perceive China as a new colonial power that exploits Africa (Lahtinen 2018: 48). This "neo-colonialism narrative" is based on three propositions: (1) "scrambling for resources," which includes disregard for sustainable development and neglect of the basic rights of workers and local residents; (2) "cheap goods for market dominance," i.e. the invasion of cheap, low-quality Chinese goods that bankrupt local enterprises and destroy the fragile African manufacturing industries; and (3) "damaging human rights," which contributes to the "prevalence of tyranny and corruption." Accordingly, China is "an amoral hegemon that sows more seeds of fear than hope" (Li 2017a: 26, 31). Critically, this leads to the perpetuation of dependency and underdevelopment and inhibits Africans' efforts to bring them to an end (Adem 2012: 144; Ziso 2018: 11): various scholars have noted that Chinese-African patterns of trade replicate and reproduce the forms of neo-colonial structural dependence first described by Raúl Prebisch and the Dependency School. Africa is treated as "a commoditized periphery" that exports to China natural resources and primary products with little added value and imports manufactured and consumer goods that undermine its nascent industrial growth (Zhao 2014: 1042–1043; le Pere 2015: 375). This has nothing to do with South-South cooperation, which is supposed precisely to shield developing countries from exploitation by industrialized nations. Africa is simply "switching from a dependency on the West to a dependency on China" (Shelton and Paruk 2008: 178; Wissenbach 2011: 24). Critically, Chinese industrial competition has led to deindustrialization and reprimarization. Econometric analyses show that the growth of Chinese manufactured product exports to sub-Saharan Africa led to "significant displacement among industries in low-tech manufacturing and reduced intra-regional and intra-sub-Saharan Africa trade" (Yap and Henson 2016: 2). Previously competitive industries such as textiles, clothing, footwear, and furniture, have "stagnated or experienced terminal decline" (le Pere 2015: 375; Zhao 2014: 1042–1043). This has affected countries with nascent manufacturing sectors such as South Africa, Kenya, Ghana, and Tanzania. States that rely on resource exports, such as Nigeria, Sudan, and Angola, on the contrary, have highly benefited from the opening of Chinese markets

(Hess and Aidoo 2015: 13). A similar development has taken place within individual African countries. Overall, China threatens their industrialization (Wissenbach 2011: 22) and pushes them back toward reliance on exports of raw materials and energy (Hess and Aidoo 2015: 13).

In addition to this negative structural impact, China has brought to Africa a business philosophy focusing on economic growth rather than on sustainable development. No attention is paid to debt sustainability or to social and environmental impacts (Wissenbach 2011: 24). In fact, Chinese firms have often been able to make better offers and win contractual bids due to their disregard for environmental standards and laws that Western companies are more likely to respect. This has led to the actual degradation of many African eco-sensitive areas (Hess and Aidoo 2015: 74). Similarly, in terms of good governance the Chinese have been accused of bringing to the continent a lack of transparency that made a disproportionate share of their aid "vulnerable to political misuse by the governing African elites" (Lahtinen 2018: 39, 46). The unconditional support for these elites also "lacks a humanitarian focus and disregards local development" (Shen 2015: 114). Beijing's willingness to cooperate with regimes responsible for human rights abuses and anti-democratic practices undermines Western and African efforts to promote democracy, good governance, and human rights on the continent as exemplified by the Chinese support for autocratic regimes in Angola, Gabon, Sudan, and Zimbabwe (Li 2017a: 26; Zhao 2014: 1039–1041; le Pere 2015: 375).

Returning to economic aspects, China's capitalism is resented in Africa as "particularly venal and brutal" (Mohan et al. 2014: 100). Chinese companies have brought controversial business practices (Lahtinen 2018: 45) related to a business culture that lacks transparency and facilitates corruption (le Pere 2015: 375). Many joint ventures with African governments or firms have been associated with shady business deals (Hess and Aidoo 2015: 14). In addition, instead of hiring mainly African workers, Chinese companies tend to bring even low-skilled laborers from China. Both categories face mistreatment and "abusive employment conditions, which fail to meet domestic and international standards and practices" (Lahtinen 2018: 6, 46). There is total disregard for labor unions and workers' rights (Hess and Aidoo 2015: 72). Moreover, Chinese employers share a racialized view of African workers as "slow" or "lazy" as opposed to their hard-working, dedicated, and productive Chinese counterparts (Mohan et al. 2014: 116). Accordingly, Chinese firms in Africa are racially segmented, with local workers unable to reach managerial, high-expertise, or better-paid positions that are reserved to Chinese nationals. This has led to labor tensions and to a toxic working atmosphere that at times has resulted in serious conflicts between local workers and their Chinese employers or coworkers, a situation that extended to concerned neighborhoods and communities (Hess and Aidoo 2015: 72, 94). All this has allowed Peter Hitchens to go as far as to claim that "China has created a new slave empire in Africa" (Hitchens 2008).

An even harsher social impact is due to the large number of Chinese entrepreneurial migrants that represent a considerable part of the one million Chinese nationals living in Africa. Their very profession is at the origin of "relatively predictable lines of conflict" (Mohan et al. 2014: 123). In ways explored in more detail in Chapter 6, Chinese traders who import large quantities of cheap Chinese consumer goods bankrupt local merchants, including those operating in the informal retail sector (Mohan et al. 2014: 110). The long-established, small turnovers businesses of petty traders are unable to survive (Röschenthaler and Socpa 2017: 178, 183), while the Chinese seldom employ locals. This leads to frequent complaints that Africans lose their jobs due to unfair Chinese competition (Lahtinen 2018: 47). This phenomenon goes beyond the trade in and production of manufactured goods: in Douala, Cameroon, Chinese prostitutes have been criticized for working for half the price charged by local ones (Röschenthaler and Socpa 2017: 172–173). Overall, the negative impact of China's economic actions in Africa dramatically affects a large part of the continent's poorest and most marginalized populations, which include manufacturing workers, miners, and petty merchants. This has resulted in considerable frustration, tensions, and conflicts with both the Chinese and the local authorities and political elites, which are perceived as protecting China's interests instead of those of the Africans (Hess and Aidoo 2015: 15). These elements as well as the complex issue of their political instrumentalization by certain African leaders are discussed in Chapter 8, where they are used to analyze similar developments in the Caribbean.

The "China Threat": A Second Order Analysis

The flood of anti-Chinese criticism is so compelling that it is not easy to ignore it and give preference to the optimists' very different views. Accordingly, the latter's response was not centered on exclusively providing empirical counter-arguments. The China-enthusiasts took the action of moving the debate from the analysis of factual elements to that of the reasons that might have motivated the skeptics' sharp criticism. They targeted the discourse about China's "offensive" presence, "new scramble," and "empire" in Africa (Lam 2017: 1), about the "greedy" or "ravenous dragon" (Li 2017a: 27–28) that is "guzzling, aggressive, an economic juggernaut, insatiably thirsty for oils and minerals, and voraciously capitalist" (Mawdsley 2008: 521; Ziso 2018: 1). This "demonization" of China—"the threat perception, the grim tableaux, and near hysteria"—is explained as an artificial construct, "a product of Western-inspired hypocrisy and arrogance that have increasingly found echoes among Africans themselves" (le Pere 2015: 361). In other words, the skeptics' criticism should be taken not as an objective depiction of reality but as part of an ideologically and geopolitically motivated Western discourse that reflects material interests and "jealous[y] about Chinese inroads to Africa" (Lahtinen 2018: 7). Deborah Brautigam, the champion of the optimistic school, has waged a crusade to "dispel many of the myths" "behind the idea that China is a 'rogue donor'" in Africa (Brautigam 2009: 19, 20). She provided a list of skeptical "myths" and of optimists' responses to them: "China Enables Sudan to Get Away with Murder in Darfur"—"Yes, but China is changing"; "China Hurts Efforts to Strengthen Democracy and Human Rights in Africa"—"Less than you probably think"; "Chinese Support Kept Robert Mugabe in Power in Zimbabwe"—"If only it was this simple"; "China Gains Business with Low Environmental and Social Standards"—"True, but this may be changing" and so on (Brautigam 2009: 281–299). But this was taken one step further by Richard L. Harris, a specialist on China's presence in Latin America who has studied the global diffusion of what he identifies as the "China Threat" concept. Building on Daniel Vukovich's work, he identifies "Sinological Orientalism" as a new form of Orientalism that combines the Cold War anti-Maoist discourse with the present Western neoliberal one about the role played in the world economy by China, which is presented as an Oriental pseudo-capitalist society that undergoes "an inevitable but imperfect process of 'becoming the same' as the West" (Harris 2015: 156; Vukovich 2012). "Sinological Orientalism" uses threatening language and imagery to promote the idea that China "represents a dragon-like threat of evil and destructive behavior" (Harris 2015: 160). The reality of China's win-win, harmonious interactions with the Global South is distorted by the use of a series of myths, misconceptions, and misinformation that find their ways into much of the academic literature and the media coverage, which further propagate anti-Chinese "biases, preconceptions, hidden agendas and fears" (Harris and Arias 2016: 509). In short, "the close link between the academic and the policy agendas in the West" was used to "create an *unfounded* Sino-phobic 'China threat'" in response to China's challenging of the Western-dominated world order (Harris and Arias 2016: 510; Hirono and Suzuki 2014: 460–461; emphasis added).

As a Constructivist, I am tempted to comment that, indeed, nobody should believe that the criticism of China's actions in Africa and elsewhere is absolutely value-free and does in no way reflect ideological, geopolitical, economic, and cultural biases. The problem with the optimists' views, however, is that because such bias exists they infer that all associated criticism is automatically void. This is a serious analytical error. To give an extreme example, when Hitlerite Germany revealed the Katyn Massacre in 1943, Stalin dismissed it as deeply biased Nazi propaganda. He was right: that was propaganda, and it was deeply biased. But it was nevertheless true. The "China threat" might well be a Western interest-motivated construct, but this does in no way necessarily mean that the issues raised by the skeptics are false. Furthermore, authors such as Brautigam or Harris cannot deny the fact that they have, be it involuntarily, joined the Chinese-initiated effort of constructing a counter-discourse. Increasing numbers of Western scholars support Beijing's views and diffuse them through the literature. Frequently, they attend Chinese-sponsored conferences or go to China as visiting professors. Are they more objective and less biased than their more skeptical colleagues? The only possible response, I am afraid, is that today the polarization of this field of study is a given and nobody can escape its constraints.

Local Perceptions of China in Africa

What can be done with a reasonable degree of objectivity, however, is to scrutinize the way Africans themselves perceive China's actions. At first view, everything is fine: perceptions of the Chinese engagement are favorable except for three countries, "which tend to be apprehensive toward the expansion of Chinese economic endeavors": South Africa, Nigeria, and Egypt (Hess and Aidoo 2015: 69). In the South African case, "general disfavor" is due to dissatisfaction with Chinese labor arrangements, balance of trade, quality of products, and environmental as well as other policies. Despite cordial diplomatic relations, uncertainty and skepticism are "reflected among the leadership and much evidently in the general population" (Hess and Aidoo 2015: 69). Perhaps it is useful to note that, given the fact that they are the first two economies of sub-Saharan Africa, Nigeria and South Africa do not share the level of dependency on foreign—and, therefore, Chinese—development assistance of most of their neighbors. Returning to regional averages, a 2016 Afrobarometer report covering 36 African countries showed that China does represent a popular model for national development. Yet, the supporters of this model—24 percent—were fewer than those of the American one (30 percent). As already mentioned at the beginning of this section, China's positive perception by Africans is mainly due to its infrastructure/development actions (32 percent), to the low cost of its products (23 percent), and to its business investments (16 percent). Negative perceptions are associated with the poor quality of Chinese goods (35 percent), with taking jobs or business away from locals (14 percent), with the extraction of resources (10 percent on average, but this is much higher in certain countries), and with land grabbing (7 percent). Interestingly, Chinese support for dictators is blamed by only 4 percent of respondents, and only 5 percent are interested in political and social considerations. At 2 percent, cultural elements can be assessed as almost negligible (Lahtinen 2018: 47; Lekorwe et al. 2016).

Africans' feelings toward Chinese nationals in their countries can be assessed as mixed. At least in part, this is due to the nature of communication between the two groups. Except in work situations, people to people relations are rare. Africans seldom have Chinese friends. The Chinese live in their compounds and are perceived as preferring their own food and habits and as not being interested in Africans and their culture. Accordingly, they are often regarded with suspicion. Things are complicated by the belief that they take Africans' jobs and destroy local small businesses. There is also the perception that they do not consider Africans to be their equals and that they adopt "a paternal, and even racist, attitude" (Lahtinen 2018: 47–48). All this leads to an ambiguous overall image of China among Africa's citizens. Development assistance, investments, and affordable goods are welcomed; China as a developmental model is also seriously taken into consideration. But actual socio-economic interactions with the Chinese seem to damage China's image instead of improving it. Overall, one gets the impression that Africans' perception of and attitude toward the Chinese they interact with are deeply discordant with the ideal-type of South-South solidarity and qualitatively not different from those toward the citizens of Western powers.

The Issue of Conditionality

This section has provided a review of the rich literature on the complex and complicated relationship between China and Africa. As shown in the following chapters, many of the approaches and instruments developed by the Chinese in their dealings with this continent were eventually employed in the Caribbean as well as elsewhere in the Global South. In this context, an important question is if and in what measure conditionality has been used in Beijing's African enterprise. The secondary literature suggests that, in different countries and under different forms, Chinese conditionalities do exist. The "no Taiwan, no Tibet, no Tiananmen Square" principle seems to be enforced. "Tied aid" is hardly unheard of. Social conditionality is well exemplified by the already mentioned Zambian and Ghanaian cases. Still, a comprehensive study is required before any generalization can be made. Conditionalities might represent the exception rather than the rule; in different countries, they might be used separately or in various combinations; their goal might be short-term profit, not international socialization; and their degree of success as well as their actual consequences might vary greatly from one country to another. This is why I refrain from drawing any conclusion on this issue.

What I can explain, however, is why scholars specialized in Sino-African relations have not addressed it. As discussed in the Introduction, there is the general trend of not questioning a "myth." Perhaps more importantly, Africa provides a long list of much more attractive topics. The infrastructure-for-resources deal associated with China's "resource expansionism" contains so many spectacular elements that scholars and journalists alike do not need to dig elsewhere. Flows of Homeric proportions connect China and Africa in terms of goods, people, and money. Dictators survive due to Beijing's veto at the UN Security Council. Testimonies on exploitation of African miners and environmental degradation can easily be obtained. The "Western plot" counter-discourse is equally exciting. Why, then, should somebody spend time and effort on writing about an abstract concept that won't sell? This is why, as already mentioned, a region deprived of such stunning developments is more appropriate for the study of Chinese conditionality. Before presenting the Caribbean, however, neighboring Latin America will be briefly scrutinized in order to have a second term of comparison.

CHINA IN LATIN AMERICA

Latin America probably represents the most popular example of China's use elsewhere in the Global South of approaches and instruments it first tested in Africa. It is also important for the Caribbean case study of this book because, at least in principle, Beijing has elaborated and conducts a common policy with regard to "Latin America and the Caribbean." Incidentally, this is a good illustration of the sub-regional diversity that China needs to take into consideration in its interactions with certain geographical regions. Chinese interest in Latin America has been explained by Evan Ellis as associated with five elements: (1) Latin America as a source of primary products; (2) Latin America as a market for Chinese goods; (3) the diplomatic isolation of Taiwan; (4) competition with the United States; and (5) a new, more confident generation of Chinese leaders. In turn, Latin America is interested in China mainly due to (1) hopes for export-led growth; (2) hopes for investment in fuel development; and (3) an alternative to US dominance (Ellis 2009: 9–32). Initially, Latin America was hardly a prime focus of Beijing's foreign policy. This has considerably changed, but as far more resources are to be gained from Africa, the latter is much more discussed than the former within the Chinese intellectual community. In fact, some of China's scholars believe that the divergence between their country and Latin America is far too large to allow for a genuinely close partnership (Shen 2015: 111).

Maoist China's interest in and assistance to Latin America were due to purely political reasons and had a strong ideological dimension (Hongbo 2017: 282). Domestically, official propaganda even succeeded in turning leftist Latin American guerilla movements and the Cuban revolution into objects of romanticization. The ideological factor, however, was dramatically downplayed when post-Mao reforms were launched (Shen 2015: 113). Mutually beneficial trade and economic cooperation began to be promoted (Hongbo 2017: 282). During the early 1980s, Prime Minister Zhao Ziyang visited Latin America and made public four principles for developing China's relations with the region: (1) peace and friendship; (2) mutual support; (3) equality and mutual benefit; and (4) the attainment of common progress (Zhang 2015: 57). But it was after the end of the Cold War and especially at the beginning of the new century that bilateral relations developed on an unprecedented scale. Mainly between 2003 and 2009, various types of strategic partnerships were established with all of the region's major countries (Shen 2015: 111). China became a member of the Caribbean Development Bank (1997), a permanent observer at the Organization of American States (2004), and a member of the Inter-American Development Bank (2008), while the China-CELAC (the Community of Latin American and Caribbean States) forum was announced in 2014 and had its first meeting in January 2015 (Roett and Paz 2015: 499). Mechanisms of dialogue were also created with various regional groupings, such as the China-Andean Community Consultation, the China-Mercosur Dialogue, and the China and Latin American Conference (Zhang 2015: 61). The key moment in this spectacular upgrading of the Chinese-Latin American relationship was represented by President Hu Jintao's November 2004 tour of Chile, Argentina, Brazil, and Cuba, during which he announced a large number of possible Chinese investment projects (Ellis 2014: 5). He returned to the region in 2005, 2008, and 2010 while Latin American natural resources became one of the main targets of Chinese state-owned firms. Except for Central America, the Taiwan factor diminished as most South American states established diplomatic relations with Beijing (Shen 2015: 111–112). Yet, non-economic factors remained important: China's presence was in part determined by the geopolitical goal of using the support of Latin American states in its effort to balance US hegemony. Beijing accordingly supported left-leaning governments in the region (Harris 2015: 153), even if it was reluctant to follow President Hugo Chavez's overtly anti-American stand. In general, anti-imperialism has been less present in China's policy toward Latin America than in the African one (Shen 2015: 113). If this was due to the will to not excessively antagonize Washington in a geopolitically sensitive region, recent Sino-American tensions might soon lead to a different approach.

Beijing's African experience led to the 2008 release of a Policy Paper on Latin America and the Caribbean identical in length, structure, and logic with the January 2006 Policy Paper on Africa. The only difference was the absence of the three-line section on the Forum on China-Africa Cooperation (Zhang 2015: 61). Yet, even this structure was eventually duplicated through the creation of the similar China-CELAC forum that first met in January 2015. The paper's key point was to make explicit the fact that, in Latin America, Beijing was not pursuing only natural resources. Its much more complex actions were related to the "growing multidimensional process of Chinese *worldization*" revolving around ideas, institutions, and interests (Haro Navejas 2013: 146). More details were added in the 2016 second Policy Paper on Latin America and the Caribbean that beautifully described the region as "a land full of vitality and hope," which "attained achievements that have attracted the world's attention" (Ministry of Foreign Affairs of the Republic of China 2016: I). Obviously, the document emphasized once more China's peaceful, win-win approach but also announced a "new stage of comprehensive cooperation" with the region. In relation to the *China-Latin American and Caribbean Countries Cooperation Plan for 2015–2019*, a new "1+3+6" framework for pragmatic cooperation was proposed that had trade, investment, and financial cooperation as driving forces, and identified energy and resources, infrastructure construction, agriculture, manufacturing, scientific and technological innovation, and information technology as cooperation priorities. A new "3x3" model for capacity cooperation was also set up that proposed to jointly build the three major "passages" of logistics, electricity, and information in Latin America, enabling "healthy interactions" among the enterprise, society, and government, and expanding the three financing channels of funds, loans, and insurance (Ministry of Foreign Affairs of the Republic of China 2016: III). Chinese scholars did not miss the occasion to hail the "open, transparent, systematic elaboration" of this policy (Hongbo 2017: 307). Well-informed Trinidadian respondents, however, expressed a very different opinion. In particular, they seriously questioned the fact that China's actual actions reflect its stated policy (more details are provided in the section *China in the Caribbean: Constructing a New Regional Order* of Chapter 4, as the two papers also cover China's involvement in the Caribbean).

For a time, nobody in Latin America cared about such discrepancies because of the impressive 2003–2013 "China Boom." The spectacular rise in bilateral trade helped reduce social inequalities, compensated for the diminished American and European economic presence due to the 2008–2009 global financial crisis, and allowed many Latin American economies to recover from that same crisis. In a decade, the "boom" turned $12 billion of trade into $289 billion. From a country representing 1 percent of Latin

America's total trade, China became the first trading partner for many of the region's biggest economies such as Brazil, Peru, or Chile (Gallagher 2016: 2, 7). This greatly increased the demand for Latin American products and, at least until the beginning of the financial crisis, the prices of many of these products (Gallagher and Porzecanski 2010: 7). This was the main factor behind the 3.6 percent annual growth rate of Latin America between 2003 and 2013, which compares favorably to the 2.4 percent of the previous, Washington Consensus-dominated two decades. In many countries the middle class grew larger while, atypically for the region, inequality diminished. However, after 2013 a number of reasons that include the beginning of China's move from an economic model based on export-led industry toward a more consumer-based economy diminished its "voracious appetite" for Latin American natural resources (Gallagher 2016: 2, 7–8). Accordingly, Chinese investment and lending that previously focused on oil, mining, and—for political and ideological reasons—Venezuela, now cover more sectors and are centered on Brazil and Argentina (*The Economist*, February 1, 2018). Critically, the "boom" came to an end, and Latin America's economic prospects took a rather negative turn (Gallagher 2016: 2).

The Chinese Deindustrialization of Latin America

The main problem, however, became evident *during* the "China Boom" and is important enough to make scholars question even that period's positive record. It is related to the structure of bilateral trade and is illustrated by the fact that, while Latin American importers and retailers have "profited enormously" from the local sale of inexpensive Chinese consumer goods, "manufacturers are being practically put out of business" (Hearn and León-Manríquez 2011: 15; Dussel Peters 2011). It is true that Latin American exports to China have also considerably expanded. Powerful Brazilian economic groups, for example, claim that close trade relations with China benefit Brazil and increase its competitiveness. This is due to the fact that they are major exporters on the Chinese markets (Jenkins 2015: 47–48). However, significant Latin American exports to those markets only concern six countries and ten *primary* commodities (Gallagher and Porzecanski 2010: 7). Imports of industrial goods from China, on the contrary, are much more diversified and have conquered all Latin American markets. It is at this point that the magnitude of the aforementioned discrepancy between China's stated policies and actual moves becomes visible. As part of Beijing's well-known win-win, South-South cooperative approach, the 2016 Policy Paper on Latin America and the Caribbean presents extensively Chinese future efforts to industrialize Latin America. Cooperation is planned in fields such as cars, energy equipment, and chemical industry. The level of industrialization of the region will be upgraded through "the joint construction of industrial parks, logistics parks, high-tech industrial parks, special economic zones and other industrial agglomeration areas" (Ministry of Foreign Affairs of the Republic of China 2016: IV.2.6). Such disinterested generosity is splendid. Unfortunately, Kevin Gallagher's and Roberto Porzecanski's "major and alarming finding" was that, in 2010, no less than 94 percent of Latin American and Caribbean manufacturers were threatened by Chinese competition, representing 40 percent of the region's overall exports and 95 percent of its high-technology exports. In the individual cases of Mexico, Costa Rica, Brazil, and Argentina, the percentages of their industrial exports under threat were 99, 96, 90, and 90 percent respectively, representing 72, 58, 39, and 27 percent of their respective total exports (Gallagher and Porzecanski 2010: 7–8, 39). Due to its lower wages, cheap fixed capital costs, low environmental and labor standards, and exchange rate policies, China "removed" Latin American light manufacturers from a number of export markets and even started to outcompete them in their own countries (Paladini 2011: 84; Gallagher 2016: 97). Shockingly, this led to Latin America's deindustrialization. Richard Harris believes otherwise (see "China and the So-Called Deindustrialization of Brazil," Harris 2015: 177–180), but there is broad agreement among scholars on China's responsibility in this process, which is in fact one of reprimarization (Ray 2017: 150). In addition to pushing Latin American manufacturers out of the market, the Chinese have vastly increased the overall demand for primary commodities produced in Latin America. In turn, this has boosted prices for those products (Ray 2017: 150; Gallagher and Porzecanski 2010: 56). Between 2003 and 2013, China accounted for only 4.2 percent of the growth in Latin American manufactured exports, compared to 19.6 percent for overall export, 40 percent for primary goods exports, and 40.3 percent for resource-based exports (Ray 2017: 150). This translated into "strong pressure to downgrade the sophistication of [Latin American] exports" (Hearn and León-Manríquez 2011: 10). In the case of Brazil, manufactured goods diminished from 53 percent of total exports in 2005 to 35 percent in 2012 due to the rise of agricultural and mineral exports (Salama 2017: 26). This "shift away from state-led industrialization back toward LAC's traditionally competitive production of raw commodities" (Ray 2017: 150) is extremely detrimental to the socio-economic development of Latin America as it hampers its "ability to climb up the value-added ladder" and compels it "to climb back down and remain focused on producing raw materials" (Hearn and León-Manríquez 2011: 5). Major social and political consequences may ensue. On the one hand, deindustrialization and reprimarization disempower organized labor because they replace factory employment with more dispersed workplaces, where it is more difficult to unionize and mobilize. Such a development leads to changes in the structure and nature of the working class and in the nature of work and job security, making nonstandard employment conditions more likely. On the other hand, deindustrialization affects negatively the interests of domestic industrial capital while reprimarization empowers landlords and mine owners as well as transnational resource-based producers (Jenkins 2015: 46; Cypher and Wilson 2015: 17). One cannot miss the nineteenth-century scent of these developments.

If the system level of analysis is taken into consideration, this reinforcement of dysfunctional patterns that Latin American states have tried to move away from for over half a century (Cypher and Wilson 2015: 5) "develop[s] along the lines of the classic center-periphery relations" (Devadason et al. 2017: 1262) studied by the Dependency Theory: "China emerges as a new centre and the countries of the Latin American and Caribbean region as a new periphery" (Rosales and Kuwayama 2012: 11; Cypher and Wilson 2015: 9). Some authors go as far as arguing that "dependence must be accepted as a permanent feature of the Sino-LAC relations," as an exploitative type of interactions "has been somewhat fixed, and is unlikely to change" (Devadason et al. 2017: 1274). This statement is perhaps too radical, at least for the time being. But it is difficult to completely reject the claim that, overall, the "increasingly asymmetrical relationship with China has made room for crisis, but not growth" (Salama 2017: 9).

Latin American Reactions and Chinese Counter-Reactions

Despite Beijing's friendly discourse, these developments led to widespread discontent that "aroused anti-Chinese sentiment" (Shen 2015: 114). Even Chinese authors acknowledge the poor image of their country by noting that, in countries like Peru and Ecuador, "China's investments in projects related to energy and mineral resources have been disturbed and even destroyed many times by the local people" (Hongbo 2017: 323). In fact, the very rise of labor movements in Latin America was associated by some observers with "the ongoing ascent of China" (Shen 2015: 114). Manufacturers' protests have been equally vocal. In response to their lobbying, protectionist measures were taken by countries such as Brazil—which adopted its first antidumping measures targeting Chinese exports back in the 1990s—or Argentina, which imposed quotas on Chinese toys, tires, and electrical equipment, including computers (Cypher and Wilson 2015: 11). Foreign exchange controls were also introduced to curb imports from China (Roett and Paz 2015: 511).

It is interesting to see the Chinese viewpoint on this situation. China's scholars—who need to reflect, at least in part, the position of their government—assess Latin American negative reactions against the background of the region's past that, in their opinion, distorts present perceptions. To them, there is no doubt that advantages brought by Chinese "trade and investment are apparent and can be shared and felt in the internal [*sic*] society." Latin Americans understand that such trade and investment "will help promote their development." It is true that Chinese exports "bring pressure on *some* countries in *some* competitive industries" (emphasis added). But, essentially, people in Latin America are "afraid of China's development due to their long-term colonial history." Fortunately, there is a solution: "to build soft power in Latin America through assistance" (Hongbo 2017: 322).

It is obvious that this instrument is less effective in the case of larger and more developed countries such as Chile, Mexico, Brazil, or Argentina. But in other parts of Latin America development assistance can play an important role, and the same Chinese author has no problem in noting that Beijing instrumentalizes its aid to Central America and the Caribbean in support of its "more political interests" while in the case of Andean countries "China's aid is more inclined towards economic interests" (Hongbo 2017: 321). In these poorer regions the Chinese approach tends to be similar to that used in the Caribbean and presented in detail in the following chapters. Here I will only mention an aspect related to the Chinese finance in Latin America. Only 1.2 percent of the total amount is represented by loans at concessional rates of interest (somewhat lower than those of the US ExIm Bank) that are offered as aid to low-income countries by the China ExIm Bank. As much as 82 percent of that bank's funding to Latin American borrowers carries commercial interest rates. The rationale is that countries in need are best served by lower-cost options consisting in blending Chinese export promotion with development aid (Gallagher 2016: 79–80). However, as illustrated by the example of Panama (see the section *The Belt and Road Initiative* of this chapter), this can lead to situations close to Sri Lanka-type debt traps.

Scholars have noted that, in such extreme cases as well as in more "normal" ones, Beijing's prime target is represented by the Latin American elites while little is done to address the negative perceptions and reactions of local societies (Shen 2015: 114). This suggests that the same pattern of socializing local political elites used by China in the Caribbean (see the following chapters) might be valid at least in the case of some Latin American countries. The logical question one is likely to ask is if similarity stops here or extends to the use of conditionality. The secondary literature suggests that states in subregions that share the Caribbean's features, such as Central America, might well be the target of Chinese conditionalities. However, in Latin America as in Africa, nobody has studied this aspect because more pressing issues capture the energies of scholars and journalists alike. In particular, the topic of deindustrialization and reprimarization is so overwhelmingly important in terms of economic, social, and political consequences that at times it tends to monopolize China-related discourses and debates. Beyond that, what is generally acknowledged is the fact that Chinese diplomats and companies are deeply "immersed in the business, social and political conditions in [Latin American] countries—and in some cases are even shaping those conditions to suit their interests" (Ellis 2012: 28). Probably the best depiction of China's overall impact on Latin America is that provided by Adrian Hearn and José Luis León-Manríquez:

> Labor disputes in the Caribbean and Central America, despair among Latin American manufacturers, and anxieties about overdependence on natural resource exports reveal that *there is nothing inherently harmonious* about the region's contemporary relations with China. These problems are systemic components of China's rise, and therefore have no simple solutions (Hearn and León-Manríquez 2011: 11; emphasis added).

CHINA IN THE CARIBBEAN

China's Latin American policy papers also cover the Caribbean. However, at a practical level, Beijing has to take into consideration the specificities of this region. This has resulted in a particular approach that has little to do with that toward countries such as Mexico or Brazil but, in a certain measure, is similar to Chinese interactions with Central America. Most of the relevant features of the Caribbean and of China's policies toward it are analyzed in the next chapters and therefore do not need to be redundantly presented here. The goal of this short section is to sketch the general framework of the Chinese-Caribbean relationship in order to show that this region is the most appropriate for the study of China's three conditionalities. As already mentioned, the latter might be at work in various parts of the Global South, but their configuration, effectiveness, and visibility vary greatly. Critically, the African and Latin American examples presented in this chapter show that, in many cases, major trade or investment issues dominate public debates and scholarly analyses, leaving little room for the study of other aspects such as conditionality.

To begin with, the following factors contribute to China's interest in the Caribbean: (1) the "diplomatic duel" with Taiwan; (2) the assertive global agenda of the new generation of Chinese leaders; (3) the associated growing rivalry between Beijing and Washington; (4) marginally, the perception of the Caribbean as a market for Chinese goods; and (5) in certain cases—that include Trinidad and Tobago—the view of the region as a source of primary products. In turn, the interest in China of Caribbean states that do not recognize Taiwan is due to (1) Chinese development assistance; (2) hopes for tourism-, investment-, and export-led growth that are frequently unrealistic; (3) the idea of South-South cooperation as an alternative to US dominance and, more generally, to Western influence; (4) the self-interested political and electoral instrumentalization of actual and potential China-related economic benefits by Caribbean political elites; (5) these elites' preference for Chinese political and economic conditionalities as opposed to Western conditionalities related to human rights, the rule of law, and good governance; and (6) citizens' positive overall perception of China (see Ellis 2009: 9–32; Montoute 2013: 112, 122–123; Bernal 2016: 5676–5807). Each of these factors deserves to be explored in detail, which is done in the following four chapters. As a general comment, there is a growing corpus of literature covering China's presence in the Caribbean. Still, almost all of it is severely undertheorized. Even the reference work on this topic, Richard Bernal's 2014/2016 book, bluntly states in its Introduction "this study does not lay claim to scholarship" (Bernal 2016: 107–114). If theory is seldom present, somewhat surprisingly—and different from other regions—almost all works add to empirical analysis abundant policy recommendations to local governments. They also emphasize the very visible Caribbean "receptivity to the expansion of economic relations with China" (Bernal 2016: 5818–5824). This can be associated with small state resilience, as out of the "myriad opportunities" provided to them by globalization (Cooper and Shaw 2009: 4; Briguglio 2007: 105), China is by far the biggest one. Accordingly, they opportunistically elaborate "appropriate strategies to meet their foreign policy goals" (Braveboy-Wagner 2008: 2): "rather than imposing itself on small Caribbean nations, China is being actively courted by these nations" (Oosterveld et al. 2018: 43). In particular, many elements that include the prospect of increasing their domestic legitimacy but also "China's flattering diplomatic demarche" (see Bernal 2016: 3162–3221) have made Caribbean political elites respond enthusiastically to Beijing's efforts to socialize them (see the section *The Socialization of Caribbean Elites* of Chapter 5). In conjunction with the relative vacuum created by American and European disinterest in the region, this has turned China into the "only game in town" in the Caribbean (Oosterveld et al. 2018: 6). Unless Washington launches an aggressive anti-Beijing campaign, it is reasonable to expect the further deepening of the Chinese engagement with the region. In turn, this will result in Caribbean countries becoming increasingly dependent on China (Oosterveld et al. 2018: 6).

In principle, many of Beijing's approaches toward the region are not fundamentally different from those presented in the sections on Africa and Latin

America. There are infrastructure-for-resources deals; but—different from the African case—hardly all countries are concerned as only a few have relevant resources. There is deindustrialization; but it only affects the few islands that do have some industry. More surprisingly, even trade is not important (Haro Navejas 2013: 144). China's exports to the Caribbean are "infinitesimal" as a percentage of its total exports (Bernal 2016: 5718–5729) and modest with respect to other sources of Caribbean imports. Chinese investments are hardly impressive, too. Accordingly, these issues do not permanently capture the attention of scholars and journalists. By far the most important—and therefore the most scrutinized—form of bilateral cooperation consists in the construction of prestige infrastructure projects financed by Chinese loans that are associated with political, economic, and social conditionalities. To the surprise of foreign observers, the Chinese-related headline scandals are about infrastructure projects and their dark world of non-transparency and failures. At the same time, given the smallness of most islands, the negative impact of the inflow of Chinese entrepreneurial migrants is even more visible than that of the million who settled in Africa. This is why the study of the three Chinese conditionalities finds in the Caribbean an excellent laboratory.

Within the region, Trinidad and Tobago's hydrocarbon-based energy resources make it the largest economy (Braveboy-Wagner 2010: 424) and, in socio-economic terms, one of the most developed states. Unlike smaller Caribbean islands, it possesses an industry that is vulnerable to Chinese competition as well as natural resources that can be—and in part already are—exported to China. Critically, it "has the highest connectivity with China in the region" (Khan 2017), which has translated into the construction of a large number of Chinese-financed and built infrastructure projects. This is to say that, within the Caribbean laboratory, Trinidad provides the best illustration of a wide range of aspects related to Beijing's multifaceted activities, conditionalities, and international socialization.

CHINA'S CONSTRUCTIVIST JOURNEY

Elements presented in this chapter allow for the understanding of China's last seven decades as a perfect illustration of a Constructivist journey through various identities, interests, and approaches toward the developing world. Under Chairman Mao, the Middle Kingdom took the identity of a communist crusader that supported Third World anti-colonial and anti-imperialist forces while trying to limit the Soviet Union's competing influence. This ideological and political approach was discarded when the reforms launched in 1978 by Deng Xiaoping turned his principle of "peaceful rise with a low profile" into a key dimension of China's new identity as a capitalist apprentice. Relations with the Third World were significantly downscaled and took a more pragmatic turn. Eventually, the quiet apprentice became a global dragon that did not have much choice in the geographical origin of primary products needed to fuel its formidable economic machine. The Global South therefore became a *destination obligée* for its merchants and diplomats. Finally, president Xi Jinping started to add the missing touch of geopolitical assertiveness. China-the-global-power is extending today its multidimensional influence all over the Global South. Its newly—and still incompletely—forged identity is accompanied by an approach toward the developing world that brings together (1) the inescapable win-win, South-South cooperation discourse; (2) a learning process illustrated, among others, by the development in Africa of instruments later used in Latin America; and (3) the combination of a general pattern of action with specific region- or state-related strategies customized to fit local conditions. Two closely related instruments are frequently used: the charm offensive targeting the political elites of the partner country; and the well-calculated use of development assistance—frequently consisting in large infrastructure projects—as an incentive.

In the Caribbean, the effectiveness of these two instruments has been significantly enhanced by the scarcity of American and European development aid. Local elites gratefully accepted "the dragon's gift" customized to fit their own political and electoral interests, despite the fact that it was accompanied by political, economic, and social conditionalities. In the process, they got socialized and started to redefine their substantive beliefs in ways compatible with the views and interests of their Asian partner. In turn, the state itself became involved in a successful Chinese-centered international socialization process. However, as shown in this chapter, the relationship of many Global South countries with China is not necessarily harmonious. Negative consequences range from unemployment and environmental degradation to deindustrialization and reprimarization. Predictably, some of them are aggravated if conditionalities are at work. This has been the case in the Caribbean, leading to popular frustration and discontent. A paradoxical situation has emerged where Beijing's efforts to socialize the state-society complex are fully successful on the state side but a failure on the society one. It is this interesting contradiction and the valuable insights it offers on China's conditionalities, strategies, and instruments that the following chapters explore.

Chapter Four

China's Political Conditionality

Previous chapters have already defined Chinese political conditionality as Beijing's use of economic incentives to shape the recipient state's China-related foreign policy preferences as well as its attitude toward democracy and human rights in China. This is well summarized by the "no Taiwan; no Tibet; no Tiananmen Square" formula. The "no Taiwan" part is hardly a secret; all works on Chinese development assistance acknowledge its importance. The only problem is that they associate it exclusively with the realm of foreign policy and treat it as a strange form of "conditionality-free" condition. The critical re-reading of this "reality" proposed by this book is little more than showing that the emperor has no clothes. The second part of China's political conditionality, however, is almost always ignored. It is true that Global South governments with doubtful democratic credentials have natural affinities with the leadership in Beijing when it comes to oppressing dissidents or minorities; in their case, such conditionality does not need to be enforced. But the Caribbean provides an excellent example of a group of consolidated democracies in the developing world that, as explained in this chapter, have made a name for themselves by vocally supporting human rights and democratic values domestically and internationally. In this case, the second part of China's political conditionality can hardly be described as irrelevant. The Caribbean example is also useful for another important aspect analyzed in this book. The political conditionality is imposed by Beijing on all the recipients of its development assistance. Nobody can hope to receive one more yuan after recognizing Taiwan, receiving the Dalai Lama in a state visit, or erecting a monument dedicated to the Tiananmen victims. But in the Caribbean, this conditionality is just the first step of a more ambitious strategy. The next section presents Chinese efforts, already analyzed in the literature, to construct nothing less than "a new regional order." Accordingly, the normative and cognitive effects of political conditionality are turned into instruments leading to the Caribbean's pro-Beijing international socialization. This conditionality is therefore much more important here than in regions not concerned by similar Chinese plans; and its close scrutiny is likely to reveal aspects that might be irrelevant or absent in other parts of the Global South.

CHINA IN THE CARIBBEAN: CONSTRUCTING A NEW REGIONAL ORDER

"Chequebook Diplomacy"

Unlike neighboring communist Cuba, Caribbean states taken into consideration in this book started to establish diplomatic relations with the communist regime in Beijing only after it replaced the government in Taipei as a member of the United Nations and as a permanent member of the UN Security Council in 1971. The first to do so were Guyana and Jamaica in 1972, followed by Trinidad and Tobago in 1974, Suriname in 1976, and Barbados in 1977 (Bernal 2016: 5697–5704). In a few cases such as that of Guyana, ideological reasons did play a significant role. However, during the ensuing four decades, the China-Taiwan "diplomatic duel" and, more specifically, the use of "chequebook diplomacy" have represented by far the determinant factor in the recognition of one or the other camp by Caribbean states. The dynamic of the "duel" has already been presented in the section *China vs. Taiwan* of Chapter 3, which has also emphasized the central role played by Central America and the Caribbean (even today, they represent half of Taipei's "diplomatic allies") and the "flip-flop allegiance" of "swing states" such as Saint Lucia or Grenada that changed sides more than once. Relevant for this chapter, in one occasion the financial logic of "chequebook diplomacy" was dwarfed by democracy- and human rights-related arguments: the 1989 pro-Taiwanese shift of allegiance of Grenada and Belize was a direct reaction to China's Tiananmen massacre (Li 2005: 81–82).

Yet, in most cases money has represented the decisive factor: "Caribbean officials generally view China's checkbook diplomacy in a positive light" (Ward 2017: 13). China's impressive economic growth led to the similar expansion of its development assistance that, in the Caribbean, "helped offset drying up funds from Western institutions" such as the IMF and the World Bank (Ward 2017: 13). Some of Taipei's "diplomatic allies" "appear[ed] to regret nailing their flag to the Taiwanese mast" (Wigglesworth 2013). Five years before his country's 2018 pro-Beijing shift, a former Dominican Republic central bank governor stated "we've missed the boat, undoubtedly" (Wigglesworth 2013). Involved amounts have indeed been impressive by local standards. Dominica's support was "bought" by Beijing in 2004 with promises for grant aid larger than a third of the government's revenue for five years, representing no less than US $1,750 for each of the island's 70,000 inhabitants (Li 2005: 88). The then new Prime Minister Roosevelt Skerrit had in fact started by asking similar amounts from the Taiwanese, who were unable to provide them. Exasperated, they publicly stated that "being young and harbouring unrealistic illusions about the PRC, he decided to yield to temptations" from Beijing (Ministry of Foreign Affairs 2004). Less than one year later, Grenada wanted Taipei to significantly increase its financial assistance, to pay the national debt on its behalf, and to increase the Five-Year Cooperation Plan to US $245 million. Taiwan's frustrated Ministry of Foreign Affairs officially stated "Prime Minister Keith Mitchell, lacking foresight, incorrectly believes that by his leaning towards the People's Republic of China, Taiwan can be pressured into significantly increasing the financial assistance we provide to Grenada;" his requests are "insatiable and beyond our capacity" (Ministry of Foreign Affairs 2005). Grenada immediately recognized China. Yet, the latter is far from having won the game. Caribbean states are aware of its larger potential, "but if they need cash, the temptation to recognize Taiwan is very strong" (Li 2005: 88). Moreover, "the fewer allies Taiwan has the more it has to spend on each" (Atkinson 2010: 410). In addition to such tactical consideration, there is also a strategic one. As already mentioned in the sections *Small States* of Chapter 2 and *China in the Caribbean* of Chapter 3, the Caribbean opportunistic exploitation of the Beijing-Taipei rivalry represents an expression of small state resilience. It is a fully rational approach that cannot ignore the fact that, if all Caribbean states recognize China and this contributes to bringing the competition to an end, there will be no reason for Beijing to "buy" their diplomatic allegiance anymore (Bernal 2016: 6546–6554). The idea has therefore been suggested that cautious Caribbean countries may actually try to maintain the China-Taiwan balance by adopting a "wait-and-see" strategy that preserves the present high levels of development assistance from both sides (Paladini 2011:85).

In any case, it is clear that China's initial interest in the Caribbean was exclusively due to the Taiwanese issue. This did not change for a very long time. At a Beijing official conference directed to a Chinese and Caribbean audience that a respondent attended some years ago, a politically well-connected Chinese scholar bluntly explained—speaking off the record—that Taiwan represents the only reason that made China involve itself in an otherwise uninteresting region: "for other than that, you can't sell anything to us and we can't sell anything to you" (Respondent 23). Things, however, have considerably changed in recent years.

China's Broader Agenda in the Caribbean

The Beijing-Taipei struggle for recognition was suspended between 2008 and 2016 due to the "diplomatic truce" enforced during the tenure of the pro-China Taiwanese President Ma Ying-jeou (Tudoroiu 2017: 206). Yet, it is precisely in 2008 that analysts place the turning point of China's policy toward the Caribbean. This was mainly due to the decline of American investment in the region triggered by the financial crisis. On the contrary, the government in Beijing intensified its support for the international expansion of Chinese companies. In the Caribbean, this led to a visible increase in investment, contracted projects, and bilateral trade. A 2014 report of the US-China Economic and Security Review Commission claimed that the Chinese were trying "to take advantage of what they see as declining US and European commercial engagement in the region in the wake of the global economic crisis" (quoted by Southerland 2017). It should be noted that Xi Jinping's first visit to the Caribbean took place in 2009, when he went to Jamaica in his capacity as Vice-President of China (Ward 2017: 16). By the spring of 2012, observers were noting the increased Chinese presence in Jamaica, the Bahamas, and other parts of the region (*The Economist*, March 10, 2012). However, it was President Xi who, only some months after taking power, considerably upgraded this presence. His May 31–June 2, 2013, visit to Trinidad and Tobago was the first by a Chinese President to the region (Ministry of Foreign Affairs of the People's Republic of China 2018) and represented "an effective and a graphic demonstration of China's growing influence and outreach in the English-speaking Caribbean" (Badri-Maharaj 2016). Moreover, the setting was spectacular. "Like a royalty holding court" (Badri-Maharaj 2016), he hosted the leaders of eight Caribbean nations at a private luncheon in Port of Spain where he stated that "China would not be a spectator to the region's economic difficulties" (Wigglesworth 2013). The President's "firm commitment to building comprehensive partnerships of cooperation" took the concrete form of the announcement of no less than US $1.5 billion of concessional loans and of US $1.5 billion of special loans for infrastructure development (Ministry of Foreign Affairs of the People's Republic of China 2018). A top Caribbean official later explained that, with respect to grants, he "told us that we don't ask for enough, but gave us a grant of $8m and begged us to spend it as soon as possible" (Wigglesworth 2013). In addition, during the next three years China would send 100 medical workers, train 100 on-service MA candidates, and offer 1,000 government scholarships. The Chinese leader also had bilateral meetings with each of his Caribbean counterparts, discussing "extensive[ly] and in-depth" bilateral cooperation in the fields of economy, trade, new energy, education, health, agriculture, tourism, aviation, people-to-people and cultural exchanges, and regional and international affairs (Ministry of Foreign Affairs of the People's Republic of China 2018). Critically, he made clear that, besides trade and investment opportunities, China also sought "strategic partnerships" in the region (Southerland 2017).

Observers took all this as "a demonstration of Beijing's ambition to cement ties with countries in America's back yard" (Wigglesworth 2013) at a time when the US was "somewhat less forthcoming with financial grants for the region" (Badri-Maharaj 2016). Chinese authors concur: the Caribbean "has a great value in terms of geo-economy and geopolitics." Investing there "is conducive to China's global agenda, and enables China to maintain the strategic benefit in the Caribbean region and its neighboring areas" (Ouyang and Qiu 2015: 7). In fact, the "geo-economy" side is hardly promising. Potential economic benefits are tiny: natural resources are not large enough to matter much to Beijing; wages are relatively high and there is heavy unionization, two factors that make massive investment unlikely; and populations are small, which limits imports from China (Wigglesworth 2013). Chinese sources report that President Xi Jinping's 2013 decisions did lead to the rapid increase of Chinese companies' investments in the Caribbean; but "due to the lack of relevant information" they could not "grasp an accurate understanding of the investment prospects and risk prediction in the area." Ultimately, "their investment behavior seems rather aimless" (Ouyang and Qiu 2015: 1). Yet, the Chinese presence continued to grow, mainly through closer diplomatic ties and substantial development assistance that took the form of prestige construction projects, "which has generated goodwill for China" (Bernal 2016: 4955–4959). At least in the beginning, locals were appreciative; but also wondered—to quote a Jamaican official—"what does China want from us? That's the big question that everyone has about this: Why?" (Ward 2017: 13–14). Most analysts agree that the answer is associated with China's "deeper strategic intent" in the region (Wigglesworth 2013). As already mentioned, the issue of Taiwan was irrelevant between 2008 and 2016. When it was reactivated, Beijing's Caribbean approach had already shifted "to a broader agenda," which "has to be seen in the context of China's global rivalry with the United States" (Southerland 2017). The local public opinion tends to share this view. Sixty percent of respondents in Trinidad and Tobago believe that the reasons for China's investments in the country are both political and economic against 27 percent who prefer the purely economic explanation. A further 13 percent opt for political reasons alone. A respondent noted that the Chinese "presence is way bigger then it should be." "It has a lot more to do with their geopolitical interest in Trinidad and Tobago;" the Chinese are "actually utilizing investment as a geopolitical tool." In fact, they have "a very, very set and pinpoint accurate view of exactly what they want from

Trinidad and Tobago. They see this as a critical pillar point for them into dominance of the Caribbean region" (Respondent 1). Such opinions seem to be supported by the impressive trajectory of China's institutional cooperation with the Caribbean.

The Chinese-Caribbean Institutional Relations

China's involvement in a large number of Caribbean organizations is interesting because its relations with the region's countries have in fact been conducted on a mainly bilateral basis (Bernal 2016: 5597–5598). The bilateral approach allows Beijing to create competition between states seeking its assistance and to have more room for setting specific conditions (Oosterveld et al. 2018: 24). However, China also engages the region both in the framework of Latin American-Caribbean organizations and in that of exclusively Caribbean ones. For the first category, China became a permanent observer in the Organization of American States in 2004 and, during the last decade, has taken part in the UN Economic Commission for Latin America and the Caribbean (ECLAC) (Oosterveld et al. 2018: 34; Roett and Paz 2015: 499). In 2008 it purchased the 184 shares available after the breakup of Yugoslavia to become a member of the Inter-American Development Bank and, at the same time, acquired 110 shares that made it a member of the Inter-American Investment Corporation. On joining, it contributed a total of $350 million that included $125 million for soft loans to Bolivia, Guyana, Haiti, Honduras, and Nicaragua, $75 million for strengthening the institutional capacity of the state, $75 million for the development of small and mid-sized private businesses, and $75 million for microenterprises. In 2013, it established with the IDB the China Co-Financing Fund for Latin America and the Caribbean that would co-finance $500 million public sector loans and $1.5 billion for private sector entities in support of sustainable economic growth (Bernal 2016: 4185–4200; Bernal 2015: 1425). However, the most visible event was the establishment of a partnership between China and the Community of Latin American and Caribbean States (CELAC). The latter had been created in 2011 as an alternative to the Organization of American States and brings together all the states of the Western Hemisphere with the exception of the United States and Canada (Harris and Arias 2016: 518). Its second, 2014 Havana summit approved the proposal for a China-CELAC Forum that was formally established later that year (Roett and Paz 2015: 499) and held its first ministerial meeting in Beijing in January 2015. A comprehensive 5-year cooperation plan was adopted that covers trade, investment, finance, infrastructure, energy, natural resources, industry, agriculture, science, and people-to-people exchanges (Harris and Arias 2016: 519).

Given the disproportion in terms of population and economies, Caribbean states obviously do not represent the main focus of this large Chinese-Latin American and Caribbean institutional framework while their features and needs are hardly identical with those of Latin America. Beijing has compensated for this situation by developing specific links with the region. The best candidate partner was the Caribbean Community (CARICOM), which represents the leading interstate regional arrangement. Yet, some of its members recognize Taiwan and, at first view, this made China look for alternative solutions. This remains a debatable reason as the Chinese did join the Caribbean Development Bank (see below), which includes the same pro-Taipei states (Oosterveld et al. 2018: 5, 24). Certain authors suggest that, in fact, Beijing simply wanted to improve its negotiating position by avoiding to deal with a cohesive and well-organized group (for a discussion see Bernal 2016: 6519–6536). The alternative solutions comprised the biennial China-Caribbean Consultations held in 2002, 2004, and 2006 (Oosterveld et al. 2018: 34; Bernal 2016: 5601–5610); China's joining as a non-regional member of the Caribbean Development Bank, to which it contributed $56 million in shares and US $33 million in the Special Development Fund (Bernal 2015: 1425; Bernal 2016: 4185–4195); the China-Caribbean Joint Business Council, "the institutional vehicle for fostering business cooperation" (Bernal 2017: 241) whose objectives were set by the declaration adopted at the September 2007 meeting in Xiamen (Haro Navejas 2011: 209); and, last but not least, the China-Caribbean Economic and Trade Cooperation Forum that met in 2005, 2007, and 2011 (Bernal 2015: 1412) and became "the platform for the announcement of China's aid policy for the Caribbean countries" (Hongbo 2017: 308). Finally, the complementary approach represented by the progressive incorporation of Caribbean states into the Belt and Road Initiative should be mentioned, even if it is based on bilateral "Belt and Road Cooperation Agreements" (Barrios 2018; see the section *The Belt and Road Initiative* of Chapter 3) and, for the time being, does not allow for a dialogue between China and the entire region.

Overall, the intensity of these interactions fully justifies Respondent 1's claim that the Chinese "presence is way bigger then it should be." It is clear that purely economic interests can in no way explain the scale of Beijing's institutional involvement in the Caribbean that is supplemented by even more important bilateral relationships. Observers of this phenomenon have come to the conclusion that, through its multidimensional and multitask policy that builds new trade, aid, and diplomacy cooperation mechanisms as well as ad hoc institutions, China is integrating itself into the Caribbean framework of economic and diplomatic governance while simultaneously transforming the parameters of engagement. By constructing its own institutional architecture and projecting political and legal power, "Beijing has set about achieving nothing less than the genesis of a new regional order, built on functioning institutions and rules (. . .): *its* regional order" (Haro Navejas 2013: 147, 203, 209–210; emphasis in the original). This book shows that the use of conditionalities and the associated process of international socialization are key elements of this Chinese regional project.

China and Trinidad and Tobago: the Highest Connectivity in the Region

In 2017, two studies released by the International Labor Organization and the Caribbean Development Bank argued that Trinidad and Tobago "has the highest connectivity with China in the region" (Khan 2017). In May 2018, the Chinese Prime Minister Li Keqiang noted that Trinidad is his country's largest trade partner in the English Caribbean (Yue 2018). It is also the largest recipient of Chinese loans: by 2015 it had already received no less than USD 2.5bn (Oosterveld et al. 2018: 67). Illustrative of the regional competition for Chinese largesse, a rivalry even developed between Trinidad and Jamaica. Richard Bernal—a major specialist on China's involvement in the Caribbean but also a former Jamaican diplomat—insists on the fact that "Beijing has accorded Jamaica pride of place because it sees Jamaica as exerting an influential leadership role in Caribbean affairs;" "China views Jamaica as the platform from which to engage the rest of the Caribbean" (Bernal 2016: 5611–5614). Trinidadian respondents made similar statements about their own country, supported by the claim that "we are the leader of the Caribbean region" (Respondent 10); "we are not the same as CARICOM. They are our markets, not peers" (Respondent 1). Anyway, back in 1971 Trinidad and Tobago was one of the Third World states that voted at the 26th UN General Assembly for China to replace Taiwan as a member of the United Nations (Hongbo 2017: 290). Diplomatic relations were established in 1974 and, for the rest of the Cold War, Trinidad received small amounts of aid and technical assistance from China (as well as from Eastern bloc countries) (Braveboy-Wagner 2008: 122). This clear choice between Beijing and Taipei was motivated mainly by moderate tensions with the United States. Ever since, there has been no debate about a possible shift of allegiance: siding with China was interiorized a long time ago as "the right thing to do." Two-thirds of respondents stated that shifting recognition to Taiwan should not be contemplated even if Taipei offers clearly more investment, development aid, loans, and grants. More surprisingly, certain respondents very closely connected to Chinese activities in Trinidad were not even aware of the fact that the Caribbean represents one of the main arenas of the "diplomatic duel." They were puzzled by the fact that a giant like China might face competition from the Taiwanese dwarf in this region. To them, the scenario of a St. Lucia-type diplomatic shift that would bring larger benefits from Taipei simply seemed absurd.

The details of the relationship with China, on the contrary, are much better known. As briefly mentioned in the section *China in Latin America* of Chapter 3, Chinese scholars hail the two Policy Papers on Latin America and the Caribbean as proof that "an open, transparent, systematic elaboration of [China's] policy was conducted" (Hongbo 2017: 30). A particularly well-informed Trinidadian respondent, on the contrary, claimed that "the Chinese have one public version of the policy paper and another one, which is not public, that they use internally" (Respondent 23). More generally, another respondent stated that "the Chinese have a way of stating to whichever region exactly what they want to hear;" but "the actual reality of how China treats with us is something completely different to their stated policy" (Respondent 1). Overall, 53 percent of respondents believe that cooperation plans presented in the two papers are beneficial to both China and the Caribbean; however, no less than 40 percent claim that they will benefit China alone.

Political elites do not share such doubts. Their perspective is similar to that of politicians in all Caribbean states that recognize Beijing, many of which happen to be heavily indebted while their economies are stagnant (*The Economist*, March 10, 2012): "China's munificence is eagerly welcomed" (Wigglesworth 2013). In the words of Freundel Stuart, Prime Minister of Barbados, "we welcome all the help we can get" (Wigglesworth 2013). Various events were organized by the government in Port of Spain to stimulate this "help," such as the Trinidad and Tobago Business Forum held at the 2010 Shanghai Expo (Bernal 2015: 1428). They were highly successful especially with respect to China's preferred field: development assistance that takes the form of prestige infrastructure projects. The largest three such projects built by the Chinese in Trinidad between 2005 and 2016 were worth US $2 billion (Khan 2017). During President Xi Jinping's aforementioned 2013 visit, he agreed to "actively advance" bilateral cooperation in the fields of energy, minerals, infrastructure development, telecommunications, and agriculture. He also announced a US $250 million loan for the Couva Children's Hospital and attended the launching ceremony of the project, which was undertaken by a Chinese company (*BBC*, June 1, 2013; Ministry of Foreign Affairs of the People's Republic of China 2018). Unsurprisingly, then Prime Minister Kamla Persad-Bissessar stated in her flattering response speech "we see in your China Dream a splendid opportunity for China to become a model for the world" (Badri-Maharaj 2016). She also described the Asian country "as a key business partner and potential new market for our energy products" (*BBC*, June 1, 2013). Trinidad is one of the largest producers of liquefied natural gas in the world, with most of its exports going to the American market. It was believed that the shale gas revolution in the US would diminish demand there, while the expanded Panama canal would allow for the reorientation of Trinidadian exports to China (Mander 2013). The Chinese President's 2013 visit was followed by a flurry of bilateral interactions. That same year alone, Trinidad received delegations of the National Energy Administration, of the Guangdong Overseas Chinese Affairs Office, of Foshan, of Chinese military officers who attended the Forum for Senior Defense Officials from Caribbean and South Pacific Countries, and of "Cultures of China, Festival of Spring," as well as the Wu Opera Troupe of Zhejiang, the Hongsheng lion dancing team, and the "Beautiful China" photo exhibition. The first China Movie Week was held while a Confucius Institute was inaugurated at the St. Augustine campus of the University of West Indies. For its part, Trinidad sent a steel drum band—accompanied by the very Minister of Culture—to the ninth International Folk Art Festival in China (Ministry of Foreign Affairs of the People's Republic of China 2018). In February 2014 it was the turn of Prime Minister Kamla Persad-Bissessar to visit China. She opened the embassy of the Republic of Trinidad and Tobago in Beijing, convinced the Chinese to deliver a long-range vessel to Trinidad's Coast Guard (see the section *The Chinese-Caribbean Security Cooperation and Its Prospects* of Chapter 7), and sought assistance on five key issues that included the construction of six new economic zones, the development of a trans-shipment port and dry dock in South Trinidad, two new hospitals, and loan agreements to finance these projects (*Power102fm News*, February 25, 2014). By mid-2017, no less than 60 China-Trinidad agreements had been concluded in fields ranging from academic to military cooperation (*Loop News*, August 10, 2017).

A new government led by Prime Minister Dr. Keith Rowley came to power in September 2015. Previously, its members had criticized the government of Prime Minister Persad-Bissessar for "giving away the country to China;" but they in no way changed the pro-Beijing policy (Oosterveld et al. 2018: 71). In the words of the new Premier, "we have to look into countries that are looking for investment opportunities abroad and China is that today" (Waithe 2018). In May 2018 he visited China, where he negotiated three projects: a supply deal between Trinidad's Lake Asphalt and Beijing Construction and Engineering Group (BCEG); a code-sharing agreement between Air China and Caribbean Airlines; and a major project—whose details were set by a memorandum of understanding signed one month later—about the construction by the same Beijing Construction and Engineering Group of the US $104 million Phoenix Park Industrial Estate in Point Lisas, an industrial park financed through a loan from Exim Bank of China (Waithe 2018). Moreover, BCEG guaranteed the presence of at least ten Chinese firms specialized in the manufacturing of glass powder, air conditioners and ceramics, paper converting operations, wood processing, communication equipment, building materials, integrated housing manufacturing, and food processing (*Trinidad and Tobago Daily Express*, June 20, 2018). In September 2018, Prime Minister Dr. Keith Rowley signed a cooperation agreement for the development of a large dry dock facility in La Brea with China Harbor Engineering Company. The latter will take a 30 percent equity in the La Brea project; the Trinidadian government will own the rest, for which it will need a new loan (Webb 2018). Finally, in 2018 five Chinese banks were invited to operate in Trinidad and Tobago. Communication Minister Stuart Young even stated "we envisage Trinidad and Tobago to be a clearing house for the Chinese currency," an initiative that "will enable T&T to be a gateway to Central America and other parts of the region" (Kowlessar 2018). However, the most important development associated with Prime Minister Rowley's visit to China was the signing of the Belt and Road Initiative memorandum that turned Trinidad and Tobago into the first Caribbean state to join BRI (Shiwei 2018; Office of the Prime Minister Republic of Trinidad and Tobago 2018; certain sources—such as Barrios 2018—wrongly attribute this to Antigua and Barbuda. In fact, the latter's memorandum was signed some weeks later, in early June; Antigua was the first member of the Organization of Eastern Caribbean States, not of the entire English-speaking Caribbean, to join Beijing's initiative). The Chinese even paid for an advertisement in Trinidad's *Daily Express* that welcomed their partner into BRI, which was described as "a public good that China offers to the world" (*Trinidad and Tobago Daily Express*, April 10, 2018).

Elements presented in this section clearly show that Trinidad and Tobago does indeed represent a case of "highest connectivity with China" and, as such, is likely to represent a good illustration of Beijing conditionality and socialization efforts. A respondent presented this situation as the result of an "opportunistic and savvy" national strategy leading to a strategic alliance that represents a "better, more lucrative way forward" (Respondent 9). The next section briefly examines the "soft power" dimension of this relationship.

CHINESE INFLUENCE AND SOFT POWER

As mentioned in the section *China in Latin America* of Chapter 3, in Latin America the main target of Beijing's influence is represented by the elites. Little is done to address the negative perceptions and reactions of local societies (Shen 2015: 114). The situation is different in Africa, where the magnitude of negative effects and ensuing harsh criticism have compelled China to "compete not only for commerce, but for public opinion" (Bräutigam 2015: xv). There has even been a discussion of the "charm defensive" launched by Chinese media on that continent that represents "a responsive tactic to clarify misrepresentations" (Li 2017a: 35). This shows that, in different regions, various approaches are used by Beijing based on the local situation and on China's regional interests. They might target or ignore specific social categories while the instruments employed range from development assistance to "a hidden world of inducements, threats and plausible deniability" used to influence sections of the political, business, academic, and legal communities, as well as the ethnic Chinese living in the target country (Garnaut 2018). Related to this latter "instrument," Beijing has created the Liaison Department of the General Political Department of the People's Liberation Army, a huge intelligence agency designed to perform international influence operations. China's Propaganda Department, United Front Work Department, International Liaison Department, and other units of the People's Liberation Army and of the Ministry of State Security are also used "to influence the perceptions and internal decision-making of foreign actors" (Garnaut 2018). An increasing number of journalists and scholars scrutinize such actions in states that one would logically expect to be targeted by Beijing, such as Singapore, as well as in others that, at first view, might represent less likely candidates, such as Australia and New Zealand (see Hamilton 2018; Garnaut 2018; *The Economist*, November 8, 2018). Overall, while actual patterns of action differ greatly from one region to the other, the Chinese influence offensive seems to be global.

In the Caribbean, China's approach is similar to that used in Latin America: the main target is represented by the political elites. As shown in the next chapter, they are socialized through the instrumentalization of the large infrastructure projects that form the bulk of the Chinese development assistance offered to Caribbean states. In Africa, Beijing's infrastructure projects have succeeded in creating a positive image of China in the society at large (Lahtinen 2018: 33). As shown in the next chapter, this is hardly the case in much of the Caribbean, where Chinese-built infrastructure projects tend to be associated with the most detrimental socio-economic effects of China's economic conditionality. Therefore, Beijing has had to rely on other forms of soft power in order to favorably influence the public opinion. Some authors even speak of "a systematic, coherent soft power strategy" amounting to a "charm offensive" (Kurlantzick 2008; Bernal 2016: 3270–3271). The intent does exist; it's just that the scale of this "offensive" is quite modest and its implementation leaves much to be desired. A large part of the Chinese efforts can be included in the large and complex category of propaganda (it should be noted that China has inherited from its communist past the aforementioned "Propaganda Department," whose name does not seem to sound inappropriate to the leadership in Beijing). The Chinese-paid advertisement published in a Trinidadian newspaper shortly after the country joined BRI represents a good example. It starts as a self-laudatory text praising the adoption of the Xi Jinping Thought on Socialism with Chinese Characteristics at the 19th National Congress of the Communist Party of China. More than half of the three columns detail the present merits and future exploits of the Chinese leadership. There is, however, place for Beijing's relationship with Trinidad and Tobago—trade, foreign direct investment, total value of contracts, and "the turnover" are presented with a visually impacting focus on words such as "million" and "billion." The inescapable "positive attitude" associated with "win-win cooperation" follows, with a slight "[trade] openness" sting toward President Trump's protectionism. Finally, BRI-as-public-good brings the promise for common prosperity (*Trinidad and Tobago Daily Express*, April 10, 2018). Not all texts of this type come as paid advertising. A regular article was published by another Trinidadian newspaper before the inauguration of the US $15 billion Hong Kong-Macao bridge. Somewhat strangely, most of the text deals with the plan for a 30 kilometers bridge between the islands of Trinidad and Tobago: Chinese construction engineers "believe it can be done." Chinese expertise and its possible use in the Caribbean as suggested by Chinese officials are presented and hailed. It is only toward the end of the article that the author acknowledges the fact that the cost of building and maintaining such a bridge could in no way be justified by Tobago's actual transportation needs, which are fully addressed by the present ferry service (Samaroo 2017). After reading the article, one cannot fail to question its logic. Given the obvious conclusion, why would a reporter spend time and energy on such a topic? The answer is perhaps related to the fact that "Guardian Media was given a tour" of the Chinese bridge located at no less than 12 time zones from the reporter's office in Port of Spain.

Part of China's Trinidad-related propaganda targets a more general Global South audience. A China Global Television report about the signing of the Belt and Road Initiative memorandum by Trinidad and Tobago proudly emphasized the fact that "the capital's landmark," the Chinese-built National Academy for the Performing Arts (NAPA), is "widely acknowledged as one of the best architectural masterpieces in the Caribbean region." For its part, the Couva Children's Hospital "became the first of its kind in Trinidad and Tobago and the wider Caribbean" (Shiwei 2018). Ironically, both NAPA and the hospital in Couva are famous in Trinidad as the most representative failures of China's development assistance. They created an extremely negative image of the Chinese contractors, which "have lost the battle in terms of the public opinion. There is generally extraordinarily negative viewpoint of Chinese firms" (Respondent 1). In turn, because it was the government in Beijing that imposed these contractors as part of its "tied aid," the NAPA and Couva issues contributed considerably to the rejection of the Chinese economic conditionality by the Trinidadian society (see Chapter 5). But China Global Television knows that nobody outside Trinidad reads local newspapers, and successfully uses footage of beautiful façades to promote the image of China-the-generous-donor in the developing world. The same thing is done by Chinese scholars. Using information provided by the Chinese government instead of widely available local sources, Sun Hongbo wrote admiratively about the same National Performing Arts Center and about another remarkable failure, the "electrolytic aluminum plant"—an aluminum smelter project cancelled years ago by Trinidad's government for reasons presented in Chapter 5; the issue is currently before the courts, with a Chinese claim that amounts to US $201 million (*CNC3*, March 3, 2018)—to illustrate the advantages "of China's preferential loans" and of "the economic cooperation between the two countries" (Hongbo 2017: 319). More modestly, he also mentioned "the free material assistance provided by China" that "has effectively made the Chinese products well-known." He gives the example of container inspection equipment generously offered to five countries in the region (Hongbo 2017: 312). The problem is that the "fixed scanner at the port of POS (Port of Spain) has yet to be operationalized by GOTT (Government of Trinidad and Tobago) almost four years after being handed over" (Respondent 30). Occasional cultural exchanges also give birth to imaginative statements in Chinese publications targeting a foreign audience. If one believes *China Daily*, "Wuju, a kind of opera in Jinhua, East China's Zhejiang province, is one of the favorites of the people of Trinidad and Tobago;" moreover, "China's acrobatics was commonly seen in Trinidad and Tobago" (*China Daily*, June 2, 2013). It is understandable that, after reading such strange claims, few in Trinidad might trust Chinese sources of information. Definitely, the Propaganda Department in Beijing should take a closer look at the actual situation of countries depicted in the reports and guidelines it distributes to China's state-controlled media.

This is not to say that Chinese-Trinidadian artistic and cultural contacts are absent. In fact, in recent years they have significantly increased in frequency as a result of China's new interest in the region. Their actual impact, however, remains limited, and there are only two truly responsive audiences: the local ethnic Chinese community (see Chapter 6) and, for obvious reasons, the Ministry of Community Development, Culture, and the Arts. Probably the most successful Chinese cultural enterprise in Trinidad is represented by the Confucius Institute, launched in October 2013 as the second such institution in the Caribbean. In many Global South countries, these Institutes "act as a countermeasure to the negativity around trade;" "the perception of what China means is very much coloured" by their actions (Respondent 4). In practical terms, the main goals are the teaching of Mandarin Chinese—students include Trinidadians scheduled to visit China for academic or professional purposes—and the promotion of Chinese culture through exhibitions, performances, demonstrations, lectures, and workshops. They include Chinese Movie Nights, Chinese Spring Festival Galas, Chinese Tea Appreciation Workshops, and Chinese Knotting Workshops. There are also two "tour to China" programs, one for local educators and one for students (The Confucius Institute 2018). Undoubtedly, there is genuine Trinidadian interest in many of these activities. But it would be highly exaggerated to claim that the Institute has achieved mass participation. Much of its audience continues to come from Trinidad's small ethnic Chinese community, which has shown particular "openness" to its activities (Respondent 4). It is perhaps relevant that the Institute's 2017 annual report has only 17 pages, many of them filled with pictures.

The main expression of Chinese soft power that has favorably influenced the local society in Trinidad and Tobago—and possibly in the Caribbean—on a relevant scale pertains to the field of academia. More precisely, it concerns the close cooperation between China and the University of the West Indies (UWI). With the University of the South Pacific, this is one of the few surviving international regional universities and "the largest, most longstanding higher education provider in the Commonwealth Caribbean." Its four campuses—in Trinidad, Jamaica, Barbados, and the Open Campus—educate over 40,000 students (*UWI Campus News*, December 16, 2016). In the 1970s it replaced educational institutions in Western Europe as the region's university of choice. Already in the early 2000s the leaders of Trinidad and Tobago, Jamaica, Barbados, Grenada, St. Kitts-Nevis, Saint Lucia, and St. Vincent and the Grenadines had been educated at UWI (Braveboy-Wagner 2008: 178), a trend that continues to be very visible. Unsurprisingly, China chose it as its key academic partner in the region and initiated a wide range of cooperation programs. In 2013 a partnership was launched between the China Agricultural University (CAU) and the UWI St. Augustine Campus in Trinidad that resulted in the 2015 creation of the UWI-CAU Agricultural Innovation Park at Orange Grove. The 200-acre farm is intended to showcase advanced intensive agricultural production methodologies and practices and to adapt them to Caribbean conditions (*UWI Campus News*, October 23, 2015). In 2016, the Jamaica and Barbados UWI campuses launched a bi-culturally designed Bachelor in Science Software Engineering program with the Global Institute of Software Engineering in Suzhou, China; Caribbean and Chinese students spend half of the program in the partner university. Chinese language and cultural training is provided as a part of the curriculum. The creation of a UWI Institute in China is also planned. Student exchanges are facilitated by the fact that in 2016 China's Ministry of Education approved the official recognition of UWI degrees (*UWI Campus News*, December 16, 2016; *UWI Campus*

News, February 7, 2018). The most important effect of this cooperation is the favorable perception of China shared by a part of the successive generations of UWI graduates who eventually become active in politics, business, mass media, or education. However, while this category is much larger than that of the political elites, it remains somewhat limited to the upper social strata of educated professionals and its views do not necessarily influence the entire Trinidadian society.

This is also the situation of technocrats directly involved in dealings with the Chinese. Two-thirds of the respondents belonging to this category had good or very good perceptions of those interactions; the remaining third were neutral. Many of them expressed genuine admiration for the Chinese they met: "they work hard (. . .) they work very well" (Respondent 24); "they are very hard working (. . .), they are much, much more industrious than locals in Trinidad (. . .). They are very efficient. Very, very efficient people" (Respondent 3). "Actually, [they are] very good to work with. The attitude is so different from what we are accustomed to in the Caribbean. They are so amenable, they are willing to listen, willing to exchange ideas" (Respondent 8). "I think they are one of the better people to liaise with in businesses" (Respondent 30). Problems can arise from the Chinese's poor command of English or from Trinidadians' lack of familiarity with the Chinese culture; but they can be solved and, overall, "I feel much more relaxed in dealing with [the Chinese]" (Respondent 24). A similarly positive perception of the same respondents concerns China as a whole: "that combination of financial might and human resources, it leaves everybody in the shade, it is just an unbeatable combination" (Respondent 5). Critically, the Chinese are perceived as having learned to respond appropriately to partners in the Global South, which is not the case of the US:

> As an institution, it has been very easy to work with Chinese organisations for two reasons: they are practical and they have money. (. . .) If I am talking to the United States, it's really, the whole world is talking to the United States and Trinidad is not a priority (. . .). The Chinese actively are looking for new opportunities. (. . .) They want to develop cooperative programmes, (. . .) they get in a plane and come here. (. . .) The entire world is in Beijing. The entire world wants to collaborate with China. (. . .) The Chinese know how to cooperate now. Their system has evolved and they are very efficient at collaboration and cooperation. And they don't have a lot of bureaucracy, and that's a big issue. (. . .) The minute you are in front of a decision-maker in China because they are there to develop a collaboration and they take a decision they stick to their word. It happens. (. . .) Collaboration is very easy with China (Respondent 23).

Of course, the respondents who made these comments are not manual laborers or cleaning ladies; they are educated professionals involved in medium and high-level interactions with the Chinese. Therefore, their views are illustrative not of the perception of Chinese-centered interactions by the Trinidadian society at large—its members seldom have direct contacts with Beijing bureaucrats or agencies—but for the more general reasons that contribute to China's positive image. The latter is only in a very small measure related to "Confucius Institutes, scholarships to study in China, training in the Caribbean, friendship associations, [and] CCTV in English," to use a list positively presented in the literature (Bernal 2016: 3263–3327). The situation is not different from that in Africa, where appreciation for Chinese culture brings the lowest contribution (2 percent) out of all favorable factors: "China's cultural agenda attached to diplomacy has not resonated with African minds" (Lahtinen 2018: 47, 85). What does resonate with Caribbean minds is the remarkable economic success resulting from China's business and managerial effectiveness which impressed the respondents. This success is unlikely to be perceived positively by, say, Vietnamese audiences, but in the Caribbean it generates undisguised admiration among technocrats and common people alike. It is due to this admiration that, despite the very serious Chinese-triggered socio-economic problems presented in Chapters 5 and 6, "a favorable view of China persists" in the region (Southerland 2017): as shown in more detail in Chapter 8, 47 percent of the Trinidadian respondents have a positive overall perception of China and 27 percent a very positive one. Yet, other soft power factors that might have a similar effect—such as aforementioned academic cooperation or the activities of the Confucius Institute—are few and concern a limited audience. Accordingly, "China's soft power in the region is very fragile. One major mishap might destroy its reputation beyond repair" (Oosterveld et al. 2018: 8). Even without such a dramatic development, the impact of Chinese soft power is too weak to change the society's negative perception of China's economic and social conditionalities. The case of the political conditionality, however, is different.

CHINA'S POLITICAL CONDITIONALITY AND ITS RECEPTION IN TRINIDAD

Previous sections have shown that China initially engaged the Caribbean in the rather narrow framework of its "diplomatic duel" with Taiwan. However, after 2008 and especially since 2013, a much broader agenda was progressively adopted. The resulting multidimensional policy towards the region has set up new trade, development assistance, and diplomacy cooperation mechanisms that are intended to project political and legal power and to construct a new institutional architecture. This shows the will of the leadership in Beijing to engage the region in a way and on a scale that are not justified by natural resources- or trade-related interests and that can only be understood as the expression of a geopolitical project. The final objective has been identified in the literature as nothing less than the creation of a Chinese "regional order built on functioning institutions and rules" (Haro Navejas 2013: 147, 203, 209–210; see the next section). In this context, it would be naïve to believe that Beijing simply expects Caribbean states to harmoniously follow its lead and spontaneously adopt policies that respond to its interests in the region. Any great power in its position knows that it needs to shape the way its presence and actions are perceived and responded to. In other words, China needs to create a cognitive and normative space favorable to its interests; and this is most easily done by imposing a set of specific conditions that partner states have to respect in exchange for economic incentives. This happens all over the region; Trinidad and Tobago represents the best case study for the analysis of this process only because it has "the highest connectivity with China in the region" (Khan 2017), which makes evidence easier to collect. Its close relationship with Beijing is promoted enthusiastically by political elites, which have good self-interested reasons to appreciate China's prestige infrastructure projects (see the next chapter) and therefore never question associated conditionalities. The society's overall perception of China is favorable, but things are very different when its response to specific conditionalities is scrutinized. For methodological reasons, I analyze the economic and social ones in separate chapters that substantiate their rejection by Trinidad's society. The limited effectiveness of soft power instruments used by China in the region contributes to this rejection and makes it unlikely to come to an end in the predictable future. However, this does not apply to Beijing's political conditionality, which is fully accepted by both elites and society.

A key element of China's propaganda effort is represented by the vocal claim that its benevolent, win-win approach is in no way related to any conditionality. The first Policy Paper on Latin America and the Caribbean clearly states that "the Chinese Government will (. . .) continue to provide economic and technical assistance to *relevant* Latin American and Caribbean countries without attaching any political conditions" (The State Council of the People's Republic of China 2008: IV.2.12; emphasis added). The "relevant" tag might leave some doubt; but it disappeared from the second policy paper: "China will continue to provide economic and technical assistance to Latin American and Caribbean countries without attaching any political conditions" (Ministry of Foreign Affairs of the Republic of China 2016: IV.2.13). The same document mentions "unconditionality" as one of the principles of its cooperation with the region (Ministry of Foreign Affairs of the Republic of China 2016: IV.7). These statements are one hundred percent correct if one adopts the Western understanding of political conditionality, i.e. the respect by a developing state of certain principles related to human rights, democracy, good governance, and the rule of law as a precondition for the validity of an international agreement related to development assistance (Dipama and Dal 2015: 112). Due to "a long and troubled history" of IMF programs, the imposition of such conditions "has become stigmatized" in Latin America and the Caribbean (Gallagher 2016: 82). In fact, a vicious circle has developed. In the words of a Global South government spokesman, such "conditions are probably well intentioned, but they are humiliating" (Gallagher 2016: 84). This leads to their rejection; yet, as noted by scholars in the region, "lack of emphasis on human rights, the rule of law and good governance may be very detrimental for the long term social and economic development of the Caribbean" (Montoute 2013: 123). For its part, authoritarian China is hardly interested in supporting democracy and human rights at home and abroad; accordingly, it takes advantage of this situation in order to present its own actions as conditionality-free. Yet, the very policy papers that proclaim the fundamental importance of "unconditionality" do not find it odd to state that "China is ready to establish and develop state-to-state relations with Latin American and Caribbean countries on the basis of the one China principle" (Ministry of Foreign Affairs of the Republic of China 2016: III). In fact, this "unconditional" condition goes further than the simple diplomatic non-recognition of Taiwan. Beijing also requires recipient states to actively oppose UN resolutions supporting Taipei's claim for sovereign status (McElroy and Bai 2008: 230). More importantly, in practical terms China's partners are prevented from accepting the Taiwanese development assistance that comes with diplomatic recognition. In this way, to quote an African author, "China has implicitly intervened in the domestic affairs of African sovereign states" (Ziso 2018: 14), a situation that repeats itself in the Caribbean and all over the Global South.

As already mentioned, the Chinese political conditionality doesn't stop at Taiwan. States receiving Beijing development assistance are also required to avoid any statement or act that might be contrary to China's domestic anti-democratic policies and practices; and to oppose UN resolutions that criticize its human rights record (McElroy and Bai 2008: 230). Due to their prolonged "diplomatic duel" with Beijing, Taiwanese diplomats are perhaps the most qualified observers of Chinese actions. François Chih-Chung Wu, the French-educated Deputy Foreign Minister in Taipei, noted that the "process may begin with a Confucius Institute, scholarships, grants, but the next thing you know you must self-censor discussions China considers sensitive" (Garnaut 2018). To give a striking example, democratic South Africa refused to issue a visa to the Dalai Lama three times in five years for fear of endangering economic ties with China. This prevented him from attending the October 2014 Cape Town 14th World Peace Summit. In response, nine former peace prize winners as well as eleven affiliated organizations boycotted the conference, which had to be canceled. Archbishop Desmond Tutu accused President Jacob Zuma of "kowtowing to China" (Lahtinen 2018: 22). If such things happen in one of Africa's richest and most developed countries, it is not difficult to imagine the situation of poorer and smaller Global South recipients of Chinese development assistance. A Trinidadian respondent accordingly noted "the conditionalities that come with Chinese money:" "there is unquestionably a package that comes with Chinese assistance and aligning to their sort of global influence" (Respondent 1). No less than 73 percent of the respondents shared this opinion. One of them also provided a comprehensive description of Beijing political conditionality: "Taiwan doesn't exist. The Dalai Lama doesn't exist. One China. Tiananmen Square doesn't exist. (. . .) I am not naive about the whole China thing" (Respondent 5). In fact, at times the Chinese even ask for more. The second Policy Paper on Latin America and the Caribbean mentions in its section on International Political Affairs efforts "to deepen exchanges and cooperation between the two sides in the UN and other international organizations and on other international platforms" and, in the section on Global Economic Governance, China's "work to strengthen coordination and cooperation with Latin American and Caribbean countries in international economic and financial organizations and mechanisms" (Ministry of Foreign Affairs of the Republic of China 2016: IV.5.1). This is to say that the general voting behavior of partner states in international fora should follow the Chinese one. Until now, such a pattern has not been generalized. Yet, Trinidad and Tobago is closely aligned with China in terms of voting at the UN General Assembly and so are most countries in the Commonwealth Caribbean (Oosterveld et al. 2018: 34, 70). This general support for Beijing's diplomatic interests, however, is—or should be—less important for the citizens of recipient countries than the "Tiananmen Square doesn't exist" topic.

The Democracy and Human Rights Issue

Based on mainly African examples, scholars have noted that "China's concept of non-intervention is quite narrow" (Ziso 2018: 13). This is well illustrated by its economic engagement with dictatorships. While doing business with such states might be taken as a purely profit-based approach that takes advantage of local natural resources in the absence of hindrances from independent unions or opposition political parties (Gurtov 2015: 78), this is also "at a minimum, a political intervention in support of the prevailing institutions, norms and political elites" (Gonzalez-Vicente 2015: 213; Ziso 2018: 13). Indeed, Beijing's economic relations with African states whose leaders have attained pariah status and, more generally, with regimes that show disrespect for democracy and human rights—the cases of Zimbabwe, Sudan, South Sudan, and Guinea are frequently quoted—change the international and domestic dynamics and allow those regimes to survive and to continue their oppressive and at times criminal practices. China's rejection of the UN demand that pressure be applied on the government of Robert Mugabe in Zimbabwe—based on the argument that such a policy would be counter-productive—simply allowed for the prolonged political survival of the African dictator (Lahtinen 2018: 25–27; Alden and Barber 2018: 3). Empirical research has shown that the democratizing effects of OECD development assistance to sub-Saharan African states have diminished due to China's dictator-friendly policies in the region (Li 2017a: 201). This is not limited to that continent. In the Caribbean basin, China has similarly undermined the respect for human rights in "Bolivarian" Venezuela by its economic cooperation with and support for the regime of Presidents Chávez and Maduro. What is surprising is the perception of such actions in the Global South: the Chinese "non-interference" support for the authoritarian regime of Zimbabwe at the United Nations "was widely welcomed publicly by African leaders" (Lahtinen 2018: 26). African common people think likewise: only 4 percent of respondents in 36 countries "blame China for its willingness to work with autocratic governments" (Lahtinen 2018: 47). One could hardly think of a better encouragement for the continuation of Beijing's support for non-democracies abroad.

Of course, this support is not directly linked to China's political conditionality. But it is related to the "Tiananmen Square doesn't exist" issue that, on the contrary, represents one of the core elements of this conditionality. Basically, the Chinese policy is "we don't criticize your human rights record, you don't criticize ours." This does lead to a mutually beneficial relationship in the case of Zimbabwean or Venezuelan dictators whose anti-democratic values resonate with those of China. In the case of democracies, however, this should raise serious ethical questions. On the one hand, such states place in their Constitution, policy documents, and school curricula solemn statements in support of the universal values of democracy and human rights. On the other hand, under Chinese pressure, they have to admit that those values are not that universal after all, and should not be invoked in relation to China's dissidents, to Tibet, or to the one million Uyghurs currently detained abusively in "reeducation camps" (The United Nations Office of the High Commissioner for Human Rights 2018). This should be highly disturbing for CARICOM states that, as already mentioned, have constantly promoted democracy and the respect for human rights domestically and internationally, an effort that has considerably increased their prestige at the United Nations (Braveboy-Wagner 2010: 422). In 1989, harsh criticism explicitly concerned Chinese policies when the Tiananmen massacre made Grenada and Belize shift their diplomatic allegiance to Taiwan. Contrary to mainland China, at that time the island had resolutely launched its process of genuine democratization (Hu 2015: 10–11; Li 2005: 82). For its part, since independence Trinidad and Tobago has been proactive on global anti-colonial and anti-racist issues and, more recently, an early promoter of the International Criminal Court. Prime Minister Arthur Napoleon Raymond Robinson was one of the key international actors who contributed decisively to the creation of the court in 1998 (Braveboy-Wagner 2010: 423). Domestically, Trinidad "has maintained a robust parliamentary democracy with a vibrant media and civil society" (Freedom House 2018). Its Freedom House political rights, civil liberties, and overall freedom ratings are 2 out of 7, where 1 stands for "most free," and 7 for "least free;" the aggregate score is 81 out of 100, with 100 representing the score of "most free" countries (Freedom House 2018). In 2010, an opinion poll showed that 67 percent of the citizens believed that democracy is preferable to any other form of government. Only 12 percent preferred an authoritarian regime. With respect to the country's actual situation, 7 percent considered that Trinidad was "very democratic," 62 percent "somewhat democratic," 21 percent "not very democratic," and 4 percent "not at all democratic" (Kirton et al. 2010: 27). Against this background, one would expect both elites and the society in Trinidad to care about democracy at home *and* abroad. Yet, when the case of China is considered, the political elites fully and uncritically accept its political conditionality. They never mention unpleasant human rights-related issues. This is hardly surprising, as they also accept the much more detrimental—in practical terms—economic and social conditionalities. The latter are rejected by the Trinidadian society; but this is not the case for the political one. Indeed, to no less than 86 percent of respondents, China's lack of democracy is irrelevant to Trinidad. It represents a seldom mentioned, unimportant issue. Moreover, in the field of development assistance a sort of division of labor has developed. The Americans and the Europeans

> are helping the country in human rights, that kind of things. (. . .) Chinese funding is really for return of investment. (. . .) If we want to improve government bureaucracy, we will do an Inter-American Development Bank loan. (. . .) If we build a highway, we check the Chinese. So there is one set of loan money for a thing and the next for the other (Respondent 30).

A respondent attributed this situation to the fact that parts of the Trinidadian society tend to associate human rights with gay rights and to perceive them as Western-imposed. In any case, the debate interests only limited groups in the academia and perhaps in the media, not the society at large (Respondent 9).

Political Conditionality and International Socialization

Besides this rather disturbing hypothesis, the overall acceptance of the Chinese-imposed "no Taiwan; no Tibet; no Tiananmen Square" way of thinking and acting can be associated with a pragmatic lack of interest in issues that are perceived as geographically remote and unable to impact the country's socio-economic situation. In fact, the specific reasons for the acceptance of China's political conditionality are less important for this book than the very existence of this conditionality as an instrument used by Beijing in its Caribbean enterprise. To remind once more of its formal definition, Chinese political conditionality represents the use of economic incentives in order to shape the recipient state's China-related foreign policy preferences as well as its attitude toward democracy and human rights in China. Because it prevents the acceptance of Taiwanese development assistance, it directly affects the domestic socio-economic situation. Because it limits the reach of the recipient state's democracy discourse, it reshapes the way that state understands its fundamental values. Consequently, it qualifies as conditionality even if the narrow definition of the latter is taken into consideration (see the Introduction). It is, however, a weak conditionality—in any case, weaker than the contrary Western political conditionality that promotes democracy and the respect of human rights. For a Global South state, the diplomatic choice between Beijing and Taipei and their respective packages of development assistance or the attitude to adopt on the issue of dissidents in China are of course of a different order of magnitude than the sudden obligation to stop rigging elections or to put an end to abusive detentions. From the Chinese point of view, however, this "weak" political conditionality has highly beneficial effects. At a general level, it enables Beijing to shape the political behavior of Global South countries in ways favorable to its foreign policy interests. This has traditionally been useful in fighting Taiwan; today, it becomes a key feature of China's newly acquired status of global power that identifies itself as a representative and a teacher of the developing world. In the Caribbean, Beijing has preserved the nature of its Global South efforts but considerably increased their intensity. Disproportionately massive development assistance has been used to set up close bilateral partnerships and regional institutional frameworks that led to a very high density of Chinese-initiated and controlled interactions. Through these "South-South" cooperation mechanisms, the entire region is made to evolve toward a Chinese-centered cognitive and normative space. Caribbean state-society complexes are taught how to think and how to act with respect to China and to its political interests. This is an obvious process of international socialization intended to ensure the adoption of collective understandings about the desirable and beneficial nature of a special relationship with China. If such beliefs are internalized as norms, they would ultimately make Caribbean state-society complexes develop new, Chinese-friendly international identities. This would of course greatly enhance Beijing's regional political influence, which confirms the aforementioned argument that China's socialization efforts in the Caribbean cannot be dissociated from the use and production of power (see the section *Socialization and Power* of Chapter 2). From this perspective, the use of political conditionality in this region has been a success as the compliance of both elites and society has been acquired. An important step has therefore been made toward the Caribbean's international socialization. However, the latter also requires the acceptance of China's economic and social conditionalities analyzed in the next two chapters.

Chapter Five

China's Economic Conditionality

China's economic conditionality was defined in previous chapters as the imposition on recipient states of "tied aid" and of the non-transparent, secretive negotiation of associated government-to-government agreements. The case study of Trinidad and Tobago used to analyze the features of this conditionality in the Caribbean is particularly relevant as almost all of Beijing's development assistance directed to this country consists in large infrastructure projects financed by Chinese loans. The content of this chapter will likely surprise many readers unfamiliar with the region as it unveils the large scale public dissatisfaction with China's imposition of its own contractors, labor, and materials for such infrastructure projects; with the very serious failures of these projects; with the exploitation by Chinese construction firms of Chinese nationals brought to work in Trinidad; and, critically, with the perceived negative impact of Chinese actions on Trinidad's good governance and democracy. In particular, China is kept responsible for the aforementioned secretive government-to-government negotiations and undisclosed agreements that the majority of citizens believe to be at the origin of the above-mentioned problems and to encourage high-level corruption. The Chinese socialization of Trinidadian and, more generally, Caribbean political elites is also discussed in this chapter as, on the one hand, it stems precisely from the close bilateral top-level interactions related to development assistance; and, on the other hand, it represents the key reason for the continued acceptation of China's economic conditionality by the state despite its rejection by the local society.

CHINA'S ECONOMIC PRESENCE IN TRINIDAD AND THE CARIBBEAN

China's Successful Economic Formula in the Global South

China's "Go out" or "Going Global" strategy is intended to provide new international market and investment opportunities (Stahl 2018: 8–9). It was initiated by President Jiang Zemin in 1999 (Hess and Aidoo 2015: 16) and was adopted by the Chinese Communist Party as part of its tenth five-year plan in 2002. It provides encouragement and support for Chinese companies that develop ties abroad in response to "the imperatives of China's economic expansion" (Ellis 2014: 5). As already mentioned in the section *The "Panda Cometh" and "Globalization with Chinese Characteristics"* of Chapter 3, this strategy significantly contributed to China's spectacular economic penetration of the Global South by setting up a particularly effective collaboration among the Chinese state, Chinese state-owned banks, and Chinese state-owned enterprises (Ellis 2013: 2). The strategy—that has already been presented in the section *China in Africa* of Chapter 3—was first experimented in Africa and then successfully extended to Beijing's interactions with the entire developing world (see Hess and Aidoo 2015: 9; Ellis 2013: 2; Ellis 2014: 8; Campbell 2014); in Latin America it started to "blossom" in 2010–2011 (Ellis 2014: 8). The fact that Chinese firms are able to secure financing from their government obviously improves their competitiveness (Oosterveld et al. 2018: 24). The fact that framework agreements are frequently concluded by the government itself—which uses concessionary loans from China Exim Bank as incentives—is even more important in ensuring the success of Chinese companies in the developing world (Lahtinen 2018: 42). In principle, these companies are state-owned, hybrid, and private, which should determine different types of interaction with China's government. In fact, the peculiarities of "capitalism with Chinese characteristics" ensure that "even hybrid and private firms depend on the government to do business in China" (Backaler 2014: 12) and even more so abroad. First, ownership is not always clear. A large state-owned corporation is led by chief executive officers at ministerial-level rank and senior staff are appointed by the state; its subordination to the government is obvious. But many "private" companies do not disclose clear information on equity structure; despite appearances, they may be controlled by a state-owned parent company. Second, in addition to ownership there is state influence. Major private firms have internal Communist Party committees that ensure their accountability to the state and adhere closely to government policy or informally specified objectives. In exchange, they have access to particular credit lines, tax breaks, priority in the allocation of key contracts, and favorable interpretation of regulations (Lahtinen 2018: 41–42). Accordingly, one should not expect them to act differently from state-owned ones in the Global South. Anyway, by 2014 no less than 180 state-owned corporations were designated by the government in Beijing to "go global" (Mohan et al. 2014: 59). The second Policy Paper on Latin America and the Caribbean explicitly stated that "China will support its strong enterprises to participate in major resources and energy development projects and infrastructure construction projects" in the region (Ministry of Foreign Affairs of the Republic of China 2016: IV.2.6). For their part, these companies "are learning how to develop their business while transforming into global industry giants at the same time" (Backaler 2014: 11). In particular, in various Global South regions and countries they create informal social networks between different Chinese actors. Firms already there facilitate the entry of other businesses from China by providing "contacts, insights, and overcoming obstacles to doing business" (Ellis 2014: 8).

All this explains the massive expansion of Chinese companies in the developing world and China's ensuing rise as a global power. However, not everything is perfect. As shown in the sections *China in Africa* (see the parts about the "pessimistic view" and the "China threat") and *China in Latin America* of Chapter 3, Chinese corporations have also encountered major obstacles and challenges that in many occasions turned them into symbols of the "particularly venal and brutal" "Chinese capitalism" (Mohan et al. 2014: 100). In a way, due to the negative depiction of their actions, "China has become [the] biggest victim" of the anti-globalization trend (Mullen 2017; Fang and Chimenson 2017: 485). In extreme cases, local frustration with the detrimental consequences of the activity of Chinese corporations even led to kidnappings and killings of Chinese nationals sent to partner countries. Some governments also adopted explicit anti-Chinese measures (Ellis 2013: 3, 4; Lahtinen 2018: 46; Hess and Aidoo 2015: 4, 136). As many of these reactions came in response to socio-economic problems, they will be presented and analyzed in the next chapter, which deals with social issues. Overall, scholars have identified three simultaneous dynamics that characterize the complex interaction of Chinese companies with the Global South: increased conflict, accelerated learning, and increased soft power due to their role as local employer, major tax payer, and member of the local business community (Ellis 2013: 4). Their outcome is critical to the evolution of China's relationships with the various regions and countries of the developing world because the poor image of its firms can limit Beijing's influence and negatively affect its political and economic interests. As shown later in this chapter, in the case of the Caribbean this poor image has had a major role in the rejection of China's economic conditionality by the societies of partner states.

China's Trade with the Caribbean

The literature has identified three main stages in the recent evolution of China's economic relations with the Caribbean. Starting with the 1990s, the main focus was on trade. Eventually, the global economic crisis led to a shift to foreign direct investment. Finally, President Xi's policies have given priority to infrastructure projects (Oosterveld et al. 2018: 22–23). These changes should not be seen as radical; over the years, all three forms of cooperation have coexisted. Infrastructure projects were constructed even during the 1990s, especially in the context of the "diplomatic duel" with Taiwan; and Chinese direct investment was rather modest even in 2008–2013, allowing other types of cooperation to preserve their visibility. Today, the main economic interactions concern "carrying out infrastructure projects, the provision of cheap and opaque loans to governments or private companies, and the purchase of fossil fuels or other raw materials, albeit on a small scale" (Oosterveld et al. 2018: 6). This suggests that China's economic relations with the Caribbean are radically dissimilar from those with neighboring Latin America. Indeed, Richard Bernal identified the following major differences: (1) the increase in bilateral trade has affected both imports and exports in Latin America while in the Caribbean only the imports grew; (2) China has become the first or second trade partner of many Latin American countries, replacing the United States, while in the Caribbean trade with the US continues to be dominant; (3) unlike in the case of Latin America, exports of agricultural commodities are not significant for the Caribbean; (4) financial flows to the Caribbean are dominated by development assistance, a situation that in Latin America exists only in the case of Central American states; and (5) due to the difference in natural resources, foreign investment in energy and raw materials is much more prominent in Latin America than in the Caribbean (Bernal 2015: 1432–1432; Bernal 2016: 4935–4952). Yet, the most important difference is that, in the Caribbean, trade occupies a marginal position with respect to infrastructure projects.

This is despite the fact that Chinese cheap goods have been very attractive to Caribbean importers, which led to a significant increase in China's exports to the region. In 2013, they reached US $4.21 billion (Campbell 2014). However, this was not sufficient to turn the Asian country into one of the region's top three trading partners (Bernal 2015: 1411, 1416, 1419). In particular, Chinese imports did not displace American and European ones, which did not decrease. Rather, they added to them, contributing to the general rise of total Caribbean imports (Montoute 2013: 119). The growth of exports to China was in no way comparable. Between 2003 and 2012 they did increase from US $120.6 million to US $705.3 million, but this evolution included a decline between 2006 and 2009. The most important markets continue to be the United States and the European Union (Bernal 2015: 1414, 1432). Accordingly, the trade deficit of CARICOM states with China increased from US $ 457.21 million in 2003 to

US $4,069.83 million in 2012 (Bernal 2015: 1416), a situation "very unhealthy and unsustainable for long term development" (Montoute 2013: 121). At times, the opinion is expressed that Caribbean natural resources—such as asphalt and gas in Trinidad, bauxite in Jamaica and Guyana, timber and minerals in Guyana, and perhaps maritime and agricultural products—might be used to increase exports to China. In fact, the largest ten CARICOM exports to that country already are in raw materials (Montoute 2013: 114, 117). The problem is that they represent only 0.012 percent of all Chinese raw materials imports and resources are too limited to allow for massive growth (Oosterveld et al. 2018: 9). Furthermore, the fact that Caribbean states import manufactured goods from China while exporting raw materials "holds the danger of replicating [the nature of the trade relationship] of the Caribbean with traditional partners" (Girvan 2011; Montoute 2013: 122)—i.e. of creating the same center-periphery relationship that nurtures the anti-Chinese discourse in Africa and Latin America as presented in Chapter 3. However, for the time being such a trend is hampered by the fact that the United States remains the Caribbean's most important trading partner (Bernal 2015: 1431–1432; Bernal 2017: 260).

Still, this does not mean that the danger of Latin American-type deindustrialization is absent. Chinese imports do successfully compete with Caribbean manufacturers and put them out of business. Kevin Gallagher found that, between 2003 and 2013, 96 percent of these manufacturers were losing export competitiveness to China (Gallagher 2016: 97) as the sector was "suffocated" by cheaper Chinese products (Haro Navejas 2011: 210). Some manufacturing such as apparel has been displaced (Bernal 2015: 1420). Losses were not as dramatic as in Latin America only because the Caribbean had already lost most of its exports of labor-intensive manufacturing goods due to its relatively high level of wages. Outside the Dominican Republic and Trinidad and Tobago the manufacturing sector is limited, with services being predominant. In the case of Trinidad, the industry is in large measure related to the niche of natural gas and oil. Moreover, it was claimed that "manufacturing of consumer goods, and food processing, have the advantage of locale, brand recognition and traditional taste" (Bernal 2015: 1419–1420, 1425–1426; Bernal 2014: 64). This latter argument is in part contradicted by the fact that even products regarded as uniquely Caribbean such as costumes for Trinidad's Carnival are now imported from China (Downs 2015; Bernal 2015: 1422). Sectors under significant threat include processed food, Tilapia fillets, Portland cement, furniture, paper and plastic products, textiles, and apparel (Bernal 2014: 64; Bernal 2015: 1412, 1420). In Trinidad, 60 percent of respondents believe that competition from Chinese imports represents an actual threat to the local industry against 27 percent who share the opposite view. As one respondent put it, "we are largely consumers of their goods. So this may actually result in China rising at the expense of our economies, which (. . .) is our fault" (Respondent 30).

Trinidad and Tobago represents an interesting case of Caribbean-Chinese trade. Unlike most CARICOM states, it has significant reserves of natural gas and oil. Accordingly, the energy sector provides a large part of its exports and GDP and, as mentioned in the section *China and Trinidad and Tobago: the Highest Connectivity in the Region* of Chapter 4, the idea is frequently expressed that liquefied natural gas might be exported on a larger scale to China to compensate for the increase in Chinese imports. In terms of actual trade, World Bank's World Integrated Trade Solution data presented in Table 1 and Figure 1 show that between 2000 and 2008 imports from China increased no less than 9.5 times. This impressive growth was followed by a brief setback, but eventually continued. However, if the ratio between imports from the United States and those from China is calculated, it becomes clear that since 2007 it has stabilized somewhere between 4 and 6 times. This might seem surprising, as most cheap manufactured goods one can buy in Trinidad are made in China. Yet, they only represent a small part of the country's imports. In the case of exports, Table 1 and Figure 2 show that those to China have been 44 to 350 times smaller than those to the United States. Accordingly, the trade deficit with China is 11 times larger than in 2000 but it remains insignificant in Trinidad's overall trade balance (see Table 1 and Figure 3). Finally, Table 2 confirms the importance of energy exports: despite year-to-year fluctuations, fuel represents a similarly large part of exports to both China and the United States. All this leads to the

Table 5.1. Trinidad and Tobago's Trade with China, the United States, and the World, 2000–20

TT Exports	*2000*	*2001*	*2002*	*2003*	*2004*	*2005*	*2006*	*2007*
Exports to China	500.18	629.3	1905.28	4169.71	2130.95	3818.82	7249.75	22279.31
Exports to US	1990776	1941805	1941805	2874955	4549395	5630869	8142757.34	7734591.58
Total exports	4273447	5113382	3853322	5241265	6517202	9611480	14018733.6	13396245.46
US/China ratio	3980.119	3085.659	1019.171	689.4857	2134.914	1474.505	1123.17767	347.1647722
TT Imports								
Imports from China	51403.1	66137.33	72145.27	97650.63	127082.7	167992.2	242342.66	355518.79
Imports from US	1170242	1242551	1242551	1202898	1683752	1660271	1787810.22	1924533.62
Total imports	3308145	3932119	3661013	3942172	4869582	5693910	6477696.08	7662830.44
US/China ratio	22.76597	18.78744	17.22291	12.31839	13.24927	9.883021	7.37719979	5.413310559
Trade Balance								
TT-China	–50902.9	–65508	–70240	–93480.9	–124952	–164173	–235092.91	–333239.48
TT-US	820534.4	699254.1	699254.1	1672057	2865643	3970598	6354947.12	5810057.96
TT-World	3103206	3870831	2610770	4038367	4833450	7951210	12230923.4	11471711.84

Author generated using data from The World Bank 2018

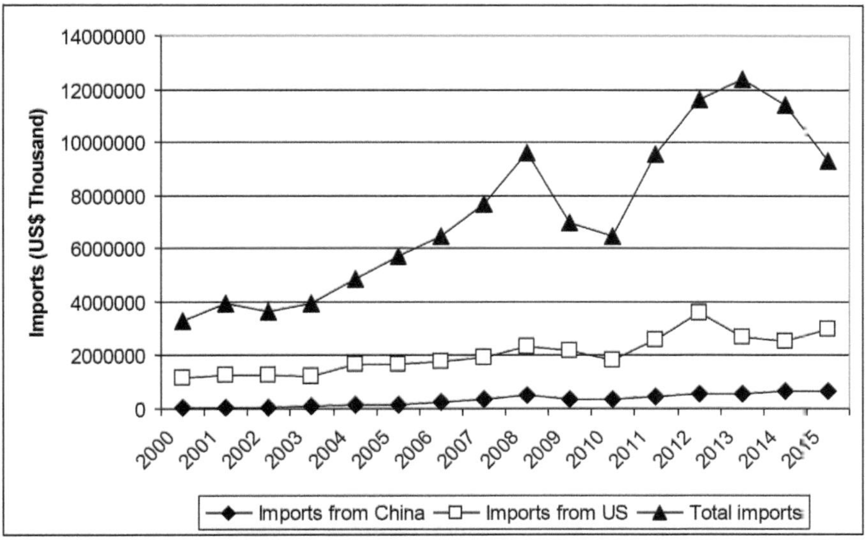

Figure 5.1. Trinidad and Tobago's imports of goods from China, the United States, and the world, 2000–2015 (US$ thousands)
Author generated using data from The World Bank 2018

(US$ Thousands)

2008	*2009*	*2010*	*2011*	*2012*	*2013*	*2014*	*2015*
12302.58	50980.27	33237.09	78841.23	18452.56	18667.08	55433.56	101806.87
8581361.24	4961654.8	5278690.54	7272992.9	5967044.23	6557567.46	6550154	4487844.8
18650425.2	9125970.63	10981679.5	14875157.9	12159202.2	16597499.2	14526145	10755571
697.525335	97.32500044	158.819275	92.2485976	323.372162	351.290478	118.16225	44.081945
486641.11	352833.31	373262.04	444589.51	549972.2	553028.71	635776.95	659698.97
2303422.73	2159313.95	1811172.39	2557696.58	3580363.52	2676434.37	2502922.5	2970789.1
9591397.38	6955437.32	6479599.29	9553307.72	11615579.6	12395843.3	11411688	9297808.6
4.73330897	6.119926574	4.85228123	5.75293956	6.51008091	4.8395939	3.9367934	4.5032495
–474338.53	–301853.04	–340024.95	–365748.28	–531519.64	–534361.63	–580343.39	–557892.1
6277938.51	2802340.85	3467518.15	4715296.32	2386680.71	3881133.09	4047231.5	1517055.8
16347002.5	6966656.68	9170507.08	12317461.3	8578838.67	13921064.8	12023222	7784782

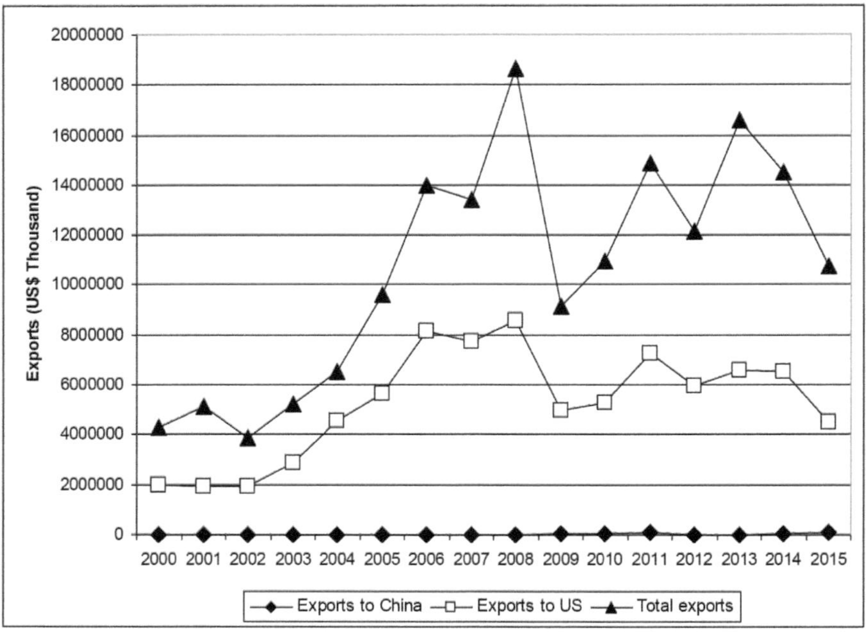

Figure 5.2. Trinidad and Tobago's exports of goods to China, the United States, and the world, 2000–2015 (US$ thousands)
Author generated using data from The World Bank 2018

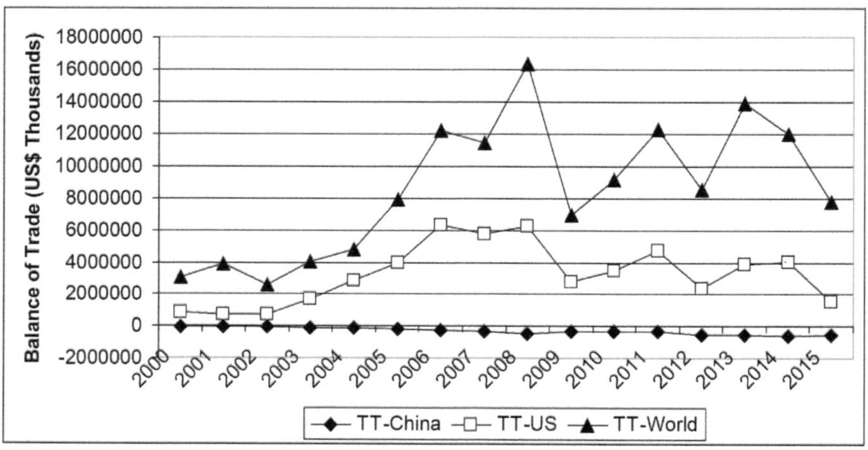

Figure 5.3. Trinidad and Tobago's balance of trade in goods with China, the United States, and the world, 2000–2015 (US$ thousands)
Author generated using data from The World Bank 2018

Table 5.2. Trinidad and Tobago's Export Product Share for Fuel (%)

	2000	*2001*	*2002*	*2003*	*2004*	*2005*	*2006*	*2007*	*2008*	*2009*	*2010*	*2011*	*2012*	*2013*	*2014*	*2015*
Exports to China	57,21	76,11	67,42	77,89	15,78	47,53	59,17	44	34,58	68,18	31,22	61,55	46,97	41,58	26,29	44,74
Exports to US	67,43	66,33	66,33	72,43	67,56	70,1	79,41	71,15	62,28	80,43	55,38	47,39	44,64	56,39	46,11	28,52
Total Exports	65,29	51,92	60,19	66,77	60,24	70,25	76,51	66,16	70	76	60,89	55,87	49,2	61,73	55,69	43,97

Author generated using data from The World Bank 2018

conclusion that the competition from manufactured Chinese goods is highly detrimental to Trinidadian producers of similar commodities, but otherwise they do not represent a major dimension of the bilateral economic relationship. This is confirmed by the fact that only 53 percent of respondents are concerned about the trade deficit with China, while 47 percent do not consider it to represent a danger. More generally, 87 percent prefer to preserve commercial relations with traditional partners while only 13 percent believe that more should be done in order to trade with China. The main consequence of this situation is the irrelevant role played by trade in Beijing's efforts to socialize Trinidad and the Caribbean.

Chinese Investment in the Caribbean

Despite the volatility associated with the consequences of the 2008 financial crisis, Caribbean states have some of the highest levels of foreign direct investment in the world. In many cases, they represent more than 10 percent of the local GDP. Accordingly, the impact of transnational corporations is much more important in Trinidad or Belize than in Brazil or Mexico. However, these investments are relatively unprofitable, especially in comparison to those in Latin America. Traditionally, the main investor used to be the United States. More recently, countries such as Canada and China have also started to significantly invest in the region. In fact, Caribbean states have adopted extensive promotion policies intended to further increase investments in the region. While their actual impact seems to be limited (De Groot and Ludeña 2014: 5, 7, 8), no less than 82 bilateral investment treaties as well as many double taxation avoidance agreements were signed with various states. China is one of the key targets. It signed such agreements with Jamaica in 1994 and 1996, respectively, and with Trinidad in 2002 and 2003. With Guyana it concluded in 2003 an Agreement for the Encouragement and Reciprocal Protection of Investment (Bernal 2016: 21). Due to these agreements and to Beijing's increasing interest in the region, between 2003 and 2012 Chinese investments in the Caribbean grew more than five times (Badri-Maharaj 2016). From 2001 to 2016, China invested US $4.9 billion in Jamaica, US $2.6 billion in Barbados, and US $1.4 billion in Trinidad and Tobago (Oosterveld et al. 2018: 21). Major projects include a US $1.5 billion mega-port in Jamaica to become a regional hub for large Chinese ships after the expansion of the Panama Canal as well as the multi-billion dollar restoration of the Baha Mar luxury resort in the Bahamas (Ward 2017: 13). China has also invested in mining and in raw materials processing industrial facilities. Examples include the US $360 million investment in a Jamaica bauxite unit as well as gold and diamond mines in Guyana (Oosterveld et al. 2018: 29).

However, despite this dynamic, Chinese foreign direct investment in the Caribbean remains very small with respect to that from the United States, Canada, and Britain (Bernal 2016: 4650–4653). By the end of 2013 it only represented less than 1 percent of the total (Ouyang and Qiu 2015: 2). Its future evolution will depend on the learning process experienced by both investors and the region's governments; the performance of Chinese companies; the contribution of transnational ethnic Chinese business networks; the local business environment; and the policies of Caribbean governments (Bernal 2016: 1). A number of key issues that seriously hamper the actions of Chinese investors have been identified: the poor macro-economic environment; the relatively low cost of doing business; the many existing obstacles to foreign investment; and specific difficulties faced by Chinese enterprises that include lack of familiarity with the Caribbean environment and of experience with investment there. Among these Chinese-centered difficulties there is also the opposition of both local and Western stakeholders that perceive China as a competitor and are therefore suspicious of its investments; and Chinese companies' lack of interest in social responsibility, which has resulted in a poor public image (Ouyang and Qiu 2015: 1, 8) as shown later in this chapter.

In fact, there is a specific sector where Chinese investment in the Caribbean is both massive and very successful; but this is not exactly what the region expects from Beijing. Financial centers such as the Cayman Islands and the British Virgin Islands are used for "round-tripping": capital is sent out of China and immediately repatriated as foreign investment, with benefits of special concessions and lower taxes. In certain years, the British Virgin Islands represented the second largest source of foreign direct investment to China while in others the Cayman Islands accounted for one-fifth of the total (Bernal 2016: 4295–4314; Bernal 2016: 30). This is beneficial to those small countries but hardly qualifies as genuine foreign direct investment to the Caribbean. Moreover, given the volatility of this type of activities there is no guarantee that financial centers elsewhere will not be preferred by the Chinese "investors."

In the case of Trinidad and Tobago, the main investors have been the United States and the United Kingdom, with smaller amounts coming from Canada (especially in the banking sector), Germany, and India. Except for some specific years, the annual investment in the oil industry has represented more than 90 percent of the total (De Groot and Ludeña 2014: 21, 46). Chinese investors have targeted the same sector. In 2009, Chaoyang Petroleum (Trinidad) (owned by the Chinese National Offshore Oil Corporation and Sinopec) paid US$780,000 for a 25.5 percent interest in the production sharing contract under Block 3A offshore of Trinidad and Tobago. It also holds a 25 percent interest in Block 2C. In 2011, China Investment Corporation (CIC) acquired for €600 million the 10 percent stake of French firm GDF

Suez in Train 1 of the Atlantic LNG natural gas plant, in addition to production payments from Trains 2, 3, and 4. It also expressed an interest in buying 30 percent of GDF Suez's Exploration and Production division. Finally, Sinopec Overseas Oil and Gas Antilles (Trinidad) has a 65 percent interest in the East Brighton Sub Block A and 45.5 percent interest in East Brighton Sub Block B (Bernal 2016: 4511–4522; Fraser 2013). At first view, this might look significant, but in fact the overall Chinese investment in Trinidad and Tobago remains very modest if compared with Western ones. Moreover, the aforementioned plans and discussions for increased exports of liquefied natural gas to China were initiated in 2013 but, six years later, have not led to any practical result. As already mentioned in the section *China's Engagement with the Developing World* of Chapter 3, a knowledgeable respondent confirmed the lack of interest of Chinese investors in Trinidad, which compares unfavorably even to Indian ones:

> The Chinese have traditionally been harder to convince to invest because their model has been generally coming and seek out EPC contracts, construction contracts, rather they would (. . .) prefer to be a vendor in the market than they would to be an investor.
>
> Greater success on the Indian side because they are now very used to being investors as opposed to the Chinese where the pipeline has been very long and, you know, they are taking a lengthy amount of time to make a decision, normally it requires us having the CEO of the company arrive in Trinidad and have their view point changed about what Trinidad and Tobago is about, they assume it is a little backward island (Respondent 1).

The conclusion is that, like trade, investment cannot represent a relevant Chinese means of influence in Trinidad and in most of the other Caribbean states, even if Jamaica or Bahamas might find themselves in a different situation.

DREAMING OF CHINESE TOURISTS

The huge majority of Caribbean politicians, technocrats, and scholars interested in China seem to have an obsession: the countless sun-and-sea-hungry Chinese tourists can and have to be convinced to visit the region. It is difficult to speak with any member of those groups about China without hearing a variation on this theme. Besides the Baha Mar complex in the Bahamas, the Chinese have constructed various tourism-related projects in St. Maarten, St. Lucia, and Guyana. Yet, these are not aimed at Chinese tourists (Oosterveld et al. 2018: 29, 31), very few of whom are willing to travel 12 time zones and to get American or Canadian transit visas in order to reach a Caribbean resort very similar to much closer ones in the western Pacific. In terms of exoticism, other regions might look more interesting to Shenzhen millionaires: even Greenland has launched a plan to attract Chinese tourists (*The Economist*, May 3, 2018). It should be noted that, despite their decades-long tradition of world travel, only 50,000 Japanese tourists visit the Caribbean every year (Bernal 2016: 4753–4772). At best, Chinese tourism to the region will be limited to a small high-end market; but even that requires considerable efforts in terms of marketing, airlift, tourism plant, and language training. Surveys show that Chinese traveling abroad expect to be attended by persons proficient in Chinese at tourist sites, hotels, and shopping centers; security from crime, which in countries like Trinidad and Tobago represents a very serious issue; and sensitivity to their cultural differences. Accordingly, 'there is much work to be done (. . .) to make [the Caribbean] 'Chinese-ready'" (Sanders 2014).

This leads to the conclusion that, at least for the time being, China can use only one effective economic instrument in its effort to socialize the Caribbean: development assistance, which is presented in the next section.

CHINA'S DEVELOPMENT ASSISTANCE

China's Development Assistance to the Global South

As explained in the section *Development Assistance and Conditionality* of Chapter 2, the Development Assistance Committee of the Organization for Economic Cooperation and Development has defined official development assistance as "grants or loans undertaken by the official sector, with the promotion of economic development and welfare as main objectives (. . .), at concessional financial terms" (Copper 2016: 1). This definition has been criticized as too narrow and restrictive as it does not take into consideration export credits, grants, subsidies, fund transfers made by private organizations, debt cancellation, preferential market access, remittances, and tariff reductions (Copper 2016: 1). Accordingly, it does not cover some of the forms of aid that are part of China's development assistance. More importantly, there is a profound divergence between the philosophy, discourse, and practice of Western and Chinese assistance to developing countries. One key difference concerns the development purpose itself. The Development Assistance Committee promotes a more comprehensive approach to development that emphasizes its social and institutional components and addresses all dimensions of poverty. The main goal is to help build the social capital and institutional prerequisites for development. For its part, China is mainly interested in the physical capital requirement of economic growth, as illustrated by its disproportionate focus on infrastructure development. Another difference is related to China's association of its assistance framework with South-South cooperation. Beijing presents itself as a development partner instead of a donor (Trinidad 2013: 38). As mentioned in Chapter 3, this stems from its historical ties with the Third World since Bandung and represents a key dimension of its "Beijing consensus"-related political discourse in the Global South. Finally, in more practical terms the aforementioned Chinese preference for infrastructure—which, in 2009, represented 61 percent of China's total concessional aid—leads to very visible differences between the sectors targeted by Western and Chinese development assistance (Trinidad 2013: 38).

Anyway, China is an old donor. During the last six decades, its development assistance has evolved in line with the shifting international landscape, its domestic situation, and associated official attitudes and policies toward the Global South presented in Chapter 3 (Trinidad 2013: 19). Following a series of reorganizations and attempts at policy innovations since 1992 (see Trinidad 2013: 32–35; Copper 2016: 18–28), today "economic assistance is the principal means of influence employed by China in its foreign policy in the Caribbean" (Bernal 2016: 5623–5625) as well as in other similar regions of the developing world. There are at least nine forms of Chinese foreign aid: medical missions, training and scholarships, humanitarian aid, volunteer programs, debt relief, budget support, complete projects, aid-in-kind, and technical cooperation (Brautigam 2009: 105; Trinidad 2013: 35–36). The main problem in assessing China's development assistance, however, is the lack of reliable data. China is not a member of the Development Assistance Committee and therefore has no obligation to make such data public. The obsession with secrecy inherited from its totalitarian past does the rest. Therefore, "it is an enigma to decipher [its] different forms of aid" (Bernal 2016: 4105–4106; Stahl 2018: 12–13; Brautigam 2009: 20) and especially the amounts granted to various states and regions. It is nevertheless believed that Chinese development assistance increased from US $1.5 billion in 2002 to US $25 billion in 2007 and that in 2009 and 2010 it was larger than that of the World Bank (Bernal 2015: 1422). I confess that I had placed great hopes in the AidData project "China's Global Development Footprint—The clearest look yet at Chinese official finance worldwide" that promised to provide a comprehensive dataset of both concessional and non-concessional Chinese financing to no less than 138 countries. This detailed study shows that the total 2000–2014 Chinese official finance amounted to US $354.3 billion, as compared to US $394.6 billion for the United States. However, in the case of China only US $81.8 billion qualify as official development assistance if the definition of the Development Assistance Committee is used against US

$366.4 billion in the case of the US. Unfortunately, the AidData study has two significant limitations. The first comes from the period covered by this vast research, which ends in 2014. China's interest in and development assistance to the Caribbean increased considerably in 2013, and therefore only the first two years of this significantly enhanced new stage are included in the database. More importantly, in the case of Trinidad and Tobago 14 projects are listed; yet, only the values of six of them are mentioned. This is of course a consequence of the scarcity of information due to Chinese and Trinidadian lack of transparency. Jamaica finds itself in a better situation, with the values of all 14 listed projects known. Still, overall the database does not seem to represent a sufficiently comprehensive source allowing for credible quantitative comparisons between the development assistance received by Caribbean countries from China.

What is much better known is how the Chinese development assistance is financed. Two state-owned banks are involved, China Development Bank and China ExIm-Bank, that "behave in a fairly similar manner to other development finance institutions (. . .), as well as other export-import banks" (Gallagher 2016: 78). Kevin Gallagher noted that the majority of Chinese finance in Latin America—which includes the Caribbean—is offered at commercial rates of interest (see the section *China in Latin America* of Chapter 3). In particular, the interest rates of China Development Bank are similar to and sometimes slightly higher than those of the World Bank, the Inter-American Development Bank, and the Development Bank of Latin America. It is China ExIm Bank that offers small subsidized loans as development aid for low-income countries. Yet, these loans at concessional rates of interest (which are somewhat lower than those of the US ExIm Bank) represent only 1.2 percent of the total Chinese finance to Latin America and the Caribbean. No less than 82 percent of China ExIm Bank's funding to the region carries commercial interest rates. In Beijing's view, it is the blending of Chinese export promotion with development aid that best serves Global South countries in need (Gallagher 2016: 77–80).

One important difference between the modalities of disbursement of Chinese and Western development assistance is the latter's participatory dimension that developed in the 1990s through the co-opting of civil society groups as intermediaries of international development. As NGOs "portray an image of altruism and flexibility," many Western donors channel an important part of their assistance to the civil society in target countries (Trinidad 2013: 38). China does not, which reflects its own state-centered vision. The leadership in Beijing believes that it is the role of the state to ensure economic development by supporting national firms (Trinidad 2013: 39; Saunders 2006). One might be tempted to think that, in terms of effectiveness, it is not very wise to allow important amounts of aid to be managed exclusively—and, frequently, non-transparently—by the governments of countries affected by high-level corruption. In terms of promoting China's influence in those countries, however, this might simply be a supplementary instrument used to socialize political elites, as explained in the section *The Socialization of Caribbean Elites* of this chapter. At times, such approaches have been contrasted with those of Taiwan, which "has become a responsible donor of foreign aid" and whose "aid model should be recognized and encouraged because it contributes to a positive cycle of aid development" (Chien et al. 2010: 1204). In fact, some scholars have studied if and in what measure Chinese development assistance is beginning to emulate international norms and practices. The response is rather ambiguous, as China's socialization into international norms varies considerably even within the narrow geographical framework of Southeast Asia (Reilly 2012: 71–72). This led certain authors to argue that, as it only seeks "money, access to raw materials, and international politics," the Chinese development assistance is "toxic" (Naím 2007: 95; Trinidad 2013: 19). A debate has developed that is part of the "China threat" one presented in the section *China in Africa* of Chapter 3. Skeptics emphasize the fact that Beijing harms the efforts of traditional donors to maximize the welfare-enhancing effects and developmental outcomes of their assistance by potentially contributing to the creation of unsustainable debts; by allowing recipient countries to postpone the necessary reforms required by other donors; and by promoting a haphazard appraisal of investments that can result in waste and unproductive capital projects (Trinidad 2013: 20; Manning 2006: 381–382). More generally, China is undermining the international aid "standard" as it de facto challenges the good governance-based values, principles, and overall philosophy of "mainstream" development assistance. For their part, optimists claim that Chinese aid has nevertheless led to economic growth, increased exports, and larger public revenues; furthermore, it can represent an alternative source of infrastructure finance (Trinidad 2013: 20). As already mentioned in the section *China in Africa* of Chapter 3, little can be done to put an end to this dispute and to the more general polarization of the China-in-the-Global-South field of study. Anyway, the goal of this book is not to decide if China's development assistance is "toxic" or not. It simply analyzes its instrumentalization in the Caribbean, a region where—as detailed in the next section—this assistance is most prominent.

China's Development Assistance to the Caribbean

As mentioned in the previous section, economic assistance—consisting in grants, loans, lines of credit, technical assistance, and donations in kind—

represents the principal means of influence employed by Beijing in the Caribbean. Much of it takes the form of infrastructure projects—highly visible buildings, stadiums, and other sports facilities—that "have boosted the prestige of several governments" in the region (Bernal 2016: 5623–5625). Appropriately called "stadium diplomacy," this Chinese way of "build[ing] goodwill and consolidat[ing] relations with Caribbean countries" (Bernal 2017: 242) has brought stadiums to Antigua and Barbuda, Bahamas, Barbados, Dominica, Grenada, and St. Lucia; a community-based cricket stadium, the Montego Bay Convention Centre, and US$400 million road construction and repair projects to Jamaica; and hospitals to Antigua and Barbuda, St. Lucia, and Trinidad, to name just a few of these numerous "highly visible symbols of China's assistance and lasting source[s] of pride for the beneficiary country" (Bernal 2017: 242; Bernal 2015: 1424; *The Economist*, March 10, 2012; Hongbo 2017: 319; Oosterveld et al. 2018: 27) and especially for its political leadership. An interesting aspect concerns the Chinese adoption of non-traditional forms of development assistance such as debt forgiveness. After being tested in Africa, the latter was used for the first time in the Caribbean in 2007, when China wrote off US $15.3 million in debt owed by Guyana for 1975–1993 loans. This was warmly welcomed in the region as most states have high levels of external debt but, as middle-income economies, do not qualify for debt relief under the Heavily Indebted Poor Countries Initiative (Bernal 2015: 1423). The enthusiasm of Caribbean political elites for new Chinese loans has increased in direct proportion with their hopes that resulting debts will never need to be paid. This, however, might be wishful thinking, and the Sri Lankan debt trap presented in the section *The Belt and Road Initiative* of Chapter 3 should inspire a more cautious approach. Elite self-interested ideas set aside, China's development assistance to the region has become particularly attractive due to the sharp decline in American foreign aid, which has turned Beijing into a key development partner (Bernal 2016: 5625–5628; Bernal 2017: 260).

Predictably, Chinese scholars obsessively repeat that "China does not offer aid for selfish interests" (Zhou 2017: vii). They like to quote Global South officials attending training in Beijing who "said that China has made an enormous self-sacrifice (. . .) to provide aid" to their countries (Zhou 2017: vii). Yet, sometimes their analyses are less idealistic. Sun Hongbo overtly acknowledged that China's aid to Latin America and the Caribbean "has served the adjustment of China's overall diplomatic strategy, (. . .) thus realizing China's national interests in this region" (Hongbo 2017: 282). Development assistance "has had a big role in promoting" bilateral relations (Hongbo 2017: 320). On the one hand, he noted the difference between investment- and trade-oriented richer Latin American states, those in Central America and the Caribbean (which "demand assistance"), and Andean countries that need assistance, investment, and trade. On the other hand, as mentioned in the section *China in Latin America* of Chapter 3, he explicitly described the different nature of China's interests in sub-regions that can be influenced through development assistance: mainly economic in the Andean countries and more political in Central America and the Caribbean. The fact that Caribbean countries "have become the key recipients" of China's various forms of aid (Hongbo 2017: 281, 321, 323) might therefore be indicative of Beijing's order of priorities in the wider region. The Chinese scholar has also made a rather atypical classification of projects that "help accumulate China's soft power" in the region: there are "morale projects" such as assistance for the agricultural sector; and "livelihood projects," mainly related to medical aid. The reader surprised by the fact that much more visible infrastructure projects are not prominently presented finds out that "the reconstruction of stadiums and other large landmark projects became a symbol of friendship" between China and the region (Hongbo 2017: 317–319).

These "symbols of friendship" were classified in two ways. Evan Ellis used the criterion of financing to identify three major categories: gifts from the Chinese government; projects paid for by Chinese investors; and those paid for by the region's governments. The second category is hardly complicated. To give an example, the huge Baha Mar casino and resort project in the Bahamas, initially evaluated at US $2.4 billion and then expanded to $3.5 billion, simply got its funding from China ExIm Bank (Ellis 2014: 53). The first category, however, is more ambiguous. Most of the Chinese "gifts" to the entire region of Latin America and the Caribbean actually consist in stadiums, government buildings, roads, and hospitals located in Caribbean states. In 2007, they amounted to $132 million, which is quite remarkable by regional standards. The problem is that many more projects are presented as being "funded by China"; which is true, except that the "funding" is done through loans, not grants. Accordingly, what is at times presented as a Chinese "gift" belongs in fact to the category of projects paid for by Caribbean governments. A case in point is that of the US $150 million Couva Children's Hospital scrutinized in more detail in the next section. In 2012, a spokesman for the government in Port of Spain stated that the Chinese were providing all of the funds (and added that, due to this, they were free to choose the contractors). But the funding came as a loan; Trinidad's debt to China for this project currently stands at TT $924.5 million (approximately US $135 million) (*CNC3*, March 3, 2018; Ellis 2014: 51). *Timeo Danaos et dona ferentes*. . . .[1]

Using a different criterion, the classification of Willem Oosterveld, Eric Wilms, and Katarina Kertysova has also identified three categories of Chinese infrastructure projects in the Caribbean: those representing "apparent signs of creating goodwill," those with an ostensible economic function, and those "likely to serve political ends" (Oosterveld et al. 2018: 27). "Goodwill" ones include stadiums, schools, and hospitals. Economically purposeful projects relate to roads, railways, ports, and airports. Both categories include cases that stirred controversy, but these are dwarfed by the criticism targeting the third one, which mainly relates to the construction of government buildings. Chinese firms have been very active in this field in Jamaica, Dominica, Barbados, and Trinidad while, as noted by Willem Oosterveld and his colleagues, a 2013 five-year ban blocked the construction of any new government building in China (Oosterveld et al. 2018: 27–28). The problem is that these categories are hardly exclusive. Chinese-built stadiums and hospitals intended to create "goodwill" as well as economically relevant roads and ports are overtly used by Caribbean political elites to increase their political and electoral legitimacy. As such, they make those elites dependent on the leadership in Beijing and implicitly "serve political ends" as much as projects in the third category. In fact, China's development assistance—of which infrastructure projects are an integral part—represents the key incentive that supports the three Chinese conditionalities and the ensuing process of international socialization of the Caribbean. Moreover, the infrastructure projects are directly linked to the economic conditionality, which is analyzed in the following sections.

CHINA'S "TIED AID" AND ITS RECEPTION IN TRINIDAD AND THE CARIBBEAN

China's "Tied Aid"

At page 149 of her *Dragon's Gift*, Deborah Brautigam explicitly and uncompromisingly states "China never has imposed economic conditions." Yet, at page 151 she starts to write about the Chinese "tied aid." Two ideas are developed: on the one hand, Beijing "is following in the footprints left by the wealthy countries"; on the other, especially in the case of China, "tied aid" represents a useful practice that reduces subcontracting costs and corruption (Brautigam 2009: 149–153). Even if all these statements were true—and this chapter shows that the one on corruption is not—it is very clear that a Global South country will receive Chinese development assistance only if it accepts it as "tied aid"; and, at least in the Caribbean, which is made up of developing small states, this has considerable detrimental consequences on the socio-economic situation of the recipient country. Indeed, a huge infrastructure project represents a considerable part of the local construction market. The fact that national contractors and laborers are excluded affects severely the business sector as well as the employment of some of the underprivileged social groups. It is important to emphasize that this is not a side effect. This is a structural component of Beijing's view of Chinese-financed infrastructure projects that represent most of its development assistance to the Caribbean as lucrative activities whose profit has to go to China's firms and not to the local economy. China simply compels the recipient government to follow a policy which shapes its economy in ways that serve Chinese interests instead of national ones. The fact that so many scholars admit that this is not economic conditionality has indeed much more to do with the uncritical assimilation of "facts" from the literature than with Beijing's actual actions.

The most common definition of "tied aid" is that provided by the Organization for Economic Cooperation and Development:

> Tied aid credits are official or officially supported Loans, credits or Associated Financing packages where procurement of the goods or services involved is limited to the donor country or to a group of countries which does not include substantially all developing countries (or Central and Eastern European Countries /New Independent States in transition) (OECD 2001/2013).

The OECD also estimates that the effectiveness of development aid is reduced by 20 to 30 percent if it is tied (Jepma 1991: 8). Of course, this only concerns the affected projects, not the aforementioned impact on the entire local economy. China first experimented "tied aid" on a large scale in Africa. Eventually, the mechanism fine-tuned there started to be used all over the Global South. Grants and preferential loans offered by China's Ministry of Commerce are tied to Chinese firms, labor, and materials. Companies eligible to bid on foreign aid project tenders must be on a list prepared in Beijing. China ExIm Bank has concessional aid guidelines that officially tie the aid at a level of 50 percent. The exporter or contractor has to be Chinese and inputs for concessional aid projects should also come from China (Brautigam 2009: 152; Lahtinen 2018: 42). In principle, local or international sub-contractors, labor, and supplies can also be used up to a certain level. Studying the case of Latin America and the Caribbean, Evan Ellis noted that this level is in direct proportion with the bargaining power of the government negotiating the deal. Especially in smaller and poorer countries, "the recipients had very little ability or inclination to demand that local contractors or laborers be used in the project" (Ellis 2014: 2, 49). In fact, in the case of all Chinese-financed projects in Trinidad the room for maneuver was so limited that, as shown later in this section, there was no tender and the Beijing-prepared "list" of eligible Chinese companies was limited to one name. Worse, that company was not always a truly reputable one.

Frustration due to the fact that Chinese companies take contracts and jobs has been visible all over the Global South. As a Kenyan journalist critical of his government's acceptance of this conditionality rhetorically asked, "why are Chinese the main builders of our roads? (. . .) What does this mean for the development of local entrepreneurship?" (Lahtinen 2018: 46). In Latin America, there have been many problems in relation to local subcontractors and labor. Protests occurred against China Water and Electric in Peru and against China Railroad Engineering Corporation in Venezuela, among others. In the Caribbean, the same thing happened in the case of China Harbor in Jamaica, of Hutchison Port Holdings in the Bahamas, and of China Jiangsu in Trinidad (Ellis 2013: 3–4). Two brief examples are relevant. After Dominica recognized China in 2004 (see the section *China in the Caribbean: Constructing a New Regional Order* of Chapter 4), it received generous concessionary terms of loans. The ExIm Bank of China provided a 20-year loan of up to US $40 million at an interest rate of 2 percent, i.e. lower than those offered by international development institutions, for the construction of the State House, the Dominica State College, the building of the Electoral Commission, and the rehabilitation of major roads. Yet, the Chinese were criticized for ignoring environmental standards, for delivering shoddy construction, and especially for the employment of their own workers. Critics complained that Beijing's generous loans actually "generated opportunities for Chinese firms and workers" (Bernal 2015: 1425) instead of contributing to the development of the local economy. For its part, Guyana recognized China in 1972 and since then has remained one of Beijing's most consistent partners in the CARICOM. In exchange, it has received significant medical, military, technical, telecommunications, and infrastructure assistance. But there has been harsh criticism of the secretive bidding process used to award all contracts to Chinese companies while local ones are shut out of projects. Like elsewhere, these projects rely primarily on Chinese labor despite initial job creation promises that had raised significant expectations among the locals. Resulting disputes have provided an "example of how China's development program can potentially sour bilateral relations" (Ward 2017: 15).

This is how Chinese state-owned companies active in the Caribbean "have become embroiled in controversy" (Ward 2017: 14). A number of factors contribute to this situation that include these companies' concentration in sectors with particularly high social and environmental impacts such as construction or extractive industries; the cultural distance between the Chinese management of the companies and local governments, workers, and communities; and their lack of experience in dealing with the region, which increases the probability that challenges arise and are managed poorly (Ellis

2014: 129). As noted by Evan Ellis, "although (. . .) Chinese companies (. . .) do not *inherently* behave worse than their Western counterparts, many *do* behave badly" (Ellis 2014: 130; emphasis in the original). Their actions "unveil a much more complicated reality where Chinese visions of development have mixed results and receptions" (Ward 2017: 14). At times, this "increases the possibilities for friction, misunderstanding, and conflict" (Ellis 2014: 129). Certain authors insist on the fact that the Chinese presence in the Caribbean (and in Latin America) "inspires a combination of racism, ignorance and resentment" (Enrique Dussel Peters quoted by Ellis 2014: 130); "the inflow of Chinese workers, poor quality of work and lack of local profit does cause resentment in Caribbean countries, inducing a rise in xenophobia"; the further increase of Chinese workers "could exacerbate social tensions and perhaps violence" (Oosterveld et al. 2018: 6). It should be added that this trend is enhanced by the socio-economic effects of the activities of Chinese entrepreneurial migrants analyzed in the following chapter. While these are two different phenomena associated with China's economic and social conditionalities, respectively, their impact on the local society tends to be similar and generates equally negative reactions.

Interviews in Trinidad confirm the general awareness of the "tied aid" issue and its perception as conditionality. China's development assistance "in part, it's positive in the sense that it presents an alternative to the established regimes of funding initiatives, but you don't get something for nothing" (Respondent 28): there are "conditionalities that come with Chinese money" (Respondent 1). Beijing's discourse about its disinterested support of developing countries is hardly convincing:

> Even in South-South cooperation, there are big players and bullies in the system. China is a big player. Essentially, it's creating a microcosm of the greater world. (. . .) the whole concept of South-South cooperation (. . .) is China saying in this instance that it is going to assist, but what kind of assistance is it, in most instances it tends to be instances where Chinese contractors are used, Chinese materials are used and there is some kind of trade arrangement connected to the deal, which in fact is no different from the initiatives used by the US and some countries (Respondent 28).

Sixty percent of the respondents share the opinion that the Chinese "*tie* you into using Chinese construction companies, Chinese workers etc. etc. So basically the money flows in and then out right back to China" (Respondent 20; emphasis added). It should be noted that the word "tied" was not suggested by the interviewer and the respondent was not aware of the terminology used in development aid studies. The power asymmetry associated with China's conditionality has also been emphasized:

> We have no bargaining power. It is stipulated in all the agreements that we have to use their contractors, their material, their labour. [We should have more bargaining power] Ideally yes, but if your hand is in the honey pot, what would you do? You have to accept (Respondent 3).

Another respondent stated that the bilateral relationship is "very very beneficial essentially to China" as it "creates a substantial amount of monopoly" (Respondent 28). The two main components of this "monopoly" represented by the Chinese laborers and the Chinese contractors are analyzed in more detail in the next two sections.

Chinese Laborers

Back in 2009, a researcher at the Zhangjiakou Academy of Agricultural Sciences explained to the National People's Congress that "sending Chinese labourers to Africa would create about 100 million more jobs and solve the problem of Chinese unemployment" (Badri-Maharaj 2016). He could have added, on the national interest side, that most of their income would be repatriated to China; and, on the effectiveness side, that their skills, hard work, and willingness to accept low wages and poor working conditions would be highly beneficial to their employers. These factors explain "China's insistence on using large numbers of Chinese (. . .) laborers on construction projects" (Campbell 2014). In the recipient countries, however, they are perceived as depriving locals of employment, which in the Caribbean has caused frustration and various forms of protests from trade unions and professional associations (Bernal 2015: 1420). Resulting hostility sometimes translates into unfounded anti-Chinese rumors being spread. In Guyana, the media claimed that convicts had been brought in from China to work on infrastructure projects, an untrue allegation previously made in various African countries (Bernal 2016: 4784–4798). The negative perception of Chinese labor is so general that it has become known even to people living in states that do not recognize Beijing. The tourism and transport minister of St. Kitts and Nevis, Ricky Skerritt, could legitimate his government's choice of Taipei as a development partner by noting that "if Taiwan lends or gives you money for an infrastructure project they (. . .) don't insist on you bringing in their engineers or workers, planting a bit of their country in the middle of ours" (Wigglesworth 2013). Active protests against the use of Chinese workers have targeted Chinese companies such as Hutchinson Port Holdings and the China State Construction Engineering Corporation in the Bahamas, China Jiangsu in Trinidad, Shanghai Construction Group in Guyana, and China Harbour Engineering Company in Jamaica (Bernal

2016: 4784–4798). In the latter country, trade unions argued that their members could have done much of the work of Chinese laborers, and this would have prevented unemployment from reaching almost 13 percent (Southerland 2017). Trade unions in Barbados blamed Chinese laborers working on construction sites for undermining the local job and construction markets. They urged the government to impose the recruitment of construction workers first from Barbados and then from the wider Caribbean while keeping the Chinese as a last resort solution (Wilkinson 2007). In the Bahamas, the very small number of local laborers used by the Chinese for the massive Baha Mar resort project was vocally criticized by the political opposition. In Guyana, the virtual exclusion of local workers from Chinese projects led opposition politicians to try to block projects to be done by Chinese companies. In Suriname, local activists blocked a project by China Zhong Heng Tai to produce palm oil on a 40,000-hectare plantation because Chinese workers would have displaced local jobs (Ellis 2014: 148).

In Trinidad and Tobago, the use of Chinese labor was criticized by trade unions (Wilkinson 2007) and by professional organizations such as the Trinidad and Tobago Institute of Architects (Bernal 2016: 4784–4798). Exact figures are difficult to find, but between 2005 and 2016 three large Chinese infrastructure projects in the country—worth US $2 billion—directly employed 4,700 persons. The total number of associated jobs (including non-construction ones) amounted to 12,700, most of which were given to Chinese nationals (Khan 2017). And 1,071 work permits were granted to Chinese citizens in 2007 and 1,756 in 2008 (against 5,103 and 7,109 received by other non-Caricom workers in those two years) (*The Trinidad and Tobago Guardian*, July 5, 2009). Out of 2,996 Chinese who obtained work permits between 2008 and 2011, 2,731 worked in the construction sector (Montoute 2013: 121). From the outside, these numbers might seem modest. But, due to the inflow of Chinese workers and entrepreneurial migrants (see Chapter 6) that send most of their income to China, Trinidad ceased to represent a net receiver of remittances after 2013 (Khan 2017). The impact on the construction market and on the level of unemployment of a country with only 1.4 million inhabitants is also significant. To quote a respondent,

> Chinese workers coming on billion dollar projects and very few locals would be hired on those projects. (. . .) Chinese nationals were coming in, they were living in squalid conditions, they wouldn't contribute to the national economy, they took jobs away from us (Respondent 12)

When asked to identify issues concerning Chinese companies involved in Trinidad and Tobago, 53 percent of respondents mentioned "giving preference to Chinese workers." Two-thirds of them joined trade unions in vocally criticizing the construction of large infrastructure projects by imported Chinese labor. This is a general opinion, widely shared within the society at large. Yet, things look very different from the government's perspective. Former Prime Minister Kamla Persad-Bissessar constantly praised China's development assistance and the effectiveness of Chinese contractors. She stated that she was aware of "concerns from the national community" about "nationals from other countries" "boxing bread out of the mouths of the citizens of Trinidad and Tobago." Still, because there are "serious shortages of skilled labour," the country's development needs to take advantage of the friendly contribution of foreign partners: "let not your hearts be troubled" (Fraser 2014b). Her concerns were contrary to those of her countrymen. On the suggestion of Chinese officials she had met in Beijing, the then Prime Minister wanted to put an end to the difficulties encountered by Chinese nationals trying to get a Trinidad and Tobago visa. Accordingly, she mentioned the plan for the visa exemption of Chinese citizens already in possession of a US or Canadian visa. This was to be the first phase of a process leading to the complete removal of visa requirements. The ensuing influx of Chinese nationals was expected to make the business and tourism sectors "grow tremendously" (Fraser 2014b). Progress was slow, but the next Trinidadian government did implement this first phase, as stated by then acting Prime Minister Colm Imbert in a May 2018 speech that praised Chinese involvement in the Point Lisas project (Douglas 2018a; see the section *China and Trinidad and Tobago: the Highest Connectivity in the Region* of Chapter 4). A complementary idea was—and still is—to connect the China to Cuba flights with one from Cuba to Trinidad (Respondent 1; Douglas 2018a), which would further increase the number of Chinese arriving in the country.

This explicit and enthusiast support for an obviously detrimental aspect of the partnership with China is the direct effect of Beijing's economic conditionality and came as a result of the socialization of Trinidadian elites presented in the section *The Socialization of Caribbean Elites* of this chapter. However, given the very different attitude of their citizens, Caribbean political elites are aware of the fact that it does endanger their legitimacy and electoral support. As already noted earlier in this section, the problem is that their very limited bargaining power severely affects the "ability or inclination to demand that local contractors or laborers be used in the project" (Ellis 2014: 2, 49). Yet, even if they are hardly spectacular, some exceptions do exist. In Barbados, the Chinese company Complan was convinced to admit a 60/40 ratio of local versus Chinese workers involved in the rebuilding of a resort destroyed by a fire in 2015. In the Bahamas, a 50/50 agreement was concluded on the building of a large resort (Oosterveld et al. 2018: 26). Surprisingly, in

June 2012 the very Labor Minister of the Persad-Bissessar government, Errol McLeod, started to speak about the creation of a foreign migrant policy intended to ensure the protection of Trinidadian workers. He explicitly mentioned "the social cost of keeping people inactive while we engage Chinese labour" and announced that he would prepare a position paper analyzing the impact of migrant workers on the local industry (Dickson 2012). But one year later President Xi Jinping visited Trinidad and raised the amount of Chinese incentives to a level that dwarfed the Minister's concerns and made the Prime Minister adopt the enthusiasm shown in the previous paragraph. This policy line predictably survived the 2015 government change. The concern for the issue of local labor in Chinese-built projects resurfaced only three years later, when the agreement on the Phoenix Park Industrial Estate was concluded one month after Prime Minister Dr. Keith Rowley's May 2018 visit to China (see the section *China and Trinidad and Tobago: the Highest Connectivity in the Region* of Chapter 4). The Trinidadian government was proud to announce that it had convinced the Beijing Construction Engineering Group to use 60 percent local labor in the construction of the industrial park (*Trinidad and Tobago Daily Express*, June 20, 2018). Similar moves were noted elsewhere in the Caribbean. Richard Bernal wrote that in Jamaica two Chinese companies "succeeded in finding a balance between local staff and Chinese staff" (Bernal 2016: 6710–6726). However, it remains to be seen if these few cases represent the beginning of a new era or just a wiser strategy that uses demonstrative examples in order to give the impression that Chinese firms have become responsive to criticism. What is clear is that, due to these limited concessions, Caribbean governments have ceased to see the need for national policies that would have protected their workers. In turn, this leaves the door for Chinese labor wide open.

Chinese Contractors and Project Failures

Similar to Caribbean workers, local contractors as well as construction-related professional associations—such as the Barbados Association of Contractors and the Trinidad and Tobago Institute of Architects (Bernal 2016: 6702–6710)—have a very negative view of their exclusion from projects financed by Chinese loans. Trinidad is the case in point as it has well-entrenched, competent construction firms and a relatively well-developed capital market that in fact can fund construction projects without the need to turn to Chinese banks. As a matter of fact, this made the advance of Chinese loan-based infrastructure projects slower here than elsewhere in the region (Ellis 2014: 79–80). Yet, local companies were powerless when non-transparent government-to-government negotiations were held between Trinidad and China and resulted in contracts being given to specific Chinese firms with no public tender. In the words of Emile Elias, a local contractor, "Chinese construction has been a disaster for national development, for the local construction sector and for local labour, and no money has been saved" (*The Economist*, March 10, 2012). Lennox Sirjusingh, the president of the Local Content Chamber, stated that he was "deeply disturbed" by the preference given to foreign contractors for building hospitals (Sookraj 2013).

This could have been a sectoral issue detrimental to the local construction industry but ignored by the general public. What turned it into a national issue was the outrageous poor quality of Chinese-built projects. All over the Caribbean, the fact that Chinese companies "do shoddy work" is a common theme (Bernal 2016: 4773–4784). In Jamaica, a US $248 million sports facility has fallen in disrepair while the Trelawny Stadium requires up to US $50 million in annual maintenance. The contractor for the huge Baha Mar resort project in the Bahamas, China Construction America, has missed deadlines and faced "numerous allegations of shoddy workmanship and poor construction quality" (Badri-Maharaj 2016; Oosterveld et al. 2018: 26–27). For its part, Trinidad can show a long series of Chinese projects that "end[ed] up over-budget, late or poorly built" (*The Economist*, March 10, 2012). It is there that "Chinese-constructed projects have stirred more controversy than perhaps anywhere else in the region" (Oosterveld et al. 2018: 67). Ironically, three of the best-known results of Beijing's development assistance—the National Academy for the Performing Arts (NAPA), the Southern Academy for the Performing Arts (SAPA), and the Couva Children's Hospital—were spontaneously indicated by two respondents as examples of success stories and major failures, respectively (Respondents 15 and 20). In a way, both were right. These buildings look impressive and, on paper, represent clear proofs of social and cultural advancement. But, as shown below, they were plagued by major technical faults that prevented their use for long periods of time and required costly repairs; and disproportionately increased Trinidad's debt to China. Less spectacular projects have also been affected. In 2008, China Jiangsu International Corporation started to build two apartment buildings worth US $ 26 million in Morvant. They were completed in late 2010; at that time, it was not revealed that cracking had been discovered one year earlier. Apparently, it was in 2011 that the government became aware that the buildings had to be demolished. This was finally decided in May 2012, after one of them began to crack open from foundations to the top story (*Trinidad and Tobago Newsday*, May 31, 2012; Raymond 2015; Bernal 2016: 4826–4833).

Yet, not even the picture of "a four storey building almost broken in two" (*Trinidad and Tobago Newsday*, May 31, 2012) could draw as much attention as the problems of the National Academy for the Performing Arts. This impressive building was described by the Minister of Community Development, Culture and Arts, Dr. Nyan Gadsby-Dolly, as "an iconic space. It is the jewel of the Caribbean" (*Trinidad Express*, November 22, 2016). These beautiful words were part of the re-inauguration speech given by the Minister at the end of a period of almost two years during which the newly built Academy was closed for repairs. The contract for NAPA was given without competitive tender to the Shanghai Construction Group due to an undisclosed government-to-government China-Trinidad agreement. In 2009, then Minister Patrick Manning opened the facility "with much fanfare" (*The Trinidad and Tobago Guardian*, August 21, 2016). But it was closed in 2014 due to structural issues. Then Arts and Multiculturalism Minister Lincoln Douglas explained that the building was deemed to be unsafe by engineers as

> tiles were falling off the building, there were plumbing failures and the foundation began failing, in terms of its design and filtration system, the moving stage showed major defects and the support stands for the stage were crumbling (*The Trinidad and Tobago Guardian*, August 21, 2016).

The cost of repairs was TT $20 (US $2.9) million as works were also needed to

> reinforce non-structural walls, improve acoustic ceiling supports, retrofit 190 timber joists on stage, retrofit concrete columns in the foundation area, re-weld 650 defective welds under the stage and 272 defective welds in the hangers and catwalk support beams, [and] test welds at critical places in the entire structure (*TTWhistleBlower*, August 31, 2016).

It should be mentioned that the outstanding debt to China for this project amounts to TT $440.3 million (US $64 million) (*CNC3*, March 3, 2018).

Less spectacular issues were encountered by the Southern Academy for the Performing Arts (SAPA). Yet, there were about 300 of them, requiring the same amount of TT $20 million in renovation (Bernal 2016: 4814–4826). In this case the outstanding debt to China amounts to only TT $180.8 (US $26) million (*CNC3*, March 3, 2018). But it is the example of the Couva children's hospital that best shows how Beijing's interest in the region, Chinese firms' interest in profit, and local leaders' interest in political legitimacy and electoral support combine in relation with the Chinese-built infrastructure projects in the Caribbean. Then Prime Minister Kamla Persad-Bissessar turned the sod for the hospital on March 2, 2012, and stated

> We are not about erecting white elephants willy nilly, we are not about creating edifices of political egos, monuments of pretentious aggrandisement at the expense of ignoring the plight of the people. We are carefully planning the de-

velopment of Trinidad and Tobago (. . .). And we are about being people centred (Office of the Prime Minister 2013).

In December 2012, a government-to-government agreement with China was concluded resulting in a US $150 million loan for the completion of the unit (*Caribbean Journal*, June 3, 2013; Office of the Prime Minister 2013). During the May–June 2013 visit of President Xi Jinping, "the project was showcased (. . .) as an example of the type of benefits provided by the P.R.C. to nations of the Caribbean" (Ellis 2014: 51). Predictably, Trinidad's government stated that the Chinese were free to choose the contractors (Ellis 2014: 51). The contract was given to the Shanghai Construction Group, which also built NAPA, with a deadline in March 2015 (Gang 2015). The hospital was officially opened by then Prime Minister Kamla Persad-Bissessar in August 2015, less than one month before general elections. However, this electoral maneuver did not prevent the opposition from winning. The new government was—or pretended to be—somewhat surprised to be criticized by the new opposition for not allocating any money in the 2016 budget for the hospital's completion. Colm Imbert, the new finance minister, noted that the hospital had already been opened and that anyway all funding should have been provided by China (Rogers 2016). Political disputes continued and it was only in April 2018 that Prime Minister Dr. Keith Rowley announced that the still not working facility would be turned into an offshore medical school under the form of a public-private partnership between the health care management firm InterHealth Canada, the University of the West Indies, and the government (Hunte 2018; Williams 2018). However, by the time this decision was taken construction faults started to be noted. A part of the roadway leading up to the hospital and the hospital's cooling tower collapsed, only two years after construction (Rogers 2016; Sookraj 2018). It is not clear if the rest of the building is secure. What is certain is that Trinidad's debt to China for the hospital amounts to TT $924.5 million (US $135 million) (*CNC3*, March 3, 2018).

These and many other smaller examples (for a list see Oosterveld et al. 2018: 67–69) suggest that China's imposition of one specific Chinese contractor for any infrastructure project it finances in Trinidad and elsewhere in the Caribbean, which is a key element of its "tied aid" and of the associated economic conditionality, has serious detrimental consequences for the recipient state. In addition to the fact that local contractors are excluded from important construction activities in their own country, costly repairs have to be undertaken by the government while for long periods of time the completed projects simply cannot be used. Of course, not all Chinese firms work poorly and when that happens there are different degrees of failure. The problem is that China's government handpicks construction firms that in many cases already have a controversial record and imposes them on the recipient government, which cannot do anything to avoid predictable problems. Probably the best example is represented by China Railway Construction Caribbean Company, which was given the contract for the Chinese-financed TT $1.6 billion (approximately US $233 million) Arima Hospital without tender, i.e. because Beijing so decided. Ironically, this company's building practices were questioned in China itself. Regulatory authorities there ordered China Railway Construction Corporation and four other firms to investigate shoddy work in the construction of railway projects and to fix structural problems on 12 rail lines, including a high-speed one where a deadly train crash occurred in July 2012 (Sookraj 2013). It should be added that the same company won the bid for the controversial TT $221.7 (US $32.4) million Curepe Interchange, which is not related to Chinese development assistance. The project—which already had a long and troubled history (see Hassanali 2017)—had an original price tag of TT $400 million. China Railway Construction Corporation got this contract because it was ready to do the work for only TT $221 million. Herbert George, the chairman of Trinidad's National Infrastructure Development Company that awarded the contract, proudly stated "so we have saved the taxpayer quite a tidy sum" (Hassanali 2017). The inquiry in China suggests that eventually there might be a price to pay for these savings.

An example of a different nature is the China Harbor Engineering Company that, as explained in the section *China and Trinidad and Tobago: the Highest Connectivity in the Region* of Chapter 4, was imposed by the Chinese as the contractor for the large dry dock facility in La Brea. This is the firm that built the controversial Hambantota port in Sri Lanka and is now constructing another useless one in Panama, thus contributing to the setting up of dangerous debt traps (see the section *The Belt and Road Initiative* of Chapter 3). Its problem is not poor work; rather, its international image has been associated with corruption. Besides illicitly funding the failed re-election campaign of the Sri Lankan President, China Harbor was blacklisted by the World Bank for some years for fraud and corruption related to construction projects in the Cayman Islands (Kakaire 2014). It was also involved in corruption in a road construction project in the Philippines (Douglas 2018b). Afra Raymond, a fellow of the Royal Institution of Chartered Surveyors and a member of the Trinidad and Tobago Transparency Institute, noted that Trinidad has procurement procedures to disbar corrupt companies and asked for details related to the China Harbor contract to be made public (Webb 2018). Predictably, his protests did not bring any change. One would expect at least Chinese firms with a poor record in Trinidad to be excluded from new contracts that are not financed by China. As shown earlier in this section, China Jiangsu International Corporation was responsible for the failures of the Morvant apartment buildings demolished in May 2012. It also performed poorly in the case of state projects that include UTT Tamana, ETeck Wallerfield, and various schools. Yet, from early 2012 onward it was allowed to compete for and to secure the contract for the Debe campus of the University of the West Indies worth more than TT $500 million (US $73 million). One is free to guess why such a thing could happen (Raymond 2015; Dickson 2012) in a country where, as shown later in this chapter, high-level corruption represents an important issue.

The most active and best-known Chinese contractor in Trinidad is Shanghai Construction Group, which presents itself as the 13th largest construction company in the world based on revenue. In 2014, the Caribbean represented one of its four main international markets and Trinidad and Tobago was envisaged as a regional base. The firm was already involved in large infrastructure projects in Barbados, the Bahamas, Dominica, Jamaica, Guyana, and Suriname. In Trinidad it had completed 13 such projects that include the aforementioned National Academy for the Performing Arts, Southern Academy for the Performing Arts, and Couva Children's Hospital in addition to the Cycling Velodrome and Aquatic Centre in Couva, a terminal of the Piarco International Airport, Prime Minister's Residence and Diplomatic Centre, the Ministry of Education Tower, the Chaguanas administrative complex, and several police stations (Fraser 2014a; Bagoo 2010; Bernal 2015: 1421). The cases of NAPA, SAPA, and the hospital in Couva have already been presented. They show how Shanghai Construction was imposed by the Chinese government and took advantage of this situation to increase its profit margins in controversial ways, to put it mildly. But in many other cases it won public tenders for projects in Trinidad that were not related to Beijing's financing. Persistent rumors attribute this to a special relationship with Calder Hart, the Canadian-born protégé of then Prime Minister Patrick Manning and chairman of the state-owned real estate development agency, the Urban Development Corporation of Trinidad and Tobago (UDeCOTT). The Prime Minister praised and defended him 45 times over two years, but Hart and his Shanghai-born wife nevertheless had to flee the country in March 2010 when proof of massive embezzlement could not be ignored anymore. The saga includes many obscure episodes, but the fact is that during Prime Minister Manning's tenure Shanghai Construction Group was awarded almost TT $2 billion (US $292 million) in UDeCOTT contracts (Bagoo 2010; *The Trinidad and Tobago Guardian*, February 20, 2012; for more details—and allegations—see Oosterveld et al. 2018: 67). Eventually, numerous construction flaws added to corruption allegations, turning the firm into a symbol of the most negative features of the Chinese contractors:

> Ask the average Trinidadian about the Shanghai Construction Group (SCG), and you will likely get an earful about it being former prime minister Patrick Manning's hand-picked contractor, an invasion of Chinese labourers, something about those funny looking multi-million dollar buildings, and of course, that National Academy for the Performing Arts (NAPA) in Port of Spain and its problems (Fraser 2014a).

When discussing general aspects of all Chinese contractors involved in infrastructure projects in Trinidad, respondents repeatedly mentioned unfair competition, business ethics issues, the fact that "in constructions, they use inferior materials" (Respondent 8), and that, more generally, "the quality of the work (. . .) in many ways it is very very substandard" (Respondent 20). The overall image is hardly positive: "I think they have lost the battle in terms of the public opinion. There is generally extraordinarily negative viewpoint of Chinese firms" (Respondent 1).

The Ecological Dimension

China-optimists sometimes speak about "China's return to greatness as an ecological civilization" (Harris 2015: 180–182), a spectacular development that, among others, will provide new export opportunities for the Caribbean while bringing there abundant Chinese renewable energy-related investments and loans (Harris 2015: 153). Everybody wishes this dream come true. For the time being, China continues to leave a prominent negative ecological footprint whose domestic cost was estimated in 2010 at 3.5 percent of the GDP, three times more than in 2004 (le Pere 2015: 376; Wong 2013). Chinese firms are frequently accused of exporting disregard for environmental responsibility all over the Global South. In Africa, "Chinese businesses have often been described as non-responsive to environmental issues," as this gives them an advantage in winning contractual bids over Western companies constrained by environmental assessment reports (Hess and Aidoo 2015: 73). Chinese extractive activities have been particularly detrimental to eco-sensitive areas, often leading to the displacement of people and wildlife that resulted in anti-China resentment (Hess and Aidoo 2015: 74). In Latin America, the World Bank estimates the annual costs of environmental degradation during the 2003–2013 "China Boom" at no less than 8.6 percent of the region's GDP (Gallagher 2016: 9). Resistance from environmental groups was frequent and even succeeded in closing down the Rio Blanco mining project in Peru, the Rio Negro agricultural one in Argentina, and the Tiejsu dam project in Ecuador (Ellis 2013: 4). In the Caribbean, vocal criticism targeted the construction by China Harbor Engineering Company of a US $1.5bn transshipment port and logistics hub on Jamaica's Goat Islands located in the Portland Bight Protected Area, which covers 1,900 sq km of mangroves, coastal swamps, cays, and coral reefs. Environmentalist groups launched a campaign to protect the indigenous flora and fauna threatened by the project, which included 22 vulnerable species such as the Jamaican iguana. A nationwide debate ensued; finally, the Urban Development Corporation decided to establish the Goat Islands as a wildlife sanctuary for endemic and endangered species (Bernal 2016: 4845–4858; Wigglesworth 2013; *The Gleaner*, December 15, 2017).

In the case of Trinidad, a not-too-well-informed Chinese scholar has recently mentioned the building of an "electrolytic aluminum plant" as a model of "taking advantage of China's preferential loans, which exemplified the economic cooperation between the two countries" (Hongbo 2017: 319). Indeed, there was a US $600 million project to build a 125,000 tons-per-year aluminum smelter, with China ExIm Bank providing a credit facility of $400 million for the construction; but it was canceled in 2010. This was announced by then Finance Minister Winston Dookeran, who mentioned health and environmental risks, to which concerns about the viability of the project and the optimal use of gas resources were added. In fact, the main dispute was on environmental issues. The project had been launched by the Patrick Manning administration and had received a Certificate of Environmental Clearance from the Environmental Management Authority. But environmentalist groups and individuals claimed that the certificate was based on flawed information and filed for judicial review. A court quashed the certificate and rejected the appeal of the Environmental Management Authority in 2010. The political decision to cancel the project was taken by a new government formed that same year; while in opposition, its members had supported the environmentalists' protests (Reuters, September 8, 2010; *The Trinidad and Tobago Guardian*, March 29, 2017). The project was relaunched in a more modest and environment-friendly form in 2017; only the production of aluminum downstream products such as pressed aluminum, coils, aluminum sheets for the vehicle industry, and wheel rims from imported aluminum ingots is now taken into consideration (*The Trinidad and Tobago Guardian*, March 29, 2017). This should make use of equipment worth US $40 million kept in a warehouse since 2010 (*Jamaica Observer*, October 25, 2017). However, the real problem is the Chinese claim for the cancellation of the initial project that amounts to US $201 million and is currently before the courts (*CNC3*, March 3, 2018). In 2016, current Prime Minister Dr. Keith Rowley stated that "we owe the Chinese a lot of money because that aspect of our attempt to diversify our economy (. . .) was rubbished by some people" (Neaves 2016).

The speech was politically flavored, but beyond that dimension environmentalist groups can find serious reasons for concern in regard to possible future industrial projects.

Unlike in Africa or Latin America, Chinese-built projects in the Caribbean have mainly been related to stadiums, government buildings, hospitals, and schools. By their nature, these do not have a significant environmental impact. Beijing's increased interest in the region, however, is likely to be accompanied by a diversification of projects. The Trinidadian example illustrates the negative ecological consequences of industrial ones. The Jamaican example is even more relevant, because the Goat Islands were to be turned into a transshipment port and logistics hub that would take advantage of the expansion of the Panama Canal (Wigglesworth 2013). All Caribbean countries hope that this expansion will significantly upgrade China's economic activities in the region, which implies a massive infrastructure effort. Fierce competition for receiving the new Chinese ports and storage facilities is likely to develop in the near future; when this happens, few governments will have ears for the warnings of local environmentalist groups.

The Ethical Dimension

Previous sections have shown that the presence of Chinese workers represents one of the most criticized aspects of China's "tied aid" to Trinidad and the rest of the Caribbean. Surprisingly, at the same time there has been genuine and widespread concern for and solidarity with such workers treated badly by their Chinese employers. The issue first became known in 2007, when an anonymous letter addressed to the government of Trinidad and Tobago was sent to a publishing company that enumerated abuses of Chinese workers. It alleged that the employer, the Shanghai Construction Group, physically abused workers, threatened them with deportation, forced them to work long hours without pay, and sent injured ones back to China without payment (Wilkinson 2007). In October 2009, a group of one hundred Chinese construction workers staged a roadside protest that caused a major traffic jam on the Uriah Butler Highway and therefore was given wide publicity. They were demanding to be allowed to return to China because they had been forced by their employer, Beijing Liujian Construction Corporation, to live and work in appalling conditions while receiving no pay for the previous two months (*China Labour Bulletin*, October 22, 2009). This triggered a number of newspaper reports and official inquiries. The then Foreign Affairs Minister, Paula Gopee-Scoon, was visibly shocked when she was shown published pictures of the squalid living conditions at Ramsaran Trace in Cunupia, where Chinese laborers were housed. Public health officials found that the workers "lived in unsanitary conditions," without private toilets and washroom facilities. They asked for the kitchen to be closed after noting the lack of proper work tables, of fly-proofing, of separate sinks to wash vegetable and hands, and of proper storage for frozen and dry food. There was no tiling of the floor and food was placed directly on the ground. For its part, Beijing Liujian—which had already rationed the laborers' food to make them return to work—asked Trinidad's Immigration Division to cancel the work permits of 32 laborers for breach of contract (*Newsday*, October 17, 2009; Honore-Gopie 2009). More recently, Shanghai Construction Group was ordered in 2017 to vacate and demolish buildings it had illegally erected next to the National Cycling Velodrome in Couva that it had completed one year earlier. The buildings—which used electricity and water illegally—housed 50 Chinese laborers, only six of whom regularly participated in the Velodrome's maintenance. The conditions of the buildings were "deplorable and unsanitary," which constituted "a health, safety and security hazard" (Javeed 2017).

The Trinidadian reaction to such news was very humane. Both the media and the general public were largely sympathetic to the concerned Chinese workers despite the very negative perception of Chinese labor involved in "tied aid" contracts. Even local trade union leaders condemned the treatment of these workers as "modern day slavery," and asked the Trinidadian government to intervene (*China Labour Bulletin*, October 22, 2009). Respondents shared these opinions; they repeatedly mentioned "slavery" and made comparisons with the colonial period. Their criticism went beyond the specific cases of Beijing Liujian and Shanghai Construction as it targeted all Chinese construction firms:

> the mistreatment of Chinese within Trinidad, (. . .) I wouldn't go so far to say slave industry, but it's close to that essentially in terms of not necessarily paying them the right amounts (. . .) and also not giving them proper housing and sanitary conditions (. . .) [this has been done] by Chinese companies (Respondent 28).

Interviews suggest that, in addition to spontaneous empathy, Trinidadians' solidarity with these workers is also due to the fact that both groups are perceived as being unjustly treated by predatory Chinese contractors: locals are deprived of work while some of the Chinese laborers that take their jobs are themselves submitted to intolerable exploitation. The general feeling is that this double injustice should not be allowed to occur.

The conclusion of this section is that China's "tied aid" has generated highly negative responses within the society at large due to the detrimental socio-economic effects of the imposition of Chinese labor and contractors as well as to image-damaging project failures, corruption allegations, environmental threats, and ethical issues. Some of these factors are also related to the other component of China's economic conditionality analyzed in the next section.

THE GOVERNANCE-RELATED COMPONENT OF THE CHINESE ECONOMIC CONDITIONALITY

This section examines the second component of China's economic conditionality. The literature strangely presents "tied aid" as a "non-conditional" condition imposed by the Chinese, but at least does acknowledge its existence. What it tends to ignore is the fact that this aid and especially its most frequent form of manifestation in the Caribbean, the prestige infrastructure projects, are non-transparently negotiated and result in government-to-government agreements that normally are not made public. This is part of Beijing's conditionality and has a clear reason: it allows for the imposition of questionable Chinese contractors (see the previous section) and of Chinese labor that, if known to the public of the target country, would likely lead to protests. In turn, this could limit the willingness of the local government to fully accept Beijing's conditions, which would be detrimental to China's economic interests. Secretive negotiations ensure that certain details are known, at best, only after the agreement is concluded; by then, it is too late for any change. The problem with this approach is that it distorts on purpose the working of democratic mechanisms in the target country and negatively affects its governance. It also encourages high-level corruption, which already is a very serious issue in the Caribbean.

Corruption

Of course, corruption itself is not part of the Chinese economic conditionality. But it represents an important side effect of the "tied aid" and is considerably enhanced by the lack of transparency analyzed in this section. Moreover, it needs to be addressed before this latter issue because it significantly contributes to the creation within the political elites and the state bureaucracy of a climate conducive to lack of public accountability and to poor governance; in turn, this climate enforces the predisposition toward secretiveness and the associated acceptance of Chinese-imposed conditions that might be detrimental to the national interest but do serve well political and electoral group interests. As shown in the previous chapter, some of the contractors imposed by Beijing in the framework of its "tied aid" to Trinidad and the Caribbean are known for corrupt practices. In fact, it is hardly a secret that "Chinese firms have often engaged in corruption, offering bribes to foreign officials to secure business deals" in the Global South (Hess and Aidoo 2015: 9). This is believed to come from Chinese business practices that center on personal relations instead of formal contracts and involve opaque state-business relations. The proliferation of such questionable Chinese practices in partner countries has been widely criticized in Africa and elsewhere in the developing world (Hess and Aidoo 2015: 14, 130). In the Caribbean, this issue is aggravated by the fact that endemic corruption is already present. One of the main causes that makes the US conduct its economic assistance programs to the region through the Inter-American Development Bank or the World Bank instead of bilateral channels is precisely the monitoring by these multilateral institutions of the use of funds. China, on the contrary, "seem[s] to be unconcerned with issues regarding either the misuse or misappropriation of funds" (Badri-Maharaj 2016). Some authors even rhetorically ask if Beijing is likely "to pour money into the leaky bucket of Caribbean state finances indefinitely" (Wigglesworth 2013). This is to ignore the fact that the Chinese actually benefit from corruption in partner countries and have little interest in stopping it. An analysis of the similar situation in neighboring Latin America leads to a very pessimistic conclusion:

> One of the less auspicious convergences between China and Latin America is a preexisting tendency on both sides of the Pacific toward informal economic and political practices. There is the real danger that informal mechanisms that prioritize personalistic ties above systemic procedures could mutually reinforce each other as Sino-Latin American relations deepen, and thereby pose a serious challenge to the rule of law (Hearn and León-Manríquez 2011: 14).

Panama is in the process of providing such an example in the Caribbean basin. Since its diplomatic recognition of Beijing in June 2017, suspicious awards in a series of public contracts involving Chinese companies have complemented the "array of [Chinese-financed and built] projects that defy economic rationale" (Ellis 2018) mentioned in the section *The Belt and Road Initiative* of Chapter 3. The Jamaican clean government activist Trevor Munroe expressed the concern of civil society organizations and of the private sector that "shadowy deals between governments and China will fuel even more graft" in his country and in the Caribbean (Wigglesworth 2013). In Dominica, two deals with China concerning military equipment concluded in 2017 and 2018 led to "a cloud of controversy," large-scale protests, and calls for Prime Minister Roosevelt Skerrit to resign as they were associated with corruption allegations related to his decision to "sell" passports, many of which are now used by Chinese intelligence officers (Oostervelc et al. 2018: 40). John Ashe, a former UN ambassador from Antigua and Barbuda and the 2013–2014 President of the United Nations General Assembly, was prosecuted in 2015 for conspiracy- and bribery-related charges. Between 2011 and 2014 he had accepted over US $1 million in bribes from Chinese businesspeople in exchange for using his UN positions to help them meet Antiguan government officials and to secure certain investments. In the words of the prosecutor, the Caribbean diplomat's shadowy relations with the Chinese "converted the United Nations into a platform for profit." Antigua was not the only target of his corrupt practices; one of the other five persons prosecuted in the same case was Francis Lorenzo, a deputy UN ambassador from the Dominican Republic (*The Guardian*, October 6, 2015; Oosterveld et al. 2018: 37).

Trinidad is hardly immune to similar temptations. The country has "a robust parliamentary democracy with a vibrant media and civil society"; but "corruption among public officials and within state institutions remains a challenge." The fact that the anticorruption legislation is "infrequently enforced" makes corruption "a pervasive problem" (Freedom House 2018). On Transparency International's scale of 0 (highly corrupt) to 100 (very clean), Trinidad's score is 41, identical with those of China, Serbia, and Suriname. Its rank is 77 out of 180 countries (Transparency International 2018). *The Global Competitiveness Report 2017–2018* of the World Economic Forum identifies corruption as the third most problematic factor (out of 16) for doing business in Trinidad (World Economic Forum 2017: 288). However, at only six percent, petty corruption is the lowest among the 20 Latin American and Caribbean countries surveyed by Transparency International in 2017 (Transparency International 2017: 14). This means that it is high-level corruption that explains the poor national average. Willem Oosterveld and his colleagues quote a local respondent claiming that "where Jamaica is a primary school, T&T is the university of corruption" (Oosterveld et al. 2018: 66). Sixty percent of Trinidadians believe that the government is "doing badly at tackling corruption" and 59 percent claim that the level of corruption has increased; but only 37 percent are willing to speak out against corruption and the same percentage considers reporting a case of corruption as socially acceptable (Transparency International 2017: 10, 12, 24). Returning to high-level corruption, penalties against public officials who refuse to disclose their assets, income, and liabilities are limited while the Integrity Commission responsible for these disclosures has been criticized for lack of effectiveness (Freedom House 2018).

Against this negative background, a correlation has been found between the decline in controlling corruption and the sharp rise of economic interactions with China (Oosterveld et al. 2018: 71). Examples in the previous sections show that the Chinese firm responsible for the failures of the Morvant apartment buildings demolished in May 2012 was nevertheless allowed from early 2012 onward to compete for and secure a US $73 million public construction contract (Raymond 2015); and that the head of the Urban Development Corporation of Trinidad and Tobago who awarded contracts worth US $292 million—including NAPA—to the Shanghai Construction Group was praised and defended by the then Prime Minister 45 times over two years before fleeing the country (Bagoo 2010; *The Trinidad and Tobago Guardian*, February 20, 2012; Oosterveld et al. 2018: 67). With such cases widely publicized in the media, it is hardly a surprise that Chinese firms are perceived as a significant source of corruption. Respondents' criticism ranges from elegantly mentioning "some level of leniency when it comes to the regulatory environment" (Respondent 1) to more directly stating that "the way China does business (. . .) is fertile ground for partnerships with Caribbean governments where members of those governments are inclined to cut corners" (Respondent 12) to bluntly explaining that, in the case of Chinese construction projects, "in the entire process of procurement there are questions related to governance and corruption" (Respondent 28). The latter respondent also took the discussion from the level of Chinese firms to that of the China-Trinidad bilateral relationship:

> in terms of unfair competition, the procurement processes used for Chinese companies seem not to be sufficiently aligned with national best practices essentially, and that might be as a result of bilateral agreements and relationships between China and Trinidad (Respondent 28).

Indeed, Chinese-related corruption cannot be dissociated from poor governance aspects that are an intrinsic part of China's economic conditionality.

Governance

In many Global South countries, the normal practice for public works projects is based on formal, competitive bidding processes. This is expected to ensure a higher degree of transparency and accountability that translates into improved governance. China prefers to set up high-level relationships and then to circumvent bidding by choosing the Chinese contractor through government-to-government agreements. The reason is mainly economic. To give a relevant example, Chinese firms have often fared poorly in Latin American countries such as Chile and Colombia where they had to participate in competitive bidding. The detail and technical quality of their proposals were not competitive while lack of familiarity with the bidding process prevented them from hiring the right legal and consulting firms. Such problems did not occur in Venezuela and Ecuador, where political affinities and ensuing cooperation had contributed to the creation of a friendlier environment, and in the small Caribbean states where Chinese development assistance had the same effect. In these cases, Beijing could directly negotiate deals with the target government without formal competition (Ellis 2012: 3, 32). In the Caribbean as elsewhere, due to tactical reasons and possibly to the Chinese business culture based on opaque state-business relations, Beijing makes sure that in these government-to-government agreements' "precise terms often remain hazy" to the public, "leaving often even local experts in the dark about the precise terms of government contracts agreed with Chinese counterparts" (Oosterveld et al. 2018: 16–24). In Latin America, these secretive dealings have drawn criticism in relation to their consequences in terms of environmental impact and labor conditions (Hearn and León-Manríquez 2011: 2). The aforementioned activist, Trevor Munroe, expressed civil society concern that in Jamaica and in the rest of the Caribbean "the hunger for Chinese investment will lead to far too many compromises" that "shadowy deals" hide from the public opinion (Wigglesworth 2013). Indeed, there is a strong temptation for political elites to secretively accept deals—mainly concerning prestige infrastructure projects—that serve their own political and electoral interests despite conditions that are perceived very negatively by the citizens. This is in fact what China counts on, and, as shown in the next section, this is how it has succeeded in socializing Trinidadian and Caribbean elites. The price is jeopardizing good governance; but in Beijing this is hardly a concern.

China's 2016 Policy Paper on Latin America and the Caribbean provides an interesting insight into this issue. The document states that Beijing is "ready to work with Latin American and Caribbean countries to strengthen exchanges in governance experience"; the two sides should "further strengthen exchanges of experience on governance." There should be cooperation "on strengthening and innovating social governance, (. . .) [to] jointly promote the modernization of governance system and governance capacity, (. . .) and ensure social *stability and order*" (Ministry of Foreign Affairs of the Republic of China 2016: III, IV.1.2, IV.3.1; emphasis added). Such exchanges and cooperation could be beneficial to China itself in its current effort to build a modern public governance system. But it is in no way clear how this interest in "strengthening and innovating social governance" might be compatible with Chinese actions in the Caribbean that, on purpose, have contrary consequences. In fact, the relevant element in these quotes is not good governance; it is Beijing's understanding of governance as an instrument that should ensure "stability and order" in partner countries. If Chinese actions in the Caribbean are assessed in this regard, it is clear that China believes that such stability and order are not necessarily associated with law-based, accountable, transparent, and participatory government—that is, with what is generally understood by good governance. Rather, they can be ensured by helping increase the legitimacy of local political elites. This is what Beijing does through its prestige infrastructure projects. Incidentally, Chinese contractors and workers get their part of profit.

As repeatedly mentioned in this book, China has frequently been accused of endangering Western-supported good governance efforts and results in Africa and in other parts of the developing world (Ziso 2018: 8; Wissenbach 2011: 21). The situation is not different in the Caribbean, where multilateral lenders that promote it are being sidelined by China's opaque loans. Moreover, a vicious circle has emerged. On the one hand, a pattern was identified whereby Chinese economic activities are more likely to target states with weak governance regimes. It is not an accident that Jamaica and Trinidad, which have some of the lowest scores for governance and rule of law indicators in the Caribbean, compete for the title of China's main partner in the region (Oosterveld et al. 2018: 35, 43, 44). On the other hand, the lack of transparency imposed as part of the Chinese economic conditionality further worsens governance in those states. The overall result is so detrimental to citizens that civil society groups are mobilizing themselves to "provide push-back against unbridled ambitions shared between Chinese firms and local elites" (Oosterveld et al. 2018: 44). Undoubtedly, when China's "legitimate and transparent forms of influence cross the line into harmful interference," "sunlight is the best disinfectant" (Garnaut 2018). To quote a very outspoken respondent,

> In terms of contracts they [the Chinese] get from Trinidad and Tobago, I think that any document that is executed on behalf of the people of Trinidad and Tobago by any government, there should be full transparency, accountability, responsibility and full disclosure (Respondent 15).

But actual reactions sometimes go one step further. Given "the strings attached to the Chinese financing" and the serious structural flaws of the associated construction projects, the benefit to the region has been assessed by some authors as "very questionable" (Badri-Maharaj 2016). In Trinidad, this opinion was shared by respondents coming from both the civil society and the general public: "not all free money or cheap money is good money" (Respondent 1). "It does not help when we get money too easily. . . . I think the citizens will suffer" (Respondent 30). "Problem: the lack of sustainable engagement, at a broad level. (. . .) Let's quantify how much money China has put in Trinidad and has resulted in what, at the end of the day? Decaying infrastructure" (Respondent 23). In extreme cases, the aforementioned view of

Chinese development assistance as "toxic" (Naím 2007: 95; Trinidad 2013: 19) took the form of radical rejection: "I don't believe Trinidad and Tobago needs [Chinese] aid. (. . .) What do you need aid for? We have a multi-billion dollar budget that we supply every year. So . . . I don't know if you need aid. I don't think we do" (Respondent 28). This was an extreme opinion. While not going that far, 93 percent of respondents nevertheless criticized fully or to a certain extent the secretive dealings and undisclosed agreements between Trinidad and China. The governance-related effects of these dealings are especially detrimental as not so long ago Trinidad and Tobago had an "interest in developing a reputation for good governance and social consciousness" (Braveboy-Wagner 2010: 423) that stands in stark contrast to the present Chinese-induced trend.

The conclusion of this section is obvious. Both components of China's economic conditionality—"tied aid" and their secretive negotiation—are unambiguously rejected by the society at large. The question remains, why does a democratic state whose citizens share such opinions nevertheless accept the Chinese conditionality. This issue is analyzed in the next section.

THE SOCIALIZATION OF CARIBBEAN ELITES

It is widely acknowledged that, in the Caribbean, the Chinese "are welcomed by local politicians" (*The Economist*, March 10, 2012): "Caribbean officials generally view China's checkbook diplomacy in a positive light" (Ward 2017: 13). In objective terms, at a time of American and European relative neglect, Beijing has become a key provider of development assistance; responsible regional leaders cannot ignore the new and growing opportunities available to their countries. But there is more than that. As in Latin America, Beijing's "prime target remains the top elites" (Shen 2015: 114). Richard Bernal appropriately wrote about "China's flattering diplomatic demarche." The Chinese exhibit particular sensitivity to all the Caribbean states, not overlooking even the tiniest ones. There are many embassies and "countless" delegations; equally important, the style of diplomacy pursued by China is more sensitive than the American one. Caribbean heads of state or government visiting Beijing "are allowed for a fleeting moment to live the illusion of respect": they meet the Chinese President and attend "elaborate ceremonies in ornate surroundings" with guards of honor and an actual red carpet, which is not necessarily the case in Washington (Bernal 2016: 3222–3223, 3230–3241). Their narcissism is further flattered by China's friendly discourse that always praises their merits, speaks only of harmony and cooperation, and never uses a judgmental tone. On the contrary, Caribbean leaders perceive occasional American criticism of their policies as inappropriate conduct and are particularly frustrated when they cannot respond aggressively because their countries depend on tourists and remittances from the US (Bernal 2016: 3230–3241). As elsewhere in the Global South, the perception of Western "lessons" and conditionality related to good governance or economic reforms is very negative: the opinion of an African official that "these conditions are probably well-intentioned, but they are humiliating" (Brautigam 2009: 149) is certainly shared by his Caribbean counterparts. They highly appreciate the fact that China does not impose such detailed and intrusive conditions: "the Chinese will not do this. They will not say 'You must do this, do that, do this!'" (Brautigam 2009: 149). Hence one respondent's explicit preference for Beijing as opposed to Washington: because it is much more pleasant to interact with them, "it wouldn't bother me if the Chinese want to increase their influence here" (Respondent 24).

Pour joindre l'utile à l'agréable—that is, to combine the pleasant and the useful—Chinese kindness comes with prestige infrastructure projects. Analysts have noted Caribbean leaders' "political compulsion of showcasing visible projects for maximizing electoral gains," which makes them "peculiarly susceptible to the allure of Chinese fiscal blandishments" (Badri-Maharaj 2016; Oosterveld et al. 2018: 66). In the words of a Trinidadian respondent, the Chinese "are willing to give [money] and politicians that really just are looking for getting headlines, they may be tempted to say OK, sign too quickly" (Respondent 30). As already shown, then Prime Minister Kamla Persad-Bissessar stated in 2012 that "we are not about creating edifices of political egos, monuments of pretentious aggrandisement at the expense of ignoring the plight of the people" (Office of the Prime Minister 2013). Yet, the following year she negotiated the purchase of a Chinese patrol vessel not because Trinidad needed it (see Chapter 7) but because it represented a "non-pretentious aggrandisement" that was deliverable prior to the 2015 election (Oosterveld et al. 2018: 66). Less than one month before that election, the same politician officially opened the Chinese-financed and built Couva Children's Hospital despite the fact that it was not complete (Rogers 2016). To be fair, this simply followed a pattern set up by the previous Prime Minister, Patrick Manning, who opened the impressive and equally Chinese-financed and built National Academy for the Performing Arts (which was completed but would eventually be closed for major repairs) in November 2009, some months before calling the early general election of May 2010. Even when elections are not imminent, the Chinese projects are routinely exploited by the members of the government for political self-legitimizing purposes. It would have been abnormal for Prime Minister Dr. Keith Rowley not to mention that the La Brea project he negotiated with the Chinese would transform one of the most depressed communities in the country into "a place of excellence that the world is looking to" (Webb 2018). Interestingly, when in opposition Dr. Rowley did criticize some of the China-related actions of the then government. Yet, this was simply part of the local political disputes; once in power, he became a champion of Beijing's infrastructure projects. He even described the 2010 scrapping of the planned aluminum smelter as the work of "some people'—*i.e.* the previous government—that was clearly detrimental to Trinidad's national interest (Neaves 2016; *Jamaica Observer*, October 25, 2017). This is to say that politicians in power are enthusiastically pro-Chinese. Those in the opposition might criticize the way their adversaries in the government use Beijing's money to acquire legitimacy and win elections, but never criticize China itself: when they come to power, they will need its projects. There is nobody in Trinidad's political elite that could be described as anti-Chinese.

It is in Chapter 8 that examples from other regions are used to analyze under what circumstances Global South opposition leaders might adopt anti-Chinese political platforms in order to capitalize on popular discontent generated by China's actions. This has not happened in Trinidad because, despite the very negative perception of its economic and social conditionalities, China preserves an overall good image among the citizens; and because, since the failed Islamist coup d'état attempt of 1990, no anti-system group has succeeded in becoming politically prominent. For their part, system-related politicians—that is, the ruling elite—have been significantly influenced by China's socialization efforts. Aforementioned Chinese flattery as well as the prestige infrastructure projects are beneficial to their narcissistic egos and electoral fortunes; such psychological factors and political incentives cannot fail to create a solid basis for cordial relations. This is pushed one step further by Beijing's use of secret diplomacy between state leaders as a tool of socialization. The previous section has presented the negative consequences of the secretive negotiations related to China's "tied aid" on Trinidad's governance and their equally negative perception by the society. However, for those involved in or directly benefitting from these negotiations—and this group includes the hard core of the country's political and bureaucratic leadership—the perspective is different. Already mentioned affinities are greatly enhanced by two tools that significantly contribute to the success of cooperative activities and are frequently used in this type of socialization: small informal groups and personalized interactions. These, and especially the latter, are seldom publicly discussed and scholarly analyzed due to their "delicate" nature (Terhalle 2011: 353–354) and to the difficulty to obtain first-hand information, which might come from memoirs published years or decades later that frequently present incomplete or distorted facts. Yet, in

2009, a former adviser to German Chancellor Helmut Schmidt, Egon Bahr, explained in what way intimate ways of communication represent the origin of developing common grounds:

> Secret diplomacy between state leaders is quintessential since it helps strengthening trust through personal relationships, while foreign offices are often too much restrained by existing protocols. This way you can exchange your views, tell the other side what is possible, what is not, what you want and what you do not want. States simply need such back channels (Terhalle 2011: 353).

President Xi Jinping's 2013 visit to Trinidad and those of successive Trinidadian Prime Ministers to China provided opportunities for both public and more discreet exchanges. They were supplemented by numerous visits of and contacts between ministers and other high officials from both countries and, critically, by the frequent negotiation of agreements related to China's infrastructure projects. The secretive character of these negotiations creates the ideal environment where politicians can overtly tell each other "what is possible, what is not, what you want and what you do not want." In time, such reiterated contacts and their positive results tend to alter the behavior, the opinions, and ultimately the substantive beliefs of leaders already sensible to flattery and political incentives. This is a rationalist process related to what Ikenberry and Kupchan call the "material components of power" (which include politicians' foreign-supported "opportunities for political advance" in their own country); but it is socialization nevertheless, as instrumental reasons drive national leaders in Trinidad—and similar states in the Caribbean—to embrace the norms and values articulated by the Asian global power. The causal chain presented in the section *Mechanisms of Socialization* of Chapter 2 is at work: external inducement leads first to policy change, which can be understood as cooperation through interest, and eventually to norm change, i.e. to cooperation through legitimacy. Indeed, Beijing has clearly been successful in making these elites accept as their own its vision of international order and of bilateral relations. In particular, the latter are perceived by Caribbean leaders as serving the national interest of their state despite the visibly negative domestic economic and social impact. This acceptance is not and does not need to be radical and complete. Not all of President Xi Jinping's ideas are perfectly mirrored in Port of Spain or elsewhere in the region. But it is sufficient that "the norms and value orientations of leaders in secondary states change and more closely reflect those of the dominant state"; this is enough for a successful Type I process of socialization to take place that allows a great power to exercise its influence on the target state (Ikenberry and Kupchan 1990: 285–286, 290, 293).

The bilateral approach that allows Beijing to closely interact with and to socialize elites in the Caribbean is complemented by China's aforementioned efforts to construct its own institutional architecture in the region. International institutions such as G20, the EU, NATO, or ASEAN are well known as frameworks that, sometimes unintentionally, help to facilitate personalized interactions (Terhalle 2011: 353). In part, this explains why the Chinese have been so active in developing various forms of multilateral cooperation in the region that, apparently, contradict their pronounced preference for bilateral interactions. Within these regional structures, China establishes "political and diplomatic linkages at every government level (congresses and political parties included)" and supports local organizations—including business-related ones—to become members (Haro Navejas 2013: 147). The state bureaucracy is also targeted: "they know [your] ministries better than you" (Respondent 30). As a result, two-thirds of the interviewed Trinidadian technocrats who had actually interacted with the Chinese had good or very good perceptions of those interactions; many expressed genuine admiration while nobody criticized China (see the section *Chinese Influence and Soft Power* of Chapter 4). One response is particularly relevant for the dynamic of their socialization:

> My overall perception [of China] is positive today, after seven or eight years of very active and substantial and deliberate engagement. I was deliberately cautious in the beginning, I was somewhat negative in the early days, not understanding Chinese culture and systems, and now that I understood it and I can navigate it better, now I think it's we're operating equal footing and that's what makes it positive (Respondent 23)

Top-level government officials adopt from the very beginning a self-interested positive attitude toward China. Bureaucrats have much less to gain from the bilateral interaction as their positions do not depend on infrastructure projects-enhanced political legitimacy. But even when negative or neutral initial positions exist, the Chinese seem to have the ability to successfully socialize them in the framework of reiterated close interactions. At times, "they even do little things that, by our standards, are unacceptable," such as making small presents (Respondent 1). Overall, the socialization of elites goes far beyond the narrow circle of state leaders. From Prime Minister to relevant mid-level bureaucrats, all those who might even slightly influence China-related national policies are targeted and convinced to adopt friendly and even admiring views. Once this happens—and, in Trinidad, it did happen—the state itself is successfully socialized and acts accordingly.

The consequences of this situation can be comprehensively analyzed only after the topic of social conditionality is addressed. Therefore, it is in Chapter 8 that I will discuss in more detail the mechanisms of socialization, the resulting elites-society gap, and its consequences. In particular, a comparison will be made with the Europeanization process in order to identify and explain differences that include the less important role played by Trinidadian bureaucrats (if compared to politicians) in the overall socialization of their state and society. For the moment, I will turn to the sensitive issue of local critics who vocally reject the socialization process. Some of them did not refrain from claiming that the Chinese "are becoming a colonial force in the Caribbean, but at least not in the traditional way," to quote a prominent Barbadian economist who insisted precisely on the deliberate acceptance of this situation by the region's governments: "it's all voluntary, there are no gunboats involved" (Wigglesworth 2013). A Trinidadian respondent echoed this view by claiming that the Chinese might "try to colonise us in different ways" (Respondent 24). Of course, this is part of the much wider debate between China-optimists and China-pessimists. But the interviews revealed that a large number of respondents tended to blame not the Chinese government or firms but local official policies ("it is the fault of [Caribbean] states for not being strategic or protective" (Respondent 17)), the leaders that promote such policies ("I think it is the fault of Trinidadians who were involved in the exercise" (Respondent 24)), and ultimately the political system that gives these leaders too much room to act against the national interest: "the problem is, I think, that they don't have robust checks and balances [on the part of Trinidad and Tobago]" (Respondent 30). One respondent explicitly mentioned "the immaturity of the state" (Respondent 15). This issue is further developed in Chapter 8. But it is relevant that no less than 80 percent of the respondents believe that Trinidad's government should be more conscious in its dealings with the Chinese government and business partners while a further 13 percent share this opinion to an extent. No matter the ultimate causes to which it can be attributed, the acceptance by the political elites of China's economic conditionality is clearly rejected by Trinidad's society.

Consequently, the case is completely different from that of the Chinese political conditionality. Unlike "no Taiwan; no Tibet; no Tiananmen Square," which does not directly impact Trinidad's socio-economic situation, China's "tied aid" prevents local workers and contractors from accessing a significant part of the construction market of their own country. The secretive nature of associated government-to-government agreements damages, on purpose, preexisting policies and practices of transparency and public accountability, which in turn encourages corruption. Unsurprisingly, both are widely rejected by citizens. A strange situation has been reached: China's economic conditionality-related socialization of the Trinidadian political elites and state is highly successful while that of the society is a total failure. This "happy government" vs. "skeptical society" situation sets obvious limits to the depth of the China-centered process of international socialization of Trinidad and Tobago's state-society complex. Moreover, this process is further hampered by the similar response to the Chinese social conditionality analyzed in the following chapter.

NOTE

1. "Beware of Greeks bearing gifts" (Virgil, *Aeneid*, II, 49), an allusion to the Trojan horse.

Chapter Six

China's Social Conditionality

This book introduces the concept of social conditionality that represents the use of incentives and sanctions to prevent the adoption by recipient states of policies that would regulate the inflow and activities of entrepreneurial migrants from the donor country despite the negative impact of their economic actions on local businesses and workers. This is a strong form of conditionality that significantly shapes the target state's domestic policies in ways that go against its national interest. In the case of China, visibly detrimental socio-economic consequences in various Global South countries have frequently resulted in large scale frustration, criticism, protests, and even riots that have been discussed extensively in the literature. It is indeed strange that the term conditionality has never been employed. The only explanation I can think of is related to the strength of the non-conditionality "myth" and to scholars' unconscious predisposition to view social reality as a reflection of the model provided by the literature. This chapter follows the opposite path.

The following sections start by providing a brief picture of China's relations with and instrumentalization of its diaspora and continue by presenting the high level of discontent generated in the Caribbean and in Trinidad by recent Chinese entrepreneurial migrant competition that endangers the survival of small local companies resulting in increased unemployment; by the fact that Chinese small companies tend to hire only Chinese nationals; by alleged Chinese-related bureaucratic corruption and illicit activities; and by Chinese cultural and social "insularity." This is contrasted with the pro-Chinese discourse and actions of the political elites that fully accept Beijing's social conditionality. Finally, the effect of this gap is assessed on the process of Chinese international socialization of the entire state-society complex.

CHINA AND ITS DIASPORA

In recent decades, the Chinese diaspora has become "an expanding social field that gradually covers virgin territory" as large numbers of new entrepreneurial migrants from China have settled "from the Marshall Islands and Kamchatka to the villages of Romania" in their tireless search for markets still unconquered by other Chinese (Haugen and Carling 2005: 640, 660). At first view, this is a spontaneous phenomenon associated with what has been referred to as "globalization from below" or "low-end globalization" (Mohan et al. 2014: 14). Yet, the Chinese state supports and uses this migratory flow to its own advantage. This is why it can be assessed as part of Beijing's "attempt to enlarge its global influence sphere more generally both from above and from below" (Röschenthaler and Socpa 2017: 183). Indeed, for a long time China's government has "celebrat[ed] migration itself as a patriotic and modern act" (Nyíri 2001: 635; Green and Liu 2017: 11). The starting point was the massive migration of Chinese nationals—including many civil servants—who lost their jobs due to Deng Xiaoping's reforms. They were encouraged to create enterprises abroad while maintaining relations with the fatherland. In 1995, President Jiang Zemin explicitly asked his unemployed countrymen to move abroad and become global actors (Röschenthaler and Socpa 2017: 167). At the same time, specific policies were developed "to keep migrants loyal to the modernization project of the PRC" (Tjon Sie Fat 2009: 137; Green and Liu 2017: 10). No less than 360 laws were adopted between 1978 and 2000 that "concern the overseas Chinese and their duties to contribute to the development of their home country" (Pokam 2015: 51, 53; Röschenthaler and Socpa 2017: 180). This is why the Chinese diaspora has become one of the largest in the world—the million people living in Africa representing only a fraction of a much larger group—and repatriates to China the largest part of its gains (Röschenthaler and Socpa 2017: 180). Today, the Chinese presence in the Caribbean and elsewhere in the Global South takes two forms. The first is represented by the "Chinese overseas state," which is relevant in diplomatic and economic terms and is responsible for bringing in professionals and laborers who form the category of state-sponsored sojourners. This "proletarian" migration—which is very visible in the case of "tied aid"—is short-term, project-specific, and state-sponsored. The second category is that of private entrepreneurial migrants accompanied by their privately sponsored family members and workers (Green and Liu 2017: 13). Members of the first category might choose not to return to China at the end of their contract and join the second category instead. But the most original feature of the new Chinese entrepreneurial migrants is their transformation into a "transnational middleman minority" in poor and transitional economies. Many of their target countries have no recent tradition of Chinese immigration, but there is "high demand for low-cost consumer goods produced by China and a lax regulatory environment" (Nyíri 2011: 145; Green and Liu 2017: 11). The migration process is based on social networks, which "engender trust that facilitates contractual arrangements that promote trade" (Rauch 2001). Every newcomer "has the potential to become a powerful link in a phenomenon of chain migration that draws relatives, acquaintances, girlfriends, and spouses in their wake" (French 2014: 6). In turn, these "begin to work as traders, offer services to Chinese workers, sell food in restaurants, open drinking spots, and so on"; as they all "strongly rely on family and clan solidarity," the transnational relationships connecting China and its diaspora are further enforced (Pokam 2015: 13, 51; Röschenthaler and Socpa 2017: 168). This is hardly the first time that Chinese traders settle abroad in large numbers; in fact, they represent "a familiar transhistorical figure." What is different from similar experiences in the past is their heavy dependence on China "in ways their predecessors were not" (Nyíri 2011: 147; Green and Liu 2017: 9). The fatherland is a critical source of labor, merchandise, and capital on which their very economic survival depends (Green and Liu 2017: 9–10). Even in Caribbean countries that recognize Taiwan, the huge majority of entrepreneurial migrants come from China and "activate transnational entrepreneurial networks with China at the center of their supply system" (Green 2012–2014: 25). In addition to the reliance on Chinese resources, the diaspora also takes advantage of the favorable conditions of agreements negotiated by the government in Beijing with the state they live in "for opening up new territories and creating enterprises" (Röschenthaler and Socpa 2017: 180). Even older Chinese communities that had not necessarily preserved significant links with their country of origin are tempted by these new opportunities.

China's government has sought to both protect and leverage new as well as old Chinese communities (Ellis 2012: 30, 33). In Cameroon, Chinese shop owners who felt they were harassed by Cameroonian fiscal and customs authorities created the Chinese General Association of Industry and Commerce that, especially on the occasion of state visits, reports harassments and other problems to Chinese officials who eventually negotiate better conditions for their diaspora (Röschenthaler and Socpa 2017: 168). In Suriname, where episodes of violence against Chinese shopkeepers took place in 2009 and 2011, China's Ambassador, Yuan Nansheng, vigorously urged the local government to protect the ethnic Chinese, and encouraged the local Chinese associations to create a single umbrella organization that became Beijing's interlocutor. When Jamaican Prime Minister Portia Simpson Miller visited China in August 2013, Vice-Premier Li Keqiang explicitly asked for the protection of Chinese shopkeepers in the Caribbean country. One week later, the required special measures were adopted by the High Command of the Jamaica Constabulary Force (Ellis 2012: 33; Ellis 2014: 184). Through such actions, the government in Beijing "encourages inter-diaspora networking among themselves and with China" (Green 2012–2014: 26; Ma Mung 2008). By far the most spectacular events pertaining to this category are the Chinese overseas rescue missions (see Thunø 2018: 191–193). To give only one Caribbean example, 462 Chinese nationals threatened by hurricane Maria were evacuated by the Chinese government from Dominica to Antigua and Barbados and, in part, eventually to China. This was heavily publicized by the authorities in Beijing "as an example of China's growing willingness and ability to assist, protect, and rescue from danger its nationals abroad" (Gao 2017; Green and Liu 2017: 27). All this can be understood as an effort to encourage the diaspora to "take advantage of the benefits of a global Chineseness under the informal and formal patronage and protection of the Chinese state" (Green and Liu 2017: 25–26). This is not a disinterested strategy. At the National Overseas Chinese Affairs Work Conference in 2011, the deputy director of the Overseas Chinese Affairs Office of the State Council of the People's Republic of China clearly stated the "three expansions," i.e. the three long-term objectives of Beijing's diaspora policies: attracting investments and talents; protecting and promoting national unity; and generating national soft power by way of public diplomacy. This is to say that the Chinese government intends to instrumentalize the diaspora as "public diplomats" (Thunø 2018: 194, 196–198) supportive of China's various political and economic objectives globally and in their country of residence. Ultimately, this is the logical consequence of the fact that "the migrants' decisions to migrate, destination choices, and relations with local host societies are intimately entangled with Chinese state policies and processes" (Huynh et al. 2010: 290; Green 2012–2014: 26).

Chinese Immigration into the English-Speaking Caribbean

During the 19th century, the main indentured labor stream to the British colonies in the Caribbean was East Indian. Only 7 percent of the more than a quarter million Chinese coolies who went as indentured laborers to Latin America and the Caribbean arrived in the British West Indies. Almost all of these 20,000 individuals went to British Guiana, Jamaica, and Trinidad. Soon, they abandoned agriculture and formed a "middleman minority" carving out a niche in the shopkeeping sector. By the 1890s, almost all of them were working as retail traders. Three more Chinese migratory processes followed: a small return migration to China, re-migration from British Guiana to the rest of the Caribbean, and a new migratory wave from China between the late 1880s and the 1930s that was particularly significant in the case of Jamaica. It was noted that most of the present Chinese in the region are descendants of these post–1890 "free" migrants, not of the earlier indentureds. The majority of the Chinese in Trinidad and Guyana are Cantonese; the Jamaican ones belong to the Hakka, an ethnic minority group. Unlike the rest of the Caribbean, these three countries are characterized by the migratory difference between the *huagong* (laborers) and *huashang* (merchants). Between 1910 and 1940, 6,000 to 7,000 members of the latter group went mainly to Jamaica and Trinidad. British Guiana, which had been the main destination of indentured Chinese, received many fewer *huashang*. Three changes ensued. First, racial mixing was important, leading to the frequent questioning of a primary Chinese identity. Second, after independence there was an exodus of Caribbean Chinese mainly—but not exclusively—to North America, which led to the considerable reduction of their numbers. Third, the important post–1980s immigration from Hong Kong and China has visibly transformed and diversified the Chinese communities in the region (Green and Liu 2017: 2–4, 8; Rajkumar 2013; Look Lai 2000).

The Chinese in Trinidad

The idea of bringing indentured Chinese to Trinidad was first launched in 1802 by Captain William Layman, who claimed that these "free civilized men" would become an example for the African slaves, thus preventing rebellion and the establishment of a Haitian-style "black empire." The first 192 immigrants arrived in 1806 on the *Fortitude*. Mortality rates and abandonment of the plantation were high, but Chinese immigration was once more organized from the 1850s to 1866 to solve the post–Emancipation plantation problems. However, many Chinese even redeemed or purchased the remaining years of their contracts in order to abandon the plantations. They became handicraftsmen, barbers, tailors, bakers, carpenters, goldsmiths, and woodcutters or they cultivated and supplied crops to the local markets. From the 1870s, they began to set up shops and small businesses, which by the end of the century represented their main activities. Lack of Chinese females led to high rates of intermarriage with other ethnic groups, which resulted in the emergence of a mixed group that was more creole in culture than Chinese. As already mentioned, a new wave of *huashang* (merchants) migrants arrived between 1910 and 1940. They triggered a process of "chain migration" by encouraging relatives and friends back in China to come to Trinidad where they provided labor for the newcomers. Because "mail order" brides were also brought from China the rate of interethnic marriages diminished (Rajkumar 2013). The community—which was mainly Cantonese—was segmented based on the region of origin and on linguistic ties (Green and Liu 2017: 4). This was reflected by the large number of Chinese associations. In terms of religion, however, most Chinese converted to Anglicanism and especially to Roman Catholicism. The Confucian community was small from the very beginning and experienced unrelenting diminution; in 1946 it had 21 members. The only mention of Taoists was in 1946, when there were two of them. The number of Buddhists was slightly higher and at times increased due to the arrival of new immigrants. But its evolution—470 in 1891, 187 in 1901, 428 in 1911, and 42 in 1946—confirms the success of Christian proselytism (Millette 1993). Moreover, second and third generation children became upwardly mobile and, as they joined the upper middle class and the business elite, they began to distance themselves from Chinese language and traditional culture. Accordingly, the Chinese associations declined visibly (Rajkumar 2013). However, in recent decades a new dynamic emerged with the arrival of new immigrants from China.

THE IMPACT OF THE NEW CHINESE IMMIGRANTS

Chinese Small Businesses

Many of the new migrants initially arrive in the Caribbean as workers for Chinese construction firms and decide not to return to China at the completion of the project. Some of them have the intention to migrate to a third country, mainly the US. Most, however, set up small trading businesses and use language capability as well as contacts in China to import goods at prices lower than those of local merchants. They also initiate processes of "chain migration." As in other parts of the Global South, this frequently results in social friction (Bernal 2016: 6739–6744). The same phenomenon has taken place on a large scale and has been well studied in Africa. The literature speaks of "relatively predictable lines of conflict" between Chinese firms that operate "more cheaply or more productively" and African entrepreneurs who had dominated the market (Mohan et al. 2014: 123). Accordingly, the very responses of sub-Saharan African countries to Chinese migration "have been framed around the notion that this represents economic competition with local enterprises," with the newcomers benefiting "at the expense of Africans" (Yap and Henson 2016: 6). Fieldwork in Ghana and Nigeria showed that the numerous Chinese traders who settled there since the early 2000s are perceived as representing "a direct challenge to locals operating in the informal retail sector" and as undermining local manufacturing (Mohan et al. 2014: 110). Cameroonian traders feel equally insecure; one of them claimed that Chinese competition "will lead to a situation whereby petty businessmen with small turnovers will no longer be able to survive" (Röschenthaler and

Socpa 2017: 178). A South African entrepreneur complained that the Chinese always offer the lowest price, thus destroying the markets for local traders (Lahtinen 2018: 48). In Nairobi, 500 Kenyan traders chanted "Chinese must go" in protest to thousands of Chinese traders who had arrived on tourist visas. "From Senegal to Kenya, African traders are furious to see unfair competition from private Chinese merchants coming into Africa" (Lahtinen 2018: 46). An extreme case is that of Douala, Cameroon, where criticism targeted Chinese prostitutes working for half the price of local ones (Röschenthaler and Socpa 2017: 172–173).

In the Caribbean basin, similar "social friction" is highly visible. In July 2013, thousands of protesters marched in Santo Domingo complaining about the 72 new Chinese shops set up in the city during the previous two years and about unfair competition from Chinese merchants they accused of not paying taxes and of engaging in other objectionable practices (Ellis 2014: 182). The cases of anti-Chinese violence in Suriname have already been mentioned. In December 2009, assaults against Chinese shopkeepers and the looting of their property in Papatam showed the extreme tensions that had developed between these traders, who have become the main suppliers of goods and store credit in many rural communities, and local ethnic groups such as the Maroons indebted to them or frustrated by their practices. The violence repeated itself in October 2011 in Maripaston (Ellis 2014: 184). In the English-speaking Caribbean, tensions have not escalated to such levels, but they do exist. Dominican journalist Thomson Fontaine wrote critically about Chinese shops "transforming the local business landscape, soaking up small businesses from retail shops to rum shops to food joints." The aforementioned intervention of China's Vice-Premier that resulted in special measures adopted by Jamaica's Constabulary Force to protect members of the Chinese community and their businesses was due to actual harassment of the Chinese by unsympathetic locals (Ellis 2014: 184, 188). In Trinidad, respondents emphasized the rapid expansion of Chinese small businesses: "It struck me how the Chinese have been able to spread so fast. (. . .) You see a building and next thing, like two months, Chinese restaurant" (Respondent 30); "what we have seen was an exponentially increasing presence of the Chinese in terms of numbers and in terms of infiltration of sectors" (Respondent 20). They also showed a certain level of frustration:

> I think the Chinese are doing more business here than us. You know, like, they live here, this is our country, but . . . Chinese come here and have been so successful compared to us (Respondent 8).

> It's basically the traders that are coming. (. . .) [They are] wiping out the involvement of local businesses in the retail sector and that can't augur well for us (Respondent 20).

Negative social consequences were mentioned: "job losses, family disruptions due to closing of businesses unable to compete with Chinese owned enterprises" (Respondent 5). A recurrent grievance was the "they only give jobs to their people" issue. Chinese businesses

> hire mostly Chinese. (. . .) they are not creating employment for us, here. They are creating employment for their people, here. And I think, honestly, that this is something that should be a major concern for us (Respondent 8).

At times, certain responses seem copy-pasted from the literature on the Chinese small businesses in Africa. Fieldwork in Cameroon showed that local shop assistants hired by the Chinese "are easily dismissed as soon as the owners have learned to communicate in the local language" (Röschenthaler and Socpa 2017: 170). In Trinidad,

> Chinese businesses don't hire local people. At a Chinese food place, for instance, you may have one local, but that is the person who will take the orders because they understand what we want. At the point when some of the Chinese nationals get to understand the menu items they have no need for the Trinidadian any more (Respondent 12).

More generally, "financially it feels as if the resources are going one way." In addition to not hiring locals, the Chinese are accused of not "invest[ing] in local producers, they import mostly all the stuff they need, they are very frugal, don't depend on local services" (Respondent 12).

This criticism of "frugality" introduces an interesting aspect of the Trinidadian perception of Chinese immigration. Generally, China's emigration is "a migration of poor people, unemployed workers, and expropriated farmers" (Röschenthaler and Socpa 2017: 167). In Africa, their efforts have been met at times with admiration. A Ghanaian teacher spoke empathically of the hard work of the Chinese migrants, most of whom come from a very poor background and do everything in their power to help their families at home. Moreover, he appreciatively noted a wider sense of national obligation that makes them "contribute their quota to the country" (Mohan et al. 2014: 130). Such opinions are hardly shared in Trinidad. Certain responses were particularly brutal:

> They live very poorly (. . .). I mean is almost like slavery (Respondent 12).

> I see China is having almost as a policy, whether is written in documents or is unspoken, of exporting poverty. And I see that Trinidad and Tobago and the wider Caribbean has been a place that China has used in order to export its poverty. (. . .) it's obviously not the educated class that is coming. (. . .) And I don't think that that adds a lot of value to Trinidad and Tobago (Respondent 20).

Alleged Illicit Activities

Criticism becomes harsher when illicit activities are mentioned. Their alleged existence is already mentioned in the literature: "there are allegations in Trinidad and Tobago that Chinese restaurants are involved in gambling, money laundering and other forms of crime" (Bernal 2016: 6710–6726). Even respondents who have a rather balanced assessment of the Chinese presence mention, on the negative side, "gambling; there is a lot of business that goes unregulated" (Respondent 30). At times, there is the perception that the Chinese take the money of naïve Trinidadians through legal but morally questionable methods:

> With the proliferation of Chinese businesses, literally every five hundred feet you see a Chinese gaming machine and there is a Chinese national sitting there whose English is limited to put money, take money, yes and no. (. . .) I don't know what they work for, but they collect the money that Trinidadians work for and at the end of the day they take it home (Respondent 12).

More frequently, Chinese "gambling" and "casino industry" are mentioned in relation to organized crime: "there is a big question of a Chinese mafia as well as money laundering in Trinidad, which is a very valid reality" (Respondent 28).

In fact, when speaking about "mafias" it should be noted that in various parts of the developing world the Chinese entrepreneurial migrants frequently represent the targets of local criminal groups. In Nigeria, for example, there are so many acts of armed robbery that Chinese businessmen avoid social interactions with co-nationals in the hope that this might limit their visibility and vulnerability (Mohan et al. 2014: 105). In Jamaica, the Chinese entrepreneurial migrants complained that they are the victims of Jamaican-acted violence and extortion (Bernal 2016: 6710–6726). Yet, it is true that the rapid expansion of Chinese migrant communities has been accompanied by a change in the nationality of criminal groups that target them. Increasingly, the expansion of criminal activity has been noted that "has its origins in the Chinese secret societies which operate in many communities of expatriated Chinese throughout the world" (Ellis 2014: 186). The study of "Chinese mafias" in Latin America and the Caribbean has shown that their activities are encouraged by the traditional reluctance of ethnic Chinese communities to report problems among their own members to the authorities of the host state. This tendency to avoid close relationships with local law enforcement prevents police from acting effectively against criminal elements. Hence the criticism of a senior officer from the Trinidad and Tobago Criminal Investigations Unit of the "culture of the Chinese (. . .) to keep things to themselves" (Ellis 2014: 186, 192). At times, this results in repulsive crimes such as the widely publicized 2012 double homicide in Trinidad (Ellis 2014: 187). Other criminal activities that have developed significantly include human smuggling from China. Often, members of established Chinese communities are made to help the trafficking organizations by providing temporary employment and lodging (Ellis 2012: 33).

The situation is aggravated by the fact that the rise of Chinese criminal activities overlaps with what has been called "the pistolization of the Caribbean": a "weaponization" of the English-speaking Caribbean associated with drug trafficking, political patronage, and armed violence. Since the first half of the 2000s, across the region, there has been a steady rise in gun homicides and in the percentage of such crimes that the authorities were unable to solve (Agozino et al. 2009). This is particularly visible in Trinidad and Tobago: its "geographic location makes it a transit point for drug trafficking, which brings with it a high level of criminality" (Coface 2018). A major spike in criminal activities, including kidnappings, took place in the 2000s. Technical help was sought from the US and the UK to counter this threat (Braveboy-Wagner 2008: 43) but failed to improve the situation. Organized crime continues to contribute to high levels of violence that create "a difficult security environment" (Freedom House 2017; Freedom House 2018). The National Operations Center Commander Garvin Heerah went as far as stating that extortion, robberies, kidnapping, and petty crimes show that "T&T is in a crime-dominant society and crime today is a business" (*The Trinidad and Tobago Guardian*, July 30, 2017). All this has predictably increased public sensitivity to organized crime. One of the unexpected consequences is that, in a certain measure, recent Chinese immigrants as a group are blamed for the existence of Chinese criminal activities. Respondents frequently mentioned "crimes involving Chinese nationals, especially robberies" (Respondent 12) as well as the fact that "there is a negative perception of Chinese. Locals (. . .) feel threatened (. . .) especially [by] what has been happening of recent with this increase in Chinese robberies" (Respondent 28). This is somewhat strange, as the targets of Chinese criminals have been Chinese businessmen, not Trinidadian ones. Yet, the "negative perception" was important enough to make the Chinese ambassador in Port of Spain state publicly that incidents involving Chinese are isolated, that there are no reasons to be alarmed, and that overall "there is no trend to indicate that the Chinese are being singled out or targeted any more than any other group in Trinidad" (Superville 2017). In fact, his speech had two objectives. One was to put an end to rumors about the Chinese mafias. The other was to deny that Chinese businesses might represent particular targets of local criminal groups. Such a situation would indicate that Chinese immigrants—or, at least, the successful ones—face serious danger in Trinidad, which could discourage potential newcomers from settling in the country. However, the opinions of at least some Chinese businessmen differ greatly from those of the ambassador. They feel threatened and even claimed that further attacks would lead to "a second exodus" similar to the one that occurred due to the 1970 Black Power riots, when "many Chinese businessmen closed up their businesses and sold their properties cheaply. They migrated to Canada" (*The Trinidad and Tobago Guardian*, July 30, 2017). It is still debated if criminal actions perpetrated by local gangs are ethnically motivated or simply target the Chinese because they "had money, did not fight back and were 'soft' targets for criminals" (*The Trinidad and Tobago Guardian*, July 30, 2017). One might note that, to the victims, this makes little difference. What is less and less debatable is the issue of Chinese mafias acting against their co-nationals in Trinidad. Ian Ramdhanie, a criminologist and the Principal of the Caribbean Institute for Security and Public Safety claimed that "it was safe to assume that the Chinese Triads were here." These groups might not be responsible for all the attacks against Chinese nationals, but they are "plying their trade." Moreover, "this had been increasing over the years and if not addressed urgently, the attacks will intensify" (*The Trinidad and Tobago Guardian*, July 30, 2017). Aforementioned Commander Garvin Heerah, who is also a senior lecturer at Anglia Ruskin University in Britain, similarly claimed that Chinese Triads are responsible for much of the crime targeting Chinese nationals: "There are big players behind this who are controlling the Chinese business industry" (*The Trinidad and Tobago Guardian*, July 30, 2017). Overall, this triads-related discourse is very convincing, and few Trinidadians perceive it as exaggerated. In turn, this has added a significant dimension to the negative local perception of recent Chinese immigrants.

Another criticism stems from the claim that the same immigrants "support" corruption. This is in part related to the more general Global South and especially African allegations that Chinese traders are more successful because they are "bypassing local laws" (Mohan et al. 2014: 110). Yet, except for the issue of Chinese mafias involved in gambling—"there is a lot of illegal activity happening, unregulated, and is being done under the nose of police" (Respondent 30)—respondents in Trinidad mainly spoke of minor Chinese-related "bureaucratic corruption":

> I know a Chinese guy, he has a driver's permit and a national ID card and can't write English and he barely speaks English. I mean, come on. We had instances where they are given firearm permits and we have businessmen here who have been waiting 20 and 30 years to get approved to carry a firearm. These businesses are being robbed but no, the Chinese come here, within 3–4 months, 6 months you get a licence to carry a weapon and you can't write English. You can't read English, how are you passing the assess? So, it smells of corruption (Respondent 12).

The only sensitive issue related to this kind of corruption is that of alleged illegal immigration:

> I question very much how is it that Chinese immigrants are able to be here seemingly legal, and that to me speaks of corruption. (. . .) It means that it supports bureaucratic corruption in Trinidad and Tobago. (. . .) the kind of relationship that the individuals and groups would have made themselves with the bureaucracy would have been able to facilitate the growing presence (Respondent 20).

Overall, these corruption allegations are dwarfed by the much better-known similar issues related to the infrastructure projects presented in the previous chapter. Yet, in conjunction with those issues they do contribute to the negative perception of China's socio-economic involvement in Trinidad.

Insularity and Sinophobia

Returning once more to African examples, the literature presents abundant cases of clear separation between the Chinese and the local community resulting in suspicion and mixed feelings on the African side. The Chinese stick together, rent shops in the same building, speak their own language, prefer their own food and habits, support only each other, rely strongly on family networks, do not seem interested in the local culture, do not mix with locals, and do not make African friends (Lahtinen 2018: 33, 48; Röschenthaler and Socpa 2017: 182–183). In Latin America, there is a similar perception of a strong "cultural separateness" between recent Chinese immigrants and the local communities (Ellis 2013: 3). Respondents in Trinidad described an identical situation, which they assessed negatively: the Chinese "increase the social divide" (Respondent 15); there is "lack of integration, culturally" (Respondent 12). Some of the newcomers "do not speak the language" and there is "a dynamic where the whole Chinese business community in terms of them kind of integrating into our community, they are still set apart" (Respondent 26). One respondent noted the huge difference between the "historical" and the present waves of immigrants: the latter "stay among themselves, they go to shop together, they don't integrate with society and it's causing bias and polarisation. So there's two Chinas in Trinidad, two distinct Chinas" (Respondent 23). One respondent explicitly stated that this "is becoming an area of concern"; recently arrived Chinese "are not integrated into the national culture and national identity. They tend to preserve their identity, which is something that we notice, there is very little mixing" (Respondent 12). Two respondents with very different backgrounds spontaneously used the word "insularity" when asked to mention any aspect related to the Chinese presence in Trinidad they dislike (Respondents 6 and 23).

One respondent, however, spoke of this perception as illustrative not of Chinese wrongdoing but of the local society's ethnic and/or racial bias: "there is an underbelly of this entire thing which has to do with discrimination against Chinese" (Respondent 28). It has been noted that the recent massive inflow of Chinese "does cause resentment in Caribbean countries, inducing a rise in xenophobia" (Oosterveld et al. 2018: 6). Historically, they have been "a discreet diasporic community" seldom engaged in inter-community frictions. Intermarriage and interethnic relationships have been much more frequent in their case than in that of the East Indians, which kept them away from tensions such as those between Indo-Caribbean and African Caribbean groups (Misrahi-Barak 2012: 9–10). Typically, they were not "implicated in the racial politics of the country" (Misrahi-Barak 2012: 12; Lowe Shinebourne 2004: 53). At present, however, anti-Chinese sentiments develop all over the Caribbean that "are grounded in a loss of economic opportunities in employment and small-scale trading" (Bernal 2016: 6732–6737). Trinidad is no exception. To quote one respondent, "I've seen on social media and just in conversation the increased polarisation [between the local perception of old and new Chinese immigrants]. Bias. Assumptions. Chinese eat dog, you know" (Respondent 23). Not all respondents bother to note such differences. Many simply state "there is this ambiguity about the Chinese community" (Respondent 28). When asked if they were aware of discontent in Trinidad and Tobago due to the presence of recent immigrants from China, respondents made comments that are part of the following line of reasoning: the displacement of locally owned small businesses has led to the loss of jobs; the social media covering of this situation has led to increased anti-Chinese bias; in turn, this has resulted in "occasional flair ups of racism" (Respondents 1, 5, 6, and 23).

This is well illustrated by a 2015 incident. It started with a video depicting the skinning of a dog allegedly at a Chinese restaurant in Trinidad. The footage went viral on social media in a heavily racialized context. The tension was exacerbated by an interview with the Health Minister, who began by associating diminishing numbers of stray dogs with the opening of many new Chinese restaurants. "I know in China, rats are eaten, dogs are eaten, rodents, cats and other things"; Chinese immigrants have brought such customs to Trinidad "and there is little that can be done to stop it." A wave of aggressive Facebook posts followed that asked the Chinese to "go back to China." There was also vocal retaliation against these racial stereotypes. However, most of it came from Trinidadian netizens of Chinese descent. Eventually, the Minister apologized; his statements had simply been due to "erroneous information" (Mendes-Franco 2015a; Mendes-Franco 2015b).

The Political Dimension

In the context of the Chinese migration to the Global South, China has been described as "a migrant-sending country with a great deal of power to exert significant political influence on the receiving countries" (Green and Liu 2017: 11). At the same time, "the Chinese diaspora is highly instrumentalised as a resource by its government" (Röschenthaler and Socpa 2017: 180). As already mentioned in this chapter, the migrants' duties to contribute to the development of the fatherland are specified in the 360 laws that concern the overseas Chinese adopted between 1978 and 2000 by the government in Beijing. The latter "keeps a strong grip on its growing global diasporic population that is increasingly well organised and allows it to gradually gain soft power influence." Ultimately, the presence of the Chinese diaspora "represents a political strategy" (Röschenthaler and Socpa 2017: 180). Yet, this is not an aspect that most respondents in Trinidad have noted. There was only one explicit comment about the fact that "the more Chinese here, (. . .) the Chinese embassy would then increase its position, increase its stature in Trinidad and Tobago" (Respondent 30). When assessing the Chinese migrants, the respondents were clearly more interested in economic, social, and cultural aspects than in political ones.

Overall, 80 percent of the respondents believe that there has been an important recent inflow of immigrants from China. Only 27 percent think that these immigrants benefit from better legal treatment due to Trinidad's special relationship with their country of origin while three quarters oppose this view; but 60 percent think they benefit more in economic terms than the citizens of Trinidad and Tobago. Eighty percent believe that most of the trade with China is conducted by these immigrants. Finally, no less than 60 percent of the respondents associate the presence of recent immigrants from China with the various negative aspects presented in this section. Almost all respondents in this group consider socio-economic issues to be the most important.

SOCIAL CONDITIONALITY

In order to avoid any confusion, it is important to emphasize the difference between social conditionality as defined in this book and the legitimate protection of overseas Chinese nationals by the government in Beijing. China's diplomatic actions undertaken in response to violence and extortion targeting

Chinese shopkeepers in Suriname or Jamaica (see above) belong to the category of normal international practices. What is slightly different is the fact that, as in Suriname, at times Beijing's protection tends to concern all ethnic Chinese, regardless of their citizenship. But even this is hardly unheard of in the actual practice of great powers. Social conditionality has no role in this. It is the result of a transactional approach described by Thomson Fontaine, a journalist in Dominica, as "an asymmetric interest where China pours in millions of dollars and in turn it exports a few thousand of its citizens to the country." This is accepted by the local government despite the fact that these entrepreneurial migrants severely impact the local economic landscape by "soaking up small businesses," in the words of the same journalist (Ellis 2014: 188). All over the Caribbean, there is widespread discontent with and criticism of the fact that "the administration didn't (. . .) develop a policy position that said listen, we are not going to allow this to happen," to quote a Trinidadian respondent. This led to "an exponentially increasing presence of the Chinese," who "infiltrated" and "became entrenched" in various sectors of the local economy (Respondent 20). When, as shown in the previous section, 60 percent of the population bears a negative perception toward the presence of Chinese immigrants, one would expect the government to pay some attention to this issue. After all, in the case of "tied aid" presented in Chapter 5, on some occasions the government in Port of Spain has attempted to show that it does want to have some local labor involved in Chinese-built infrastructure projects. Yet, nothing similar happened in the case of Chinese migrants. On the contrary, as already mentioned, then Prime Minister Kamla Persad-Bissessar publicly stated that during her February 2014 visit to Beijing "visa restrictions were a main concern for Chinese officials." In response, she initiated a process ultimately intended to achieve the complete removal of visa requirements for China's nationals. She argued that Jamaica had already taken this step: "what does that mean? Their business and tourism sectors will grow tremendously from the influx of Chinese who will come to invest and visit" (Fraser 2014b). This is certainly true for the business side, but the kind of "investment" concerned is precisely that criticized by the local population. Moreover, the proposal is frequently mentioned to arrange a connection between the flights from Beijing to Havana and those between Havana and Port of Spain (Respondent 1) that would further encourage the arrival of Chinese migrants. The irony is that this benevolent attitude is not shared by the part of Trinidad's bureaucracy that deals directly with the Chinese newcomers: the immigration authorities. The latter are "automatically suspect" of any Chinese national landing at Piarco airport. Arrangements were made with airlines—including foreign ones—to prevent the Chinese who intend to work in Trinidad from boarding the plane unless they show the original work permits. This never happens with any other country's nationals. Still, the reason has nothing to do with anti-Chinese sentiments. A knowledgeable respondent explained that this is simply related to the high number of past cases of forgery and corruption:

> The Chinese are viewed with great suspicion. (. . .) Because automatically, when Immigration sees China they automatically expect that the documents aren't authentic, that there is some measure of fraud, there is some measure of corruption, and they are particularly severe with the Chinese (Respondent 6).

This may be the only situation where Chinese nationals are treated in an unfriendly manner by Trinidadian authorities. The mainstream attitude is one of full compliance with China's demands that its entrepreneurial migrants be allowed to settle and set up businesses no matter the impact on their local competitors. This is hardly surprising. The Chinese officials demanded that visa restrictions be eliminated for their nationals during Prime Minister Persad-Bissessar's visit to Beijing. From the Trinidadian perspective, the goal of that visit was to seek assistance on the construction of six new economic zones, on the development of a trans-shipment port and dry dock in South Trinidad, on two new hospitals, and on loan agreements to finance these projects (*Power102fm News*, February 25, 2014; see the section *China and Trinidad and Tobago: the Highest Connectivity in the Region* of Chapter 4). The Chinese received favorably these demands and the corresponding projects were eventually initiated, even if in some cases the beneficiary was the following Trinidadian government. Given these incentives, both old and new governments have had good reasons to ignore the issue of public discontent with Chinese entrepreneurial migrants. The situation is identical to that described by the Zambian former Finance Minister Fred Mutesa already presented in the Introduction: "we are making so many friendly gestures to your country (. . .). We would consider it a friendly gesture if you did not enforce such strict immigration controls on our citizens" (French 2014: 83). If the development assistance conditionality terminology presented in Chapter 2 is used, this is positive conditionality: compliance with Chinese-imposed conditions is rewarded with increased assistance. I could not find Caribbean examples of negative social conditionality, i.e. situations where sanctions are adopted to secure compliance (Hughes et al. 2005: 14; Dipama and Dal 2015: 114). This is likely due to the fact that the region's economies are so small that, in comparison, Beijng's foreign aid looks impressive; accordingly, no government can afford to miss it, especially after its members have been socialized as shown in the previous chapter. Yet, negative social conditionality has clearly been employed by Beijing in the case of Ghana. This example has already been briefly presented in the Introduction, but some supplementary details may be useful to better understand the mechanism at work. The close partnership between the governments of China and Ghana is well illustrated by the $3 billion loan from the China Development Bank to finance twelve development projects that included the reconstruction of railways, the construction of fishing harbors, irrigation projects, and oil and gas infrastructure. This cooperative climate led to a significant increase in the number of Chinese entrepreneurial migrants who successfully competed against Ghanaian small-scale entrepreneurs and petty traders. Local textile traders and their industry were particularly affected. In response, a public and media discourse emerged that presented Ghanaians as hard-working, law-abiding individuals who fall prey to "large scale Chinese manufacturers engaged in illegal modes of production (including the use of counterfeits and child labor)" (Hess and Aidoo 2015: 50–51, 52). Chinese traders and, more generally, Chinese entrepreneurial migrants in Ghana were considered to represent key elements in this unfair competition. Against this negative background, illegal artisanal gold-mining ('galamsey') by a group of illegal Chinese immigrants from Shanglin County, Guangxi, was met with public outrage. The government in Accra, similar to those in the Caribbean, had no intention of damaging its profitable relationship with Beijing by taking action against Chinese nationals, even if they were illegal immigrants performing illegal economic activities on its soil. But public pressure was so strong that, finally, the Chinese were arrested and deported to their home country. China immediately retaliated by stalling payments from the US $3 billion loan, trying to renegotiate the terms and tenets of this loan, and changing visa requirements for Ghanaian citizens (i.e. small traders) entering China (Hess and Aidoo 2015: 51, 52). Without a shadow of a doubt, this is negative social conditionality at its purest. There are few such examples simply because Beijing's partners fully understand its ability and willingness to protect its entrepreneurial migrants and do everything in their power to avoid Ghana-type situations. Indeed, Cecilia Green and Yan Liu noted that China "often does not have to lift a finger to make its influence felt" in the Caribbean. The region's governments systematically adopt a "hands-off approach" of issues concerning Chinese entrepreneurial migrants, who are perceived as "carrying a risk of alienating the overseas Chinese state if pressed" (Green and Liu 2017: 26). This results in the "failure to install institutional mechanisms for dealing with citizen and immigrant concerns and relations" and in the absence of any official effort "for establishing transparency around this new economic enclave" (Green and Liu 2017: 27).

The full acceptance by Caribbean governments of China's social conditionality resulting in total compliance with its entrepreneurial migrant-related demands and expectations is perceived by the public all over the region as negatively as it is in Trinidad. Associated frustration has resulted in anti-Chinese prejudice and various misconceptions. The most popular one—revealed by fieldwork in Dominica, St. Kitts, St. Vincent, and Antigua—is the widespread conviction that a conspiracy exists among China, Caribbean governments, and the Chinese entrepreneurial migrants. The latter are perceived "as sponsored agents and secret ambassadors of the Chinese government" (Green and Liu 2017: 24–25). The same theme of an "elite conspiracy" is popular in many African states. In some of them, it even takes the form of an alleged Chinese policy of providing financial incentives or other benefits to the local government in return for employing convicts from China's overcrowded prisons (Mohan et al. 2014: 123; Li 2017a: 28); the same untrue story was vehiculated by the media in Guyana (Bernal 2016: 4784–4798; see the section *China's "Tied Aid" and Its Reception in Trinidad and the Caribbean* of Chapter 5). Leaving aside such unfounded rumors and returning to the more general Caribbean case, the idea of a "conspiracy" among Beijing, its migrants, and local governments may seem ridiculous but ultimately does reflect some actual characteristics of Chinese-Caribbean relationships. First, there is the issue of the relation between China and its migrants. On the one hand, the claim that "the Chinese state orchestrates all of the activities of Chinese businesses" (Mohan et al. 2014: 110) is of course absurd, despite its diffusion in various developing countries. Chinese entrepreneurial migrants are "autonomous of the Chinese government's policy and aid framework" (Yap and Henson 2016: 5) as they "have interests of their own that diverge from Beijing's desires, and Beijing has lacked the capacity to control them" (Hess and Aidoo 2015: 9). On the other hand, however, the absence of strictly defined "control" does in no way mean that the complex relationship between Beijing and its growing diaspora described earlier in this chapter has come to an end. This relationship assumes different forms in different regions and countries. In the Caribbean, it includes social conditionality, which places the Chinese migrants in a privileged position, but also ties them to Beijing's policies and actions. If their dependence on labor, merchandise, and capital from the fatherland as well as the fact that they repatriate most of their gains to China are added, it is not absurd to claim that, in a certain measure, they represent de facto Chinese "agents."

Second and more important for this book, there is the issue of the alleged collusion between the Chinese and Caribbean governments. Obviously, "conspiracy" is an inappropriate term; but what this chapter has depicted is a situation where political elites socialized through means that include secret diplomacy shape their state's domestic policies in accordance with China's demands that protect the economic interests of its entrepreneurial migrants and harm those of local citizens. This implies a redefinition of the national interest that few in the local society agree with. The resulting gap between state and society is identical to that due to the Chinese economic conditionality presented in the section *The Socialization of Caribbean Elites* of Chapter 5. One of the consequences is that, in the Caribbean as in other parts of the Global South that experience similar situations, "rather than Chinese migrants or foreigners per se, it is overwhelmingly the state that is the target of resentment" (Mohan et al. 2014: 134). This can represent "a dangerous potential for conflict and revolts" (Röschenthaler and Socpa 2017: 184) of which governments should be aware. This important aspect as well as the way governments and political elites in the developing world have reacted to similar challenges are discussed in Chapter 8, because this is a complex topic that goes beyond the specific issue of social conditionality. At this point, I will only attempt to provide an explanation of the difference between the behavior of Caribbean governments—including that of Trinidad and Tobago—with respect to Chinese economic and social conditionalities, respectively. As already shown, in the former case some very "soft" attempts were made to ensure that "tied aid" ceases to be associated with the total absence of local labor from Chinese-built infrastructure projects. In the latter case, absolutely no official initiative has ever been launched or contemplated that would limit the negative impact of Chinese entrepreneur migrants on local small businesses. This may simply reflect Beijing's economic interests and the associated willingness to make concessions in certain fields. In the case of "tied aid," there is some hope that local laborers might begin to be hired, in limited numbers, in some infrastructure projects as long as contractors, materials, and most of the workers will continue to come from China. If this happens, the loss for the Chinese will represent only a small percentage of the overall cost of the infrastructure project. This is a reasonable price to pay for an improved public image that might help Chinese construction firms to further expand their activities in the region. In the case of the entrepreneurial migrants, on the contrary, Beijing seems to believe that there is an all-or-nothing situation. If Caribbean governments start to limit their settlement or their economic activities, they could simply move to more hospitable places. In turn, this would hamper China's effort to expand its influence in the region "both from above and from below" (Röschenthaler and Socpa 2017: 183).

Ultimately, the Chinese social conditionality in the Caribbean can be assessed as representing precisely an instrument of influence "from below" that complements the "from above" approach embodied by the political and economic conditionalities. The problem is that, as in the latter case, it has been fully embraced by the political elites, which has resulted in the successful socialization of the state; but it is vocally rejected by the society. At times, this rejection is passionate and almost violent. A respondent who was not personally affected by this conditionality nevertheless critically enumerated its detrimental consequences before stating "I find it very negative and distasteful" (Respondent 20). Obviously, this situation seriously hampers the advancement of the Chinese-centered international socialization of the entire state-society complex.

Chapter Seven

Too Early for Conditionality

The Geopolitical Dimension

As shown in previous chapters, China's initial interest in the Caribbean was related to the "diplomatic duel" with Taiwan. However, the considerable expansion of its involvement in the region during the 2008–2016 "diplomatic truce" between Beijing and Taipei was explained as a response to US anti-Chinese actions in the South China Sea and, more generally, as an aspect of the increasingly visible Sino-American rivalry. China's global aspirations do represent a complementary cause of its Caribbean enterprise, but it should be noted that the aforementioned rivalry stems precisely from these aspirations. This is to say that, despite obvious economic interests, the process of Chinese-centered international socialization of the Caribbean that incorporates the three conditionalities studied in this book has a major geopolitical dimension. This chapter explores it by emphasizing the case of Trinidad and Tobago, whose partnership with China does include a military component that might surprise readers unfamiliar with the region. The possibility of the emergence, in the medium- and long-term, of a significant Chinese military involvement in the Caribbean as well as its probable regional and global impact are then analyzed.

THE CHINA-CARIBBEAN-UNITED STATES GEOPOLITICAL TRIANGLE

Caribbean states have a special relationship with the United States. However, this is a "historical hegemonic relationship" (see Maingot and Lozano 2005: 1–17) strongly marked by a long and well-remembered series of American interventions (for a recent presentation see McPherson 2016). Like elsewhere in the hemisphere, a strange situation has developed. On the one hand, the

US provides widely appreciated cultural products that range from Hollywood movies to academic education. It has also represented an important destination for Caribbean migratory flows and, by far, the main economic partner. On the other hand, however, America-as-a-great-power is hardly popular. The radicalism of the Cold War might have dissipated, but "you cannot compare Castro with Hitler" is a frequent remark in any discussion in the region—including academic ones—touching totalitarianism. Why? "Because Castro fought the Americans." In Trinidad it is not unusual to see shop assistants watching RT (formerly Russia Today) on a small TV while working in a store. Anti-Americanism likely represents one of the reasons that made more than one hundred Trinidadians travel to Syria and join ISIS, a disproportionately high number for a country with approximately one hundred thousand Muslims. On the American side, the post–9/11 orientation of Washington's military and diplomatic efforts toward the Middle East and Eastern Europe as well as the consequences of the financial crisis have greatly diminished the interest in and the resources allocated to the region. Considerable assistance continues to be provided in support of the fight against drug trafficking and in judicial and law-enforcement. Yet, the United States has become "an absentee superpower" in the Caribbean: "many sense a slow and steady erosion of Washington's position as the region's leading power" (Wigglesworth 2013). Critically, "in the absence of financial largesse, the US is no longer seen as a favourite ally by the region's elite." An alternative is emerging: "it is into this fiscal vacuum that China has stepped" (Badri-Maharaj 2016). Its tempting infrastructure projects are welcomed by political elites that choose to see Beijing "as a voice for Southern countries" and, more realistically, as "an emerging counterweight to the economic and political influence of the EU and the USA" (Montoute 2013: 112).

America vs. China

Historically, China has been aggressive only when "operating from a position of overwhelming strength" (Ellis 2012: 33). Otherwise, its foreign policy has been cautious and sought to avoid open conflict. When resistance was encountered, Beijing has been willing to back down. In most cases, it has sought to reach its long-term objectives through multiple alternative paths. Its favorite approach has been to build "positions of influence that it can later use to achieve outcomes in its favor" (Ellis 2012: 33). This is a good description of both global and Caribbean Chinese strategies. In the former case, it has been widely acknowledged that "China seeks to be a reformer within the international system, not a revolutionary" (Gurtov 2015: 84). Its reinsertion into the American-centered global order was based on the acceptance, not the challenging of its rules. During the pre-Xi Jinping era, the Chinese discourse and actions were based on the use of soft power in view of accelerating the peaceful transition toward a multipolar international system. Theoretical approaches emphasizing political psychology and the role of the personality traits of individual leaders in foreign policy obviously associate the change that has become visible since 2013 with the present Chinese President's personal leadership style and ambitions. Structure-oriented approaches, however, are more pessimistic: they assign Beijing's assertiveness and expansionistic plans to structural factors that, unlike the incumbent President, might not change for decades. Offensive Neorealists such as John Mearsheimer argue that the rise of China will necessarily result in its transformation into a counter-hegemon that will overtly challenge the United States. No great power can rise peacefully; accordingly, the shifting transpacific balance of power can only have deeply antagonistic consequences. The Chinese—who are not more principled, more ethical, less nationalistic, or less concerned about their survival than the Americans—will act as the US did at its time: they will try to gain regional hegemony by pushing the US out of the Asia-Pacific. As American strategic primacy in the region will disappear, Washington will have to increase its presence and adopt a Cold War-style strategy of containment. Asian states threatened by Chinese expansionism such as Japan, Vietnam, South Korea, India, and then Russia should be convinced to join the Washington-led alliance. This might well result in a new Cold War, fought mainly in Asia and in the Middle East (where Iran looks forward to such an opportunity); it is only Europe that will have little reason to play an active role. There will even be an important risk of escalation into "hot" war, possibly as a consequence of a Taiwan-related incident (Mearsheimer 2010: 381, 389–393; Tudoroiu 2018: 136–137). It should be noted that all this was first written years before President Xi Jinping came to power and at a time when China tried hard to show a smiling face. But there already was a "flood of literature" about world power shifting from the Atlantic to the Pacific while the epoch was becoming "post-Western" (Sakwa 2010: 11; Simón and Rogers 2010: 58). Politically, the first major American response to the rise of China that, at least in part, followed Mearsheimer's neorealist logic came—surprisingly—from the rather liberal President Obama. The first US self-styled "Pacific President" (Dobson and Marsh 2014: 673) launched the famous "pivot" because, as stated by Secretary of State Hillary Clinton in November 2011, the "future of politics will be decided in Asia (. . .) and the United States will be right at the center of the action." Being "right at the center" meant to stand up to Beijing's challenge to American leadership (Hallams and Schreer 2012: 314). Economically, the previously initiated negotiation of the Trans-Pacific Partnership was reoriented to isolate China and limit its economic growth. Strategically, the Air-Sea Battle Concept was adopted, the Asia-Pacific region was redefined, and many US Asian bases were repositioned. General Martin Dempsey, the Chairman of the Joint Chiefs of Staff, spoke about his country having to "overtly confront China as it faced down the Soviet Union in the past" (Copper 2014: 102–103, 105). Yet, President Obama never unequivocally acknowledged the anti-Chinese nature of his plans and actions; the "pivot" was even relabeled "rebalancing" to suggest non-belligerent intentions (Löfflmann 2016: 95). This lack of consistency, the inability to fully disengage from the Middle East, and the need for renewed American diplomatic and even military presence to counter Russian expansionism in Eastern Europe ultimately made the "pivot" to Asia irrelevant. While they failed to contain the Chinese, American plans and actions had the unintended effect of making the leadership in Beijing fear hostile US moves and adopt geopolitical and economic counter-measures in the region (Löfflmann 2016: 92–93). Ironically, President Obama unwillingly contributed to making China's foreign policy increasingly similar to that of a revisionist power such as Russia (Tudoroiu 2018: 138–139).

In many regards, President Trump's foreign policy has been the opposite of that of the previous administration. Yet, despite its lack of clear guidelines and its disorienting incoherence, it has been relatively constant in one respect: identifying China as an adversary. This is not due to neorealist power-based reasoning or to a full understanding of such complicated things as structural power. The President's mind seems to be uninterested in abstract aspects. His businessman, zero-sum view of world affairs only allows for the strong belief that net exporters win while net importers lose (*The Economist,* November 9, 2017). This automatically turns China, Germany, South Korea, and Mexico into adversaries (Zoellick 2017). The largest American trade deficit is due to the Chinese; this implicitly makes them the main enemy, which deserves a harsh treatment: "They keep beating us. We have to beat them" (McAdams 2016). In accordance with President Trump's self-proclaimed preference for unpredictability, the bilateral relationship has experienced confusing ups and downs, surprising turns, threats, and incipient trade wars. Yet, in November 2017 nascent plans for Asia started to be unveiled. They were based on an "Indo-Pacific strategy" first suggested by the Japanese and mentioned one month earlier by then Secretary of State Rex Tillerson, who praised India and condemned China for "undermining the international rules-based order" and for "provocative actions" in the South China Sea (Sevastopulo 2017). Even today it is not yet clear what this strategy exactly means and how does it compare to Mearsheimer's views and to President Obama's "pivot." But it is containment-flavored, and this has already contributed to the further tensioning of bilateral relations. Analysts agree that, if implemented, it will add to trade conflicts and naval disputes in the South China Sea to increase instability and possibly lead to proxy struggles or even to limited Sino-American warfare (Borroz and Marston 2017: 615).

On the other side of the Pacific, these dark prospects are scrutinized by a much less vocal but equally ambitious leader. Since he came to power in November 2012, President Xi Jinping has promoted an assertive foreign policy that has nothing in common with the "low profile" promoted by Deng Xiaoping and his successors. American threats are unlikely to impress him. Moreover, during the last part of 2018 an important change was noted in the debates at the top of the Chinese government. Those believing that the US "would not tolerate China growing larger under any circumstances" and that "America has become a foe so implacable that there is no point making concessions to it" were on the point of having the upper hand (*The Economist*, October 18, 2018). In the national-security establishment a "febrile mood" was detected: there was "genuine excitement over the prospect of a great-power contest in which China is one of the protagonists." The very limited public space open for discussion is dominated by strident anti-American nationalists. Chinese military experts even contemplate favorably the possibility of an expensive arms race as they believe that the long-term potential of their economy is superior to the US one (*The Economist*, October 18, 2018). All this shows that the Sino-American rivalry has already become a matter of concern and might further worsen. Importantly for this book, it begins to have significant consequences for the Global South in general and for the Caribbean in particular.

China vs. America in Latin America and the Caribbean

The December 2017 *National Strategy of the United States of America* reflecting the foreign policy vision of the Trump administration places China among the first "set of challengers": that of "revisionist powers." Beijing is accused of having expanded its power at the expense of the sovereignty of others and of spreading features of its authoritarian system, including corruption and the use of surveillance. With Russia, it challenges American power and influence while trying to "shape a world antithetical to U.S. values and interests." In the developing world, it uses massive investments in infrastructure to expand influence and gain competitive advantages against the United States (President of the United States 2017: 25, 27). In Africa, Chinese practices undermine long-term development by "corrupting elites, dominating extractive industries, and locking countries into unsustainable and opaque debts and commitments." In the Western Hemisphere—which includes the Caribbean—"China seeks to pull the region into its orbit through state-led investments and loans." But democratic states there "have a shared interest in confronting threats to their sovereignty" (President of the United States 2017: 51). This, however, is not exactly the way Beijing's advances are perceived by most of the Caribbean governments. To them, China represents an "alternative source of influence" (Zhang 2015: 61) which formulates a "criticism of the Western-dominated international system and its governing institutions [that] strikes a strong chord with the developing world" (Oosterveld et al. 2018: 11). Accordingly, its "new alliance" with Latin America and the Caribbean "is seen as a challenge to the United States, a nation that has long considered the Americas its backyard" (Gallagher 2016: 3). For their part, Chinese scholars claim that Washington's relations with the region "are now entering a state of adjustment [due to] the decline of American hegemony in the Western Hemisphere" (Hongbo 2017: 322). A key event was President Xi Jinping's 2013 visit to Trinidad, which also included stops in Mexico and Costa Rica; ironically, the last part of this journey took him to California, where he met President Obama. Previously, "it was (. . .) conventional wisdom that China would act cautiously in the US 'backyard' to avoid exacerbating its concerns." The 2013 visit was conceived by the new Chinese leader as a strong signal to the region and to the world that "China need not be concerned about the US reaction to its growing presence" in the Caribbean and in Latin America as "there is little that the United States can do to preclude" it (Roett and Paz 2015: 509). The Obama administration did its best to change this perception. In anticipation of the Chinese visit, Vice-President Joe Biden went to Brazil, Colombia, and Trinidad—his fourth visit to the region since taking office—while President Obama traveled to Mexico and Costa Rica in April 2013 (Roett and Paz 2015: 509). But American goodwill gestures came to an end under President Trump, who "has insulted Mexico, El Salvador and Haiti" and discouraged investment in the former at a time when China was proud to offer a "strategy of mutual benefit and shared gain" to the region (*The Economist*, February 1, 2018). In the words of a Trinidadian respondent, "Donald Trump has been a boon to China in many ways because, you know, there is such a distrust of, you know, what's the American influence comes with" (Respondent 1). A good indicator of recently increased Chinese assertiveness in the region is represented by the evolution of BRI-related plans Initially, Beijing was reluctant to "connect nations in America's backyard to a Maritime Silk Road under Chinese influence" as this was likely to turn the Caribbean into "a stage for clashing Chinese and American visions of global politics" (Ward 2017: 13). At that time, Panama was the only country in the hemisphere invited to join the Belt and Road Initiative as "China [wa]s aware that signing up more countries 'would create a strong reaction' in the United States" (*The Economist*, February 1, 2018). As shown in the section *The Belt and Road Initiative* of Chapter 3, such caution was eventually abandoned and in January 2018 the "Special Declaration on the Belt and Road" signed during the Second China-CELAC Ministerial Forum opened the initiative to the entire region (Barrios 2018). Richard Bernal has noted that China's Caribbean enterprise "has elicited little attention and no discernable foreign policy response from the United States" and expressed his belief that Sino-American rivalry will not "become contentious" in this region "as security issues are not of primary concern." Washington will not alter the present policy of "peaceful coexistence with a new but subsidiary partner" (Bernal 2017: 238, 258, 259). Yet, he acknowledges the existence of an important caveat: there are no "potentially volatile issues" in the region, "but this comfort level could be disturbed by repercussions from contentious issues outside" the Caribbean, and more precisely in the South China Sea (Bernal 2017: 260, 243–244). Indeed, many scholars believe that "China's increased presence in Caribbean affairs can be understood as a subtle jab at American Western Hemisphere dominance" in response to US involvement in Beijing's own backyard (Ward 2017: 17). A part of the literature perceives "China as a challenger to the U.S. hegemony over Latin America and the Caribbean" (Su and Delgado 2017: 4; for a review of this literature see pp. 4–6). There are authors who claim that Beijing "might, indeed, be seeding the field for a series of political alliances that, once unleashed, would endanger American security" (Santibañes 2009: 18). At present, China's "growing presence in the Caribbean poses no immediate military threat" to the US (Oosterveld et al. 2018: 45), but military alliances might develop in the future, especially if the process of Chinese-centered international socialization analyzed in this book is fully successful. If that happens and a military confrontation ignites in the South China Sea, Beijing's protégés in the Western Hemisphere "might feel obliged to back their new patron" (*The Economist*, February 1, 2018). Even if such extreme scenarios do not materialize, China's geopolitical advances in the Caribbean combined with the "slow but deep changes in the political and economic architecture of the region" cannot be overlooked: they are "effectively challenging US leadership in ways that no single actor, including the Soviet Union, has before" (Haro Navejas 2011: 204). For the time being, "the combination of economic, political, military, and structural power of the USA remains unmatched" (Lairson 2018: 50). But Beijing's message is clear: "America is the past, China is the future" (Garnaut 2018).

THE CHINESE-CARIBBEAN SECURITY COOPERATION AND ITS PROSPECTS

The People's Liberation Army does not have alliances or basing agreements in the Caribbean, but this hardly means that there is no military cooperation with the region's states (Southerland 2017). The 2016 Policy Paper on Latin America and the Caribbean even has a title on Military Exchanges and Cooperation that speaks of "actively" carrying out military exchanges and cooperation and of increasing "friendly exchanges between defense and military leaders from the two sides." Explicit mention is made of "deepening" exchanges in military training and of enhancing the cooperation in military trade and military technology (Ministry of Foreign Affairs of the Republic of China 2016: IV.6.1). In general, Beijing's approach has been "very circumspect" in order to avoid provoking the Americans. In 2011, a Chinese Navy hospital ship toured Cuba, Jamaica, Grenada, and Trinidad where it provided medical services to local people and to military and administrative personnel. Most of the military cooperation consists of Chinese gifts of vehicles and equipment and in the provision of military training (Oosterveld et al. 2018: 39, 44). In 2017, the Royal Bahamas Defense Force received a donation of US $1.2 million in military equipment while the Guyana Defense Force received two Harbin Y-12 planes as well as training for their pilots and technicians and other military equipment worth US $1.2 million. For their part, Dominica was given US $4.3 million in military vehicles; Grenada received 37 police vehicles valued at US $2 million. Military assistance and training were provided to Antigua and Barbuda and to Suriname (Oosterveld et al. 2018: 40). The case of the most important Chinese partner, Trinidad and Tobago, is discussed below. There are also numerous scholarships offered to military officers throughout the Caribbean to help them study in China (Southerland 2017). This is part of a "determined effort to court the military and the bureaucratic elite in the region" parallel to that targeting the political elite. Some analysts claim that the substantial number of Chinese-trained Caribbean officers has led to an "attendant increase in influence over their military leadership" (Badri-Maharaj 2016).

The China-Trinidad Security Relationship

Within CARICOM, "Trinidad and Tobago can certainly claim some leadership and influence" on security issues as, after the organization's upgrading in 2001, the government in Port of Spain assumed the responsibility for regional security. Accordingly, it set up a coordinating security secretariat, "oversees the operations of a new regional security architecture characterized by inter-agency collaboration and intelligence-sharing," and has involved itself in efforts to solve a number of regional crises (see Braveboy-Wagner 2010: 418–419). At the same time, the Trinidad and Tobago Defense Force has initiated in 1999 a relationship with the People's Liberation Army that "has since gradually deepened" (Oosterveld et al. 2018: 69; Wigglesworth 2013). This trend was stimulated by the diminishing of US military aid in retaliation to Trinidad's refusal to exempt American citizens from the International Criminal Court, whose creation was significantly influenced by former Prime Minister and President Arthur Napoleon Raymond Robinson (see the section *China's Political Conditionality and Its Reception in Trinidad* of Chapter 4). In order to "assist in advancing initiatives between our military establishments," the government in Port of Spain created the position of Military Attaché at the embassy in Beijing (*Loop News*, August 10, 2017). There have been multiple reciprocal military staff visits, such as that of high ranking Chinese military officers who met in 2016 Major General Kenrick Maharaj, the Chief of Trinidad and Tobago Defense Staff. At Trinidad's 50th independence anniversary in 2012, the band of the People's Liberation Army played at the Chinese-built NAPA (before the building had to be closed for major repairs). Trinidadian military officers have been trained in China. Beijing also provided military aid, which has included the outfitting of the National Operations Center of Trinidad and Tobago (Wigglesworth 2013; Oosterveld et al. 2018: 70; *Loop News*, August 10, 2017; Tack 2007).

Significantly, Trinidad has been involved in "one of [China's] most controversial arms sales" representing "a major breakthrough" for Beijing in the Caribbean (Southerland 2017; Badri-Maharaj 2016). As briefly mentioned in the section *Socialization and Power* of Chapter 2, during her February 2014 visit to China then Prime Minister Kamla Persad-Bissessar added to the long list of Trinidadian demands for development assistance a rather unusual item: the purchase of a long-range maritime patrol vessel facilitated by Chinese concessional loans. Such an agreement had been rejected by a previous Trinidadian government, the Chinese vessel was selected against technical advice, and many questioned the very need for this purchase (Southerland 2017; Badri-Maharaj 2016). The nature of this "need" becomes obvious if the expected timing of delivery—prior to elections—is taken into consideration (Oosterveld et al. 2018: 66). For the then Prime Minister, this was nothing more than another Chinese-built and financed prestige project likely to bring an increase in political and electoral legitimacy. But this was also "the first sale of a non-Western military hardware to the Caribbean nation since the end of the Cold War" (Badri-Maharaj 2016) and nobody could be sure of the American reaction. This is why initially the Chinese were rather cautious. They promised the vessel, but the framework agreement for the provision of the associated loan was signed only in 2017, when escalating tensions with the United States had significantly diminished Beijing's willingness to show a permanently smiling face to its trans-pacific rival. It is certain that this was one of the Chinese moves in the Caribbean basin that made President Trump criticize China in the *National Strategy of the United States of America* made public in December of that year as "seeking to expand military linkages and arms sales across the region" (President of the United States 2017: 51). Accordingly, "it is expected that there will be a limit to what the US can accept with respect to Chinese military involvement" (Oosterveld et al. 2018: 70). Both China and Trinidad are fully aware of the red line and, for the time being, are not ready to cross it.

Local Perceptions and Scenarios for the Future

It is interesting to see the local perception of this situation. No less than 93 percent of the respondents in Trinidad view China as a rising superpower. Forty-seven percent believe that it tries to become the only superpower in the international system and a further 27 percent think that such a plan is possible. Eighty-seven percent share the opinion that Beijing is using developing countries, and particularly those of the Caribbean, to expand its influence around the world. Things get more ambiguous when the effects of this development on the Caribbean need to be assessed, with a large number of respondents being unable to give a clear answer. The few who do either speak of a "win-win situation" (Respondent 5) and clearly state "I don't see them as being this force of evil" (Respondent 30); or take the contrary view: "I won't use the word ally, (. . .) China's objective is more in terms of being godfather to countries like ours" (Respondent 20); it "becomes almost imperialistic" (Respondent 27), "a rising imperial power" challenging similarly imperial rivals (Respondent 24). A certain balance also exists when the China-Trindad-US triangle is examined. Forty percent of the respondents believe that the further improvement of the relations between Trinidad and China will not create tensions with the United States, the main reason being that "we are not important enough" (Respondent 23). Fifty-three percent, however, believe otherwise: "you can't serve two masters. (. . .) Increasing Trinidad-China relations would increase tensions with the US" (Respondent 28). Accordingly, when asked to suggest a type of behavior for Trinidad in its relationship with China many respondents employed terms such as "cautiously" and "carefully." There was only one respondent whose radical views left no place for *Realpolitik* compromise:

> I think we have a lot of opportunities to benefit from the relationship but too much of it is built on fear. What if they come to take over the world, you know, what would the United States say, what if the US get upset, what if we depend on the Chinese and then, you know, other countries that do business with us cut off because they don't like China, you know? Those kind of fears aren't founded on anything too important right now (. . .) We certainly need to be less afraid. Fear is part of our culture. In the past (. . .) [we had] colonisation, neo-colonialism, imperialism (. . .) So, once we see a big country, oh my God, who's next? and what are they coming for now? What are they going to take and leave

> (. . .) I think that this is our default position but we need to have a better, more mature and sophisticated understanding of relationships and not be daunted by size (Respondent 6).

This is a luxury that, for the time being, Caribbean governments and political elites aware of the aforementioned "red line" cannot afford no matter how effectively they have been socialized by the Chinese. This brings the discussion to the title of this chapter. In the Caribbean, a hypothetical Chinese geopolitical conditionality—and even a less ambitious but nevertheless significant Chinese military involvement—can only exist in association with the evolution of the Sino-American rivalry toward open confrontation. Short of being ready to engage the US in a Cold War that might considerably damage its own economy and international status, Beijing has to limit its actions in the region to "subtle jabs" at American dominance. Basically, major Chinese military involvement in the Caribbean has two prerequisites: Cold War-style tensions with the US as a reason and the complete Chinese-centered socialization of host countries as a means. If both conditions do materialize, the temptation to challenge America within its *chasse gardée* might be overwhelming. The Soviet-Cuban relationship shows that such a challenge can be successful. However, 1983 Grenada provides the opposite example. No matter the final outcome, such developments would signal a dangerously tense global and regional environment and would most likely result in the serious destabilization of the Caribbean. The point, however, is not to make speculations about an unclear future. The hard fact relevant for the topic of this book is that Beijing cannot successfully follow Nikita Khrushchev's Cuban example without fully socializing partner state-society complexes in the region. This is why the issue of China's three conditionalities and their acceptance or rejection by political elites and by the society represents a critical issue for the geopolitical future of the Caribbean.

Chapter Eight

Analysis and Conclusion

China's use of conditionalities in the Caribbean can be considered to stem from two factors. On the one hand, there is its transformation into a global power that has developed an interest in the region for one general and one specific reason. The former is the "attempt to enlarge its global influence sphere more generally both from above and from below" (Röschenthaler and Socpa 2017: 183). The latter is the Taiwan- and, more recently, US-related geopolitical rivalry (which cannot be dissociated from Beijing's enhanced international status). On the other hand, there is the limited effectiveness of the soft power instruments China has used in order to facilitate its regional enterprise (see the section *Chinese Influence and Soft Power* of Chapter 4). This made the leadership in Beijing use economic incentives to promote its interests. Prestige infrastructure projects have successfully been used as inducements to shape to China's advantage a number of policies of the Caribbean states that recognize Beijing. These states have been compelled to reject a source of valuable foreign aid (Taiwan) and to give up their long-standing vocal support for democracy and human rights abroad when Chinese issues are concerned. They have to prevent their own construction firms and laborers from taking part in Chinese-financed infrastructure projects that represent a large part of the local construction market. They have been made to damage pre-existing good governance policies and practices by accepting non-transparent negotiations and secretive government-to-government agreements. Finally, they are forced to restrain from regulating the inflow and economic activities of Chinese entrepreneurial migrants despite the latter's deeply detrimental consequences for local small businesses and workers. This is the clear depiction of an "arrangement" by which Caribbean governments have taken "certain policy actions" in support of which Beijing has provided "specified amounts of financial assistance" (Killick 1998: 5–6). This is the word-for-word reproduction of Tony Killick's narrow definition of conditionality and is of course equally compatible with the more general definition proposed by Olav Stokke (Stokke 1995/2006: 11–12).

This conditionality is *ex ante*, meaning that China's conditions have to be met prior to entering into the assistance relationship (Stokke 1995/2006: 12). The promise for infrastructure projects materializes only after the target Caribbean country recognizes Beijing and signs the associated "tied aid" secretive agreements. Until now, China has exclusively employed positive conditionality in the Caribbean: compliance has been rewarded with increased assistance. Given the present dynamic of its involvement in the region, it is highly unlikely that negative conditionality—i.e. adopting sanctions to secure compliance (Hughes et al. 2005: 14; Dipama and Dal 2015: 114)—will need to be used in the predictable future. Part of the conditionality is formal, meaning that it is based on publicly stated preconditions (Hughes et al. 2005: 26). The issue of diplomatic recognition is explicitly mentioned in all relevant bilateral and multilateral documents under the form of the acknowledgment of the "One China" principle. The concessional aid guidelines of China ExIm Bank officially tie the aid at a level of 50 percent (Brautigam 2009: 152). But another part is informal, i.e. based on "operational pressures and recommendations" (Hughes et al. 2005: 26). Understandably, the "no Tibet, no Tiananmen Square" principle cannot be put on paper. The precondition of secretive negotiations is equally discreetly suggested. When the issue of the elimination of visas for Chinese nationals was raised by Beijing, only the Trinidadian Prime Minister spoke about it publicly. China's leadership has never mentioned overtly any element related to its social conditionality. But lack of publicity does in no way mean lack of enforcement. Both formal and informal conditions have to be respected in exchange for Chinese development assistance.

The fact that many conditions are informal has contributed to the construction of the "myth" analyzed in this book: it is easier to ignore something that is not publicly acknowledged by the concerned actors. Yet, a more important factor is the huge difference between the Chinese and Western philosophy, discourse, and practice of development assistance discussed in the section *China's Development Assistance* of Chapter 5. In turn, this difference is due to the very different historical genesis of the two approaches. The West has tried to use development assistance in order to impose democracy, the respect of human rights, good governance and, in the context of the "Washington consensus," a neo-liberal reshaping of economic structures. A key goal has been to help build the social capital and institutional prerequisites for development. This has influenced even the modalities of disbursement, which since the 1990s include a participatory dimension represented by the co-opting of civil society groups—that "portray an image of altruism and flexibility"—as intermediaries of international development (Trinidad 2013: 38; see the section *China's Development Assistance* of Chapter 5). All this constitutes an extremely intrusive approach especially in the case of Global South countries characterized by neopatrimonial regimes and relatively traditional societies. Its complete success would amount to nothing less than a fully fledged political, social, cultural, and economic revolution. Critically, Western donors could set such an ambitious objective because, historically, they have acted from a position of power that the end of the Cold War turned into almost absolute hegemony.

The genesis of China's development assistance, on the contrary, was strongly marked by Beijing's weak international position. Itself a recipient of Soviet foreign aid for a decade, Maoist China had to cope with very limited resources and with the competition of overwhelmingly superior Western and Soviet rivals. When present-day China launched its ambitious expansion in the Global South it still had to compete from an obviously non-hegemonic position with well-entrenched Western donors. The result is an approach that necessarily reflects some of China's own features but was conceived mainly in order to exploit the rival's weak points. Where the West is a hegemonic donor that gives lessons, China is a Global South development partner that promotes win-win cooperation. Where the West preaches aggressively democracy and human rights, China only asks for silence on its own Tibet and Tiananmen Square. Where the West supports good governance that undermines the very foundation of neopatrimonial regimes, China brings in secretive government-to-government agreements. Where the West imposes neoliberal structural adjustment programs, China ignores overindebtment. Unlike the West, Beijing in no way promotes a revolution; its transformative impact is kept to a minimum. The enthusiastic reception of its advances shows that this emphasis on material progress through political, social, cultural, and economic continuity does respond to the needs and hopes of a large part of the Global South, or at least to those of its political elites. Unsurprisingly, when such welcoming elites face Beijing's narrow, non-revolutionary conditionalities, as in the case of the Caribbean, they tend to pay little attention to something they—and many external observers—perceive as "normal," negligible concessions to be made for the greater good.

This aspect highlights once more the analytical advantage of using the Caribbean as a case study. China's development assistance approach was initially set up in a mainly African context. This is why it is particularly appropriate for dealing with neopatrimonial regimes that are not necessarily champions of democracy, respect for human rights, or good governance.

This is not to claim that all African states are in such a situation; simply, neopatrimonialism does exist on that continent. In the case of these regimes, issues such as preventing the support for democracy in China or eliminating pre-existing local policies and practices of transparency and public accountability become irrelevant. If employed, Chinese conditionalities can take a simplified form; therefore, they are easier to accept and less visible. On the contrary, the Caribbean is made of vibrant democracies that do criticize lack of democracy and infringement of human rights abroad and do have well-established policies of good governance. This compels Beijing to expand the repertoire of its conditionalities, which makes them more visible and easier to study. But, of course, even in the Caribbean Chinese conditionality is much less intrusive than the Western one, which explains in part its full acceptance by the region's political elites.

Strictly speaking, an inquiry limited to the title of this book could stop here. In fact, as already mentioned in the Introduction, the example of one country would have been sufficient to show that China does impose conditionalities, thus putting an end to the "myth." Undeniably, Trinidad and Tobago is subject to Beijing's political, economic, and social conditionalities; *ergo*, the "myth" is false. *Quod erat demonstrandum.*[1] Yet, once the Caribbean is chosen as a case study, the fact becomes clear that Chinese conditionalities are used in this region for much more than possibly uncoordinated short-term benefits. The disproportionate density and the surprising magnitude of bilateral partnerships and multilateral frameworks constructed by Beijing in the region can in no way be justified by the region's meager material resources. China's Caribbean enterprise is of a different nature; as shown by Francisco Javier Haro Navejas, it targets "nothing less than the genesis of a new regional order, built on functioning institutions and rules" (Haro Navejas 2011: 210; see the section *China in the Caribbean: Constructing a New Regional Order* of Chapter 4). This ultimately geopolitical project is too important to be left aside simply because, strictly speaking, it falls outside the "myth." If its exploration is envisaged, the process of Chinese-centered international socialization of the Caribbean cannot be ignored.

ANALYZING INTERNATIONAL SOCIALIZATION

Beijing's socialization of the Caribbean was defined in the section *International Socialization* of Chapter 2 as the process of inducing both states and societies in concerned countries to adopt collective understandings about the desirable and beneficial nature of a special relationship with China, to internalize such beliefs as norms, and ultimately to develop a new international identity as a Chinese-friendly state-society complex. Both cognitive and normative levels are involved, leading to attitudes and actions favorable to China's government, companies, and citizens. As shown in previous chapters, this is a great power-led process of socialization of much weaker partners that is intended to increase the socializer's regional and global reach and status. Conditionalities represent its engine; they ensure that, in exchange for material inducements, sustained compliance based on the internalization of new norms develops in the target state-society complexes, which adhere to shared understandings of appropriate behavior and switch from a logic of consequences to one of appropriateness (Checkel 2005: 804; Park 2014: 337). The best studied similar phenomenon that is at the origin of much of the literature on international socialization is of course the European Union's Eastern enlargement and the associated process of "Europeanization." China's Caribbean venture is in many regards very different. Its reach and depth are much more limited, as it does not intend to bring about the fundamental political, economic, and social changes experienced by Europeanized post-communist countries. Yet, it cannot be dissociated from the same logic that includes the critical difference between Type I, role playing socialization, and the more advanced, fully interiorized Type II one. The first stage has already been reached due to Chinese material incentives and might allow for a purely rationalist explanation. However, this book is based on a Constructivist view that claims that further progress toward Type II socialization is not only possible but represents the actual goal of the leadership in Beijing. In many regards, this is the opposite of Frank Schimmelfennig's "institutionalist" rationalist theory. The latter acknowledged, in the case of the EU enlargement, the key role played by three "socialization agencies" represented by the institutional and cultural international environment, the normative content of international socialization, and strong international organizations (all of which were also studied by Constructivists); but rejected the key idea that the target states can change their identity, speaking instead of "strategic socialization" simply based on the rationalist maximization of utility, i.e. on purely material incentives (Schimmelfennig et al. 2006: 6, 9). Two of the three socialization agencies—the institutional and cultural international environment as well as strong international organizations—are missing in the Caribbean case, simply because the socializer is a remote great power and not a neighboring organization that progressively incorporated the candidate countries into an impressively dense network of institutional arrangements and cultural interactions. This is not to say that China chose to completely ignore this path. On the contrary, it did construct or join a disproportionately large number of regional organizations and used various soft power instruments to promote its culture. Yet, the constant preference given by Beijing to bilateral relationships over regional frameworks severely diminished the latter's effectiveness while cultural interactions remain extremely weak. Critically, Brussels' Association Agreements with East European candidate countries succeeded in turning the Copenhagen criteria (democracy, market economy, and the capacity to cope with competitive pressure within the Union) into a normative standard that was successfully implemented through a multitude of institutionalized mechanisms that connected the European Union to all sectors and levels of the candidate countries' state apparatus, which in turn directly impacted the society. This was an approach much more "revolutionary" and intrusive than Western conditionality in the Global South. In fact, to quote once more James Hughes, Gwendolyn Sasse, and Claire Gordon, enlargement conditionality was simply a "gargantuan extension" of the pre-existing EU external developmental strategy targeting the Africa-Caribbean-Pacific countries (Hughes et al. 2005: 12, 13; see the section *Development Assistance and Conditionality* of Chapter 2). For its part, China has been the prisoner of both its preference for bilateral relationships and of its low-profile conditionality presented in the previous section. Instead of the highly intrusive, conditional, and effective EU Associations Agreements and Copenhagen criteria, Beijing has limited its socialization instruments to weak regional intergovernmental organizations, non-transparent government-to-government negotiations, and never-acknowledged, narrow conditionalities. Accordingly, out of Schimmelfennig's three socialization agencies, the institutional and cultural international environment as well as the strong international organizations could not bring their contribution to China's socialization of the Caribbean; and this likely contributed to the more modest results of this process.

Only the third has been present: the normative—and, at a deeper level, cognitive—content of Chinese-centered international socialization. On the one hand, it comprises a set of universal principles ultimately inspired from China's Five Principles of Peaceful Coexistence (see the section *China's Engagement with the Developing World* of Chapter 3). The second Policy Paper on Latin America and the Caribbean of 2016 mentions equality, mutual benefit, common development, world peace, sincerity and mutual trust in the political field, win-win cooperation on the economic front, mutual learning in culture, and close coordination in international affairs (Ministry of Foreign Affairs of the Republic of China 2016 II, III). On the other hand, it includes a set of more practical elements concerning the actual bilateral relationship between Beijing and each Caribbean state. They start from the key idea that the partnership with China is highly beneficial and serves the national interest; and continue with the content of the three conditionalities. This is very similar to the EU case, which also invoked general principles but emphasized the very practical Copenhagen criteria. What is different is the way this normative content of international socialization was transmitted to the recipient state-society complexes. In Europe, it represented a socialization agency that added to strong institutional mechanisms in successfully socializing the candidate countries, which allowed for the creation of the "institutionalist" rationalist theory. In the Caribbean, the overall role of institutions has been much more modest; accordingly, an institutionalist approach cannot provide a reasonable explanation of the present stage of socialization. The vehicle used for normative transfer in this region is that studied, in the case of Europeanization, by Constructivist authors: the transformation of the social and subjective dimensions of persons—who act as particular kinds of political, economic, and social beings—in line with the socializer's particular vision of the political-economic life (Shelton 2015: 41–42). More specifically, Heather Grabbe showed how such a transformation took place in Eastern Europe due to the key role played by the socialized states' political institutions. These were Europeanized at a micro-level as their staff was progressively socialized by the European Union (Shelton 2015: 41–42; Grabbe 2006: 198–199; see the section *Development Assistance and Conditionality* of Chapter 2). In the Caribbean, the same phenomenon took place, but its scale is more limited. Not all the staff of political institutions was socialized because the EU-type intrusion into all sectors and levels of the state apparatus was replaced by China's marked preference for discreet or even secretive interactions, which concerned only a very limited part of the target state's institutions. Yet, those involved in such interactions have been successfully socialized. As shown in the section *The Socialization of Caribbean Elites* of Chapter 5, the material incentives represented by China's prestige infrastructure projects, the psychological factors associated with its "flattering diplomatic demarche," and the use of personalized interactions that include secretive negotiations as a tool of socialization resulted in a transformative process within which external inducement led to policy change (i.e. cooperation through interest) and then to norm change (i.e. cooperation through legitimacy). Due to social learning—which is an expression of normative persuasion (Park 2014: 337)—the behavior, the opinions, and ultimately the substantive beliefs of concerned persons were altered in ways favorable to China and to its regional interests, which resulted in the full socialization of the Caribbean political elites. The state bureaucracy has also been targeted. Its members involved in one way or another in China-related national policies have been convinced to adopt friendly and even admiring views of the partnership with the Asian power (see the section *The Socialization of Caribbean Elites* of Chapter 5). However, the reach of this process cannot be compared to the East European one. There, bureaucracies were socialized in their entirety. Accordingly,

Constructivist authors mentioned "bureaucratic power" as a form of EU power comparable with the economic and normative ones (Hughes et al. 2005: 12). In the Caribbean, because of Beijing's choice of a non-intrusive approach, those parts of the state apparatus not concerned by the relations with China—i.e. its huge majority—were not targeted and have not been socialized. Critically, the resulting limited number of Chinese-socialized bureaucrats made them unable to contribute significantly to the socialization of the society, which remained the task of the sole political elites.

Indeed, once they were socialized, these elites turned themselves into the main actors of the second stage of the international socialization process targeting their country. They became "norm entrepreneurs" trying to diffuse the norms they have internalized. These norms were institutionalized through the legal and bureaucratic state apparatus and led to the adoption of corresponding national discourses, policies, and practices that resulted in the socialization of the state. At the same time, domestic micro-processes have been used to similarly shape the normative beliefs of citizens. Potential choices include persuasion and various forms of social influence such as shaming, rewards, and coercion (Park 2014: 338; see the section *Mechanisms of Socialization* of Chapter 2). The Caribbean elites' China-related problem is that shaming—shunning, excluding, and demeaning those who do not behave in accordance with their expected role and identity—is irrelevant; rewards for conforming to role expectations are limited; and coercion is out of the question. The only instrument they could and did use is persuasion: changing attitudes through ongoing, iterative interactions. For many years now, in all Caribbean states that recognize Beijing there has been a deluge of official speeches and statements praising the merits of the partnership with China and its remarkable effects on national development and welfare. The problem is that these speeches and statements always emphasize the close association between one specific government and the Chinese development assistance received by its country, which is proudly presented as the result of its tireless efforts. This is useful for electoral purposes, but it also suggests to the society at large that China's socialization inducements are partisan in nature. Unlike the European Union's technocratic penetration of all sectors of the state apparatus, which leads to numerous and major policy changes that affect the entire society of candidate countries, the Chinese look like giving NAPAs, hospitals, and patrol vessels to Caribbean politicians who need to win an election later that year. One should not be surprised by the population's unwelcoming reception of such methods. In conjunction with the negative socio-economic impact of Beijing's economic and social conditionalities, it explains the elites' failure to ensure the Chinese-centered socialization of their society.

THE STATE-SOCIETY GAP AND POPULISM

In Trinidad and the rest of the Caribbean, the rejection by the society of China's economic and social conditionalities fully embraced by the government creates obvious difficulties for the overall socialization of the state-society complex. But this state-society gap can also become an important domestic issue and, in extreme cases, can develop in ways detrimental to the very stability of the country. As shown in the section *The Socialization of Caribbean Elites* of Chapter 5, Trinidadian respondents resentful of China's conditionalities tended to blame not the Chinese but the non-"protective" local official policies, the leaders that promote them, and ultimately the political system that gives these leaders too much room to act against the national interest. One respondent even spoke about "the immaturity of the state" (Respondents 15, 17, 24, and 30; see the section *The Socialization of Caribbean Elites* of Chapter 5). No less than 93 percent of the respondents shared fully (80 percent) or to an extent (13 percent) the opinion that their government is not conscious enough in its dealings with the Chinese government and firms. It was even claimed that "the general Trinidadian population is extraordinarily weary of whether the Trinidad and Tobago government is selling out the country to the Chinese" (Respondent 1). Elsewhere in the region, Dwyer Astaphan, a lawyer-businessman and ex-minister from St. Kitts (which recognizes Taiwan), similarly stated that it is not the fault of China for acting in its own interests. He criticized poor leadership and "intellectual vacuum" in the target countries and expressed the hope that Caribbean governments "sign proper deals to make sure they don't sell out their patrimony" (Green and Liu 2017: 28). Identical situations and comments have been signaled in other Global South regions. In many African countries, issues of local governance are "consistently highlighted as the most pressing problem" in the context of large-scale dissatisfaction with Chinese actions: "it is overwhelmingly the state that is the target of resentment" (Mohan et al. 2014: 134). In Nigeria, "most anger" was directed at local political elites (Mohan et al. 2014: 123); in Cameroon, a similar situation seems to create "a considerable risk for the future of the country." More generally, the gap between the political elites and the state they control, on the one hand, and the society, on the other, "might create a dangerous potential for conflict and revolts" (Röschenthaler and Socpa 2017: 184). At first view, one might be tempted to assess the situation in relation to the level of democracy of the target state. It seems logical to believe that a responsible and accountable government will follow the will of the people; tensions may occur only when authoritarian regimes give preference to their own selfish interests over those of the simple citizens. Deborah Brautigam explained that in stable and relatively well-governed countries civil society watchdogs and democratic pressure "will push to ensure that costs of competition or displacement are spread across society" and responsible governments "will be choosier when presented with the options for engagement offered by Beijing." China's engagement is much less likely to produce broad gains only in "highly corrupt, unstable, authoritarian countries" whose "governments are far less accountable" (Brautigam 2009: 21). Yet, Caribbean states tend to prove the contrary. They are consolidated democracies with vocal civil societies and well-established policies and practices of transparency and accountability (that, as shown in this book, China is damaging in order to promote its own interests). Still, their governments—controlled by Chinese-socialized political elites—have not appropriately responded to anti-Chinese popular demands. This aspect was analyzed by Steve Hess and Richard Aidoo, who used African examples to show convincingly that the democracy/authoritarian dimension is less relevant than the issue of political opportunity structures. The two authors did not study Chinese conditionality, but took as examples states meeting two conditions also present in the Caribbean: on the one hand, their governments established extensive aid, investment, and trade relationships with Beijing; on the other, the detrimental socio-economic consequences of China's presence led to "visible resentment against unwanted Chinese competition from various sectors of society" that included manufacturers, small businesses, and laborers (Hess and Aidoo 2015: xviii). These countries experienced similar state-society gaps and one would have expected consequences to be different based on the democratic or authoritarian nature of their regime. Indeed, findings showed that the "backlash has varied in nature and degree" based on the type of regime; but differences were due to something more than the democracy/authoritarianism divide. They stemmed from the uneven room of maneuver of political entrepreneurs—that is, opposition politicians—"to play the China card in mobilizing regime opposition" (Hess and Aidoo 2015: xvii, 138) against the pro-Beijing government. In closed autocratic regimes that include Ethiopia, Sudan, and Angola, tight restrictions on political activism prevented anti-regime politicians from taking advantage of anti-Chinese grievances. Coercion, censorship, and political control were used effectively by "ruling parties aligned closely with Beijing" to intimidate and silence activists who tried to promote "criticisms and resistance to the negative aspects of China's engagement." As these issues could not be placed on the legitimate political agenda, they started to be addressed in the framework of noninstitutionalized politics. Street protests were organized and, in extreme cases, insurgent groups even staged attacks against Chinese nationals and property, which became proxy targets for the regime itself (Hess and Aidoo 2015: xviii, 138–139). But these have remained marginal events that did not influence the features of the continued relationship with Beijing and the preservation of the state-society gap.

In open, democratic regimes very different mechanisms were at work; yet, the final outcome was not entirely dissimilar. Freedom of expression allowed for the frustration with the negative socio-economic consequences of the Chinese engagement to be articulated in popular discourse. In principle, concerns were channeled into the institutionalized politics of the party system and then addressed through legislation. However, free and fair elections make opposition politicians perceive their coming to power as a very plausible scenario. They also know that, once in office, they will need the economic support of China and are unwilling to position themselves against a useful future partner (Hess and Aidoo 2015: xviii, 138). Consequently, the Caribbean path of not initiating significant anti-Chinese measures is likely to be followed. Obviously, the ensuing combination of pro-Beijing government *and* opposition is hardly conducive to major changes in China's policies toward and their consequences on the concerned country. Similar to the previous case, this tends to preserve the state-society gap.

While neither the dictatorships nor the democracies surveyed by Hess and Aidoo fully addressed this gap, a third type of regime seems more apt to create conditions that turn it into a central question of domestic politics. In transitional regimes where the opening of the political system is in flux, ruling parties do restrict but cannot entirely eliminate opposition politics. Therefore, entrepreneur politicians willing to take advantage of the anti-Chinese sentiment can bring together various societal actors in coalitions that target the alleged nefarious collusion between China and the incumbent regime. This is likely to jeopardize future cooperation with Beijing; but the coming to power of such opposition politicians is highly uncertain, which makes them accept long-term costs in exchange for immediate electoral success (Hess and Aidoo 2015: xvii, 138). A case in point is that of Zambia, where the Movement for Multiparty Democracy was the dominant political party for two decades. Yet, opposition parties were given limited political space to operate. At the same time, a strong partnership was developed with China. This did have positive consequences but, on the negative side, widespread anti-China sentiments stemmed from a range of issues that included competition between Zambian and Chinese small merchants; closing down of plants due to Chinese imports; labor disputes between local workers and Chinese mining companies; and industrial accidents. Critics claimed that Chinese traders were taking over key sections of the economy (Mohan et al. 2014: 100; Hess and Aidoo 2015: 21; Power et al. 2012: 178). This situation was exploited by Michael Sata, an entrepreneurial opposition leader who, between the 2006 presidential campaign and his election as President in 2011, steadily won a growing vote share by playing the anti-China card. In a country plagued by ethnically and regionally based divisions, he succeeded in forming a diverse political coalition prominent in both Lusaka and the Copperbelt that supported his vocal rejection of the Chinese and of their alleged infiltration of the ruling party (Hess and Aidoo 2015: 20). The Movement for Multiparty Democracy responded by rejecting Sata's "racism"; but it was clear that it had a vested interest in maintaining good relations with the Chinese government and investors. While politicized by Sata, concerns about "losing out to the Chinese" were genuine, and their instrumentalization ultimately brought him to power (Power et al. 2012: 178).

The conclusion is not very optimistic. Both democracies and dictatorships do not seem to be able to solve the issue of the state-society gap, which preserves its destabilization potential. If, for whatever reason, a process of political transition emerges, it is likely that opportunistic political entrepreneurs will exploit it. Predictably, their actual goal is not genuine concern for citizens' socio-economic difficulties. They simply want to instrumentalize popular frustration in order to take power. In the process, a discourse of hatred is likely to emerge and to impose itself on a wide part of the electorate. At a time when the populist wave has submerged countries as diverse as the United States, Poland, Brazil, and Italy, the fact that Chinese-related frustration in the Global South can be instrumentalized by local populists to take power and implement their nefarious political platforms can have considerable negative consequences. For the time being, Caribbean states are consolidated democracies not predisposed to political shocks. Accordingly, transitional regimes or situations are unlikely to develop. But these are also vulnerable, fragile small states easily affected by regional and global developments. Unexpected policy changes adopted by the Trump administration or an escalation of Sino-American tensions could have disproportionately negative effects in the region. Populist leaders-in-waiting would certainly try to take advantage of the new situation, and the existing state-society gap would represent an instrument too tempting to ignore.

LEGITIMACY, POWER, AND SELF-INTEREST

Returning to the Chinese side of the process of international socialization of the Caribbean, the issue of power discussed in the section *Socialization and Power* of Chapter 2 has to be addressed in the specific context of Beijing's actions. It is important to note that the more general debate between China-optimists and China-pessimists (see the section *China in Africa* of Chapter 3) frequently scrutinizes China's expansion in the Global South in a perspective strongly influenced by the issue of legitimacy. Journalists and scholars speaking about "neocolonialism"—especially with respect to Africa—implicitly delegitimize Beijing's enterprise. Their adversaries emphasize "the fact that the expansion of the Chinese economy in Africa is legitimate" due to "consent between Chinese agencies and national and regional bureaucracies and local populations." This legitimacy is "fragile" because consent "may not have been achieved in all cases"; but ignoring the "weight of sovereign governments" is a detrimental "habit that lies deep in the colonial psyche" (Li 2017b: 32–33). In fact, this debate itself can be described as a consequence of a post-colonial psyche. To a Neorealist—who takes into consideration only power-related aspects—the rise of a new global power such as China has nothing to do with legitimacy or lack thereof. Power is self-legitimizing. If Beijing has the potential to impose a new regional or world order it will do so in a way that is not and cannot be more or less legitimate than Washington's similar attempt after World War II. By giving a prominent place to the issue of legitimacy, the China-optimists and pessimists implicitly place their respective discourses in the context of postcolonial debates strongly marked by moral and ethical values. Within the theory of International Relations, post-positivist approaches in general and Constructivism in particular probably provide the most appropriate framework for the analysis of this aspect. Yet, under a Constructivist magnifying glass, invoking the "weight of sovereign governments" as proof of legitimacy is too simplistic an analysis; in order to have a comprehensive understanding of the situation, the construction of those governments' agreement also needs to be scrutinized. The section *Chinese Influence and Soft Power* of Chapter 4 has mentioned the various influence and soft power instruments used by China in different geopolitical contexts. In Singapore, this is about "planting or nurturing" words and ideas that would "tilt the strategic decision-making landscape in a particular direction." Policymakers should be made to adopt China-friendly decisions "of their own volition" (Garnaut 2018). In the Caribbean, similar results have already been reached due to the socialization of political elites through the use of the three conditionalities. These and other instruments do acquire the consent of "sovereign governments" for China's enterprises in much of the Global South, Africa included. But this consent is little more than the consequence of the creation of a Chinese-centered cognitive and, in the Caribbean case, normative space that ultimately represents a projection of Chinese power. This, of course, is "soft" power, which makes it largely preferable to the brutal instruments employed by the two superpowers during the Cold War. But it is power nevertheless, which makes the legitimacy debate much less relevant than it might seem at first view.

Power, therefore, cannot be ignored when analyzing China's presence in the Caribbean. This is obvious when Beijing's objective of "achieving nothing less than the genesis of a new regional order, built on functioning institutions and rules" (Haro Navejas 2011: 210) is discussed. But it also has to be taken into consideration when the very use of conditionalities is assessed. In fact, as explained in the section *Development Assistance and Conditionality* of Chapter 2, development assistance itself is always associated with "an extremely asymmetric power relationship" (Stokke 1995/2006: 33). By definition, such assistance is based on "power flows" that connect donors in pursuit of their own interests and recipients subject to donor conditionality, which therefore find themselves in a position of dependency (Hughes et al. 2005: 3, 14; see the section *Development Assistance and Conditionality* of Chapter 2). Beijing's ability to provide material incentives in exchange for Caribbean states' compliance with conditions dictated by its political, economic, and social interests represents a clear example of such "power flows." The very rivalry between China and Western donors in the Caribbean can be understood in terms of power. The fact that Beijing's already abundant and further increasing (especially due to BRI) development assistance makes the region's states welcome its conditionalities illustrates a power dynamic on which the West in general and the United States in particular hold only limited control.

Conditionality constitutes a form of power projection. International socialization is more than that. As explained in the section *Socialization and Power* of Chapter 2, China's socialization efforts in the Caribbean cannot be dissociated from both the use and the *production* of power. The Constructivist definition of power—"the production, in and through social relations, of effects that shape the capacities of actors to determine their circumstances and fate" (Barnett and Duvall 2005: 42)—obviously places it at the origin of the change in normative beliefs brought by socialization. Rationalists' power is causal; that of Constructivists is both causal and constitutive, as it leads to the constitution of new rules, knowledge, positions, and identities (Skovgaard 2011: 446). As shown earlier in this chapter, out of the three types of power that led to the successful Europeanization of East European countries the bureaucratic one played a minor role in China's socialization of the Caribbean. The other two, however, have been very effective. One is the economic power illustrated by the use of economic incentives as inducement for compliance. As its nature is causal, both rationalists and Constructivists acknowledge its importance. The second is China's normative power (Hughes et al. 2005: 12), to which rationalist scholars are seldom sensible. Yet, it is this type of immaterial power that explains in part Beijing's success in its Caribbean enterprise and, in the long term, might allow it to construct "a new regional order" (Haro Navejas 2011: 210). It should be reminded that international socialization has been studied precisely as a process related to the creation, reproduction, and diffusion of a social order (Schimmelfennig 2000: 112; Park 2014: 341; see the section *Socialization and Power* of Chapter 2). If this process is successfully completed, the socializer becomes the center and coordinator of a regional system that serves its interests: international socialization leads to the production of power, and this is a form of structural power. This is to say that, in the Caribbean, the Type I socialization of state-society complexes is the result of Chinese power but also represents a source of power for China. At present this might not be very visible because the depth of the socialization process is still limited. Accordingly, more advanced Type II socialization necessarily represents the long-term objective of Beijing. Should it succeed, a situation similar to the Soviet-Cuban partnership would be multiplied on the scale of the Caribbean, turning the latter into a highly relevant source of structural power that China could use in its relations with the United States and as a component of its overall action in the Global South.

The geopolitical consequences of such a development have been discussed in the previous chapter. The main issue, however, is Beijing's inability to secure the socialization of the society in the case of its economic and social conditionalities, which in turn prevents the full socialization of the targeted Caribbean state-society complexes. This failure dramatically limits China's use of international socialization as a source of regional and, ultimately, global power. Therefore, its importance cannot be overstated, which brings the discussion to the reasons that make the Chinese impose counter-productive conditionalities. Indeed, it is clear that significantly reducing the "tied" component of aid combined with a self-imposed limitation of the flow of Chinese entrepreneurial migrants would turn Beijing into a unanimously admired benefactor that would encounter no obstacle in imposing itself as the benevolent socializer of Caribbean societies and of their state-society complexes. Yet, China seems ready to make only minimal concessions in the case of "tied aid" and none with respect to its social conditionality. Most likely, this is due to the fact that Beijing is hardly running a charity. Its use of international socialization as a source of structural power, which only applies to a limited number of states of the Global South, is accompanied by the much narrower pragmatic interest in material gains for Chinese firms and nationals that is obvious in China's interactions with all states. As *The Economist* unsympathetically stated, "in foreign policy, as in all things, China is the distilled essence of self-interest" (*The Economist*, October 4, 2018). Making an exception for the Caribbean would create a precedent that the leadership in Beijing assesses as an unneeded and perhaps dangerous deviation from the present, overwhelmingly successful strategy. Its impression seems to be that, despite some difficulties, the use of the three conditionalities will result in both fully-fledged socialization and more immediate material gains. Chinese obsessive insistence on similar narrow interests in other parts of the developing world has made Robert Rotberg appropriately note that "China hardly wants to colonise, but it has immense mercantilist ambitions" (Rotberg 2008: 1). Ultimately, it is the contradiction between this undeniably selfish approach and the claimed generosity and disinterest of Beijing's cooperative, "win-win" discourse that represents China's greatest enemy in the Caribbean.

CHINA'S IDENTITY AS A GLOBAL POWER

The discrepancy between Beijing's sophisticated strategy of international socialization that could lead to the complete and sincere support of targeted state-society complexes, on the one hand, and its unscrupulous pursuit of material gains, on the other, is well reflected by the frequently conflictive views expressed by respondents pertaining to the two groups diversely impacted by their respective effects. To a member of Trinidad's political elite, the Chinese "mean well. (. . .) I believe they have everyone at heart, yes" (Respondent 3). To a simple citizen, Beijing's actions are "very negative and distasteful" (Respondent 20; see the section *The Socialization of Caribbean Elites* of Chapter 5). Yet, as already mentioned in the section *Chinese Influence and Soft Power* of Chapter 4, the widespread negative perception of the economic and social conditionalities does not prevent 47 percent of the respondents from having a positive overall perception of China and 27 percent from having a very positive one. All respondents would like to visit China and to have their children learn Chinese as a foreign language; all but one ("it is too far") would send their children to study in a Chinese university. The explanation for this surprisingly favorable attitude is suggested by the fact that no less than 93 percent of the respondents view China as a rising superpower. Moreover, 53 percent believe that its expansion will ultimately lead to the rise of the developing world as a whole, which will fundamentally change the dynamics of the international system; a further 27 percent see this as a possibility. Accordingly, rejecting Beijing's friendly advances would be to "miss the opportunity for something that could be a real investment into the future, and that would be very sad" (Respondent 6). More than the abundance of their development assistance, it is this "America is the past, China is the future" idea (Garnaut 2018) that places the Chinese in a position of psychological superiority in the Caribbean. But again, the negative perception of Beijing's self-interested conditionalities replaces what could have been a Type II, completely interiorized and fully welcomed partnership with a more cautious, calculated approach. No less than 87 percent of the respondents believe that China is using developing countries, including those of the Caribbean, to expand its influence around the world. Ultimately, both the Chinese and the Americans impose "some kind of (. . .) arrangement connected to the[ir] deal." Therefore, "the question is which devil are you willing to deal with, because you have to deal with one" (Respondent 28). A state-society complex where such ideas are legitimately formulated can engage in Type I, role playing socialization, and can play its role very well; this is the case of all Caribbean countries that recognize Beijing. However, for the time being the potential for the advancement toward Type II socialization is clearly lacking.

This should be understood as a partial failure, as China's goal in the Caribbean has been the construction of a cognitive and normative space conducive, in the long term, to the creation of a new regional order that should be politically friendly, economically profitable, and socially open to the Chinese government, companies, and citizens. This ambitious plan, which would expand Beijing's structural power, cannot be completed as long as Caribbean state-society complexes do not develop new international identities associated with their full incorporation into the aforementioned regional order. Consequently, the predictable future will continue to be marked by the present, more modest Type I socialization. On the positive side (from the Chinese point of view), even this type of socialization allows Beijing to exercise a certain degree of structural power in the region while "tied aid" and entrepreneurial migrants continue to send back home the more traditional material benefits China is accustomed to obtain from its Global South partners. Still, the issue of how much the rising global power can gain or lose from this hybrid situation is less relevant than the way the Caribbean experiment can influence China's own identity. As mentioned in the section *Socialization and Power* of Chapter 2, this identity—the role-specific understandings about self of the Chinese state-society complex—is still very fluid. Both state and society are undergoing a tremendous transformation that, in one generation, took them from the level of a large but rather poor Third World country to that of a potential global counter-hegemon. The way this identity is shaped will influence greatly the world politics of tomorrow. Many factors contribute to the way new China perceives itself and its future global role, but the relationships between Beijing and the Global South is one of the most important. Two diverging trends are visible. One is based on the obsessive pursuit of material gains in ways that do not exclude predatory policies such as the setting of Sri Lankan-type debt traps. The other is closer to the official "win-win" discourse and does pay attention to the welfare of partner states. China's Caribbean policies are somewhere at the crossing of these two trends and the way they evolve is a significant indicator of the future profile of the Chinese global power. Less selfish efforts of international socialization would ultimately increase the ability of Caribbean and other Global South Lilliputians to socialize in turn their Chinese partner (see the section *Socialization and Power* of Chapter 2), ideally helping it to evolve toward something very different from a classic neo-colonial power. If, on the contrary, the "immense mercantilist ambitions" have the upper hand, new China will develop as a predatory global actor hardly different from those that have placed the Global South in its unenviable present situation.

Tiny Caribbean islands might look negligible when the great issues of world politics are scrutinized. Yet, they provide solid proof that the "no strings attached" nature of Beijing's development assistance is nothing more than a myth. More importantly, the evolution of their complex relationship with China represents a key test for the latter's willingness and ability to develop into a responsible global player that prefers the actual implementation of its "win-win," cooperative discourse to the exclusive pursuit of selfish material interests. In large measure, the very nature of tomorrow's international system depends on this choice.

NOTE

1. What was to be shown (Latin).

Bibliography

Abi-Habib, Maria (2018) "How China Got Sri Lanka to Cough Up a Port," The *New York Times*, June 25, https://www.nytimes.com/2018/06/25/world/asia/china-sri-lanka-port.html.

Adem, Seifudein (2012) "China in Ethiopia: Diplomacy and Economics of Sino-Optimism," *African Studies Review*, 55(1), pp. 143–160.

Agozino, Biko, Ben Bowling, Elizabeth Ward, and Godfrey St. Bernard (2009) "Guns, Crime and Social Order in the West Indies," *Criminology and Criminal Justice*, 9(3), pp. 287–305.

AidData (2018) "China's Global Development Footprint," https://www.aiddata.org/china-official-finance.

Alden, Chris (2008) "Africa without Europeans," in Chris Alden, Daniel Large, and Ricardo Soares de Oliveira (eds.) *China Returns to Africa: A Rising Power and a Continent Embrace*, London: Hurst and Company, pp. 349–360.

Alden, Chris, and Laura Barber (2018) "Introduction: Seeking Security: China's Expanding Involvement in Security Cooperation in Africa," in Chris Alden, Abiodun Alao, Zhang Chun, and Laura Barber (eds.) *China and Africa. Building Peace and Security Cooperation on the Continent*, Cham, Switzerland: Palgrave Macmillan, pp. 1–10.

Ampiah, Kweku, and Sanusha Naidu (2008) "The Sino-African Relationship: towards an Evolving Partnership?," in Kweku Ampiah and Sanusha Naidu (eds.) *Crouching Tiger, Hidden Dragon? Africa and China*, Scottsville, South Africa: University of KwaZulu-Natal Press, pp. 329–339.

Atkinson, Joel (2010) "China-Taiwan Diplomatic Competition and the Pacific Islands," *The Pacific Review*, 23(4), pp. 407–427.

Ayers, Alison J. (2013) "Beyond Myths, Lies and Stereotypes: The Political Economy of a 'New Scramble for Africa'," *New Political Economy*, 18(2), pp. 227–257.

Backaler, Joel (2014) *China Goes West. Everything You Need to Know About Chinese Companies Going Global*, New York: Palgrave Macmillan.

Badri-Maharaj, Sanjay (2016) "China's Growing Influence in the Caribbean," August 3, *Institute for Defence Studies and Analyses*, New Delhi, https://idsa.in/idsa comments/china-growing-influence-in-the-caribbean_sbmaharaj_030816.

Bagoo, Andre (2010) "Zhang's $5mn House, *Trinidad and Tobago Newsday*, December 19, http://archives.newsday.co.tt/2010/12/19/zhangs-5m-house/.

Barnett, Michael, and Raymond Duvall (2005) "Power in International Politics', *International Organization* 59(1), pp. 39–75.

Barrios, Ricardo (2018) "China's Belt and Road Lands in Latin America," *China Dialogue* (London), July 11, https://www.chinadialogue.net/article/show/single/en/10728-China-s-Belt-and-Road-lands-in-Latin-America.

BBC, June 1, 2013, "China leader Xi Jinping in Trinidad and Tobago," http://www.bbc.com/news/world-latin-america-22744040.

Bernal, Richard L. (2015) "The Growing Economic Presence of China in the Caribbean," *World Economy*, 38(9), pp. 1409–1437.

Bernal, Richard L. (2016) *Dragon in the Caribbean: China's Global Re-Dimensioning—Challenges and Opportunities for the Caribbean* (Revised and Updated Edition), Kindle Edition, Kingston, Jamaica: Ian Randle Publishers.

Bernal, Richard L. (2017) "Central America and the Caribbean: Relations with China and the United States: Contrasting Experiences! Converging Prospects?," in David B. H. Denoon (ed.), *China, the United States, and the Future of Latin America*, New York: New York University Press, pp. 232–267.

Bhambra, Gurminder K. (2010) "Historical Sociology, International Relations and Connected Histories," *Cambridge Review of International Affairs*, 23(1), pp. 127–143.

Borroz, Nicholas, and Hunter Marston (2017) "How Trump can Avoid War with China," *Asia & the Pacific Policy Studies*, 4(3), pp. 613–620.

Brautigam, Deborah (2009) *The Dragon's Gift. The Real Story of China in Africa*, Oxford and New York: Oxford University Press.

Bräutigam, Deborah (2015) "Foreword," in Carla P. Freeman (ed.) *Handbook on China and Developing Countries*, Cheltenham, UK; Northampton, MA, USA: Edward Elgar Publishing, pp. xv–xvi.

Braveboy-Wagner, Jacqueline (2010) "Opportunities and Limitations of the Exercise of Foreign Policy Power by a Very Small State: the Case of Trinidad and Tobago," *Cambridge Review of International Affairs,* 23(3), pp. 407–427.

Braveboy-Wagner, Jacqueline Anne (2008) *Small States in Global Affairs. The Foreign Policies of the Caribbean Community (Caricom)*, Basingstoke, Hampshire: Palgrave Macmillan.

Breslin, Shaun (2007) *China and the Global Political Economy*, Basingstoke: Palgrave Macmillan.

Briguglio, Lino (2007) "Economic Vulnerability and Resilience: Concepts and Measurements," in Eliawony Kisanga and Sarah Jane Danchie (eds.) *Commonwealth Small States: Issues and Prospects*, London: Commonwealth Secretariat, pp. 101–109.

Brown, Melissa J. (2010) "Changing Authentic Identities: Evidence from Taiwan and China," *Journal of the Royal Anthropological Institute*, 16, pp. 459–479.

Callahan, William A. (2016) "China's 'Asia Dream': The Belt Road Initiative and the New Regional Order," *Asian Journal of Comparative Politics*, 1(3), pp. 226–243.

Campbell, Caitlin (2014) *China's Expanding and Evolving Engagement with the Caribbean*. U.S.-China Economic and Security Review Commission Staff Report, May 16, http://origin.www.uscc.gov/sites/default/files/Research/Staff%20Report_China-Caribbean%20Relations.pdf.

Caribbean Journal, June 3, 2013, "China to Fund $150 Million Children's Hospital Project in Trinidad," https://www.caribjournal.com/2013/06/03/china-to-fund-150-million-childrens-hospital-project-in-trinidad/#.

Checkel, Jeffrey T. (1999) "Social Construction and Integration," *Journal of European Public Policy*, 6(4), pp. 545–560.

Checkel, Jeffrey T. (2005) "International Institutions and Socialization in Europe: Introduction and Framework," *International Organization*, 59(4), pp. 801–826.

Chen, Rou-Lan (2012) "Beyond National Identity in Taiwan: A Multidimensional and Evolutionary Conceptualization," *Asian Survey*, 52(5), pp. 845–871.

Chien, Shiuh-Shen, Tzu-Po Yang, and Yi-Chen Wu (2010) "Taiwan's Foreign Aid and Technical Assistance in the Marshall Islands," *Asian Survey*, 50(6), pp. 1184–1204.

China Daily, June 2, 2013, "China-Trinidad and Tobago Cultural Relations Expanding," http://www.chinadaily.com.cn/china/2013xivisit/2013-06/02/content_16556013.htm.

China Labour Bulletin, October 22, 2009, 'Chinese Construction Workers Protest in Trinidad and Tobago," https://clb.org.hk/content/chinese-construction-workers-protest-trinidad-and-tobago.

Clay, Edward, Matthew Geddes, and Luisa Natali (2009) "Untying Aid: Is it Working? An Evaluation of the Implementation of the Paris Declaration and of the 2001 DAC Recommendation of Untying ODA to the LDCs," Synthesis Report, Copenhagen: Danish Institute for International Studies, https://www.cdi.org/publications/5532-untying-aid-it-working-evaluation-implementation-paris-declaration-and-2001-dac-recommendation.

CNC3, March 3, 2018, "TT Owes China $2.229 Billion in Loan Debts," http://www.cnc3.co.tt/press-release/tt-owes-china-2229-billion-loan-debts.

Coface (2018) "Trinidad and Tobago," January, http://www.coface.com/Economic-Studies-and-Country-Risks/Trinidad-and-Tobago.

Commonwealth Consultative Group (1985) *Vulnerability: Small States in the Global Society*, London: Commonwealth Secretariat, https://www.thecommonwealth library.org/commonwealth/economics/vulnerability_9781848593985-en.

Cooper, Andrew F., and Timothy M. Shaw (2009) "The Diplomacies of Small States at the Start of the Twenty-first Century: How Vulnerable? How Resilient?," in Andrew F. Cooper and Timothy M. Shaw (eds.), *The Diplomacies of Small States. Between Vulnerability and Resilience*, Basingstoke, Hampshire: Palgrave Macmillan, pp. 1–18.

Copper, John F. (2014) "America's Asia Pivot: What Does It Mean and Will It Succeed?," *East Asian Policy*, 6(2), pp. 99–107.

Copper, John F. (2016) *China's Foreign Aid and Investment Diplomacy, Volume I. Nature, Scope, and Origins*, Basingstoke, Hampshire: Palgrave Macmillan.

Cox, Robert (1986) "Social Forces, States and World Order" in Robert Keohane (ed.), *Neoreolism and Its Critics*, New York: Columbia University Press, pp. 204–254.

Cypher, James M., and Tamar Diana Wilson (2015) "Introduction. China and Latin America. Processes and Paradoxes," *Latin American Perspectives*, 42(6), pp. 5–26.

De Groot, Olaf, and Miguel Pérez Ludeña (2014) *Foreign Direct Investment in the Caribbean: Trends, Determinants and Policies*, ECLAC Subregional Headquarters for The Caribbean Studies and Perspectives 35, Santiago, Chile: United Nations ECLAC.

Dent, Christopher M. (2011) "Africa and China. A New Kind of Development Partnership," in Christopher M. Dent (ed.), *China and Africa Development Relations*, Abingdon, Oxon, and New York: Routledge, pp. 3–20.

Devadason, Evelyn S., V. G. R. Chandran, and Shujaat Mubarik (2017) "Sino-LAC Ties: Trade Relationships, Trade Potentials, and Asymmetric Dependency," *Emerging Markets Finance and Trade*, 53(6), pp. 1262–127.

Dickson, Dixie-Ann (2012) "At What Cost, Chinese Labour?," *Trinidad & Tobago Guardian*, June 7, http://www.guardian.co.tt/business-guardian/2012-06-06/what-cost-chinese-labour.

Dipama, Samiratou, and Emel Dal (2015) "The Effectiveness of Political Conditionality as an Instrument of Democracy Promotion by the EU: Case Studies of Zimbabwe, Ivory Coast and Niger," *Perceptions*, 20(1), pp. 109–131.

Dobson, Alan P., and Steve Marsh (2014) "Anglo-American Relations: End of a Special Relationship?," *International History Review*, 36(4), pp. 673–697.

Douglas, Sean (2018a) "Imbert: US$104m Chinese Complex for Pt Lisas," *Trinidad and Tobago Newsday*, May 24, https://newsday.co.tt/2018/05/24/imbert-us104m-chinese-complex-for-pt-lisas/.

Douglas, Sean (2018b) "Moonilal: Review China Harbour Deal," *Trinidad and Tobago Newsday*, September 12, https://newsday.co.tt/2018/09/12/moonilal-review-china-harbour-deal/.

Downs, Kenya (2015) "Carnival Made in China: Trinidad's Annual Festival Faces a Generational Divide," *WLRN*, November 24, http://wlrn.org/post/carnival-made-china-trinidads-annual-festival-faces-generational-divide.

Duke, Simon (2017) *Europe as a Stronger Global Actor. Challenges and Strategic Responses*, Houndmills, Basingstoke, Hampshire: Palgrave Macmillan.

Dussel Peters, Enrique (2011) "China's Challenge to Latin American Development," in Adrian H. Hearn and José Luis León-Manríquez (eds.), *China Engages Latin America: Tracing the Trajectory*, Boulder, CO: Lynne Rienner, pp. 91–102.

Ellis, Evan (2018) "The Evolution of Panama-PRC Relations since Recognition, and Their Strategic Implications for the U.S. and the Region," *Global Americans*, September 21, https://theglobalamericans.org/2018/09/the-evolution-of-panama-prc-relations-since-recognition-and-their-strategic-implications-for-the-u-s-and-the-region/.

Ellis, R. Evan (2009) *China in Latin America: The Whats and Wherefores*, Boulder, CO: Lynne Rienner.

Ellis, R. Evan (2012) "Learning the Ropes," *Americas Quarterly*, 6(4), pp. 28–33.

Ellis, R. Evan (2013) "China, S.A. as a Local Company in Latin America," *Regional Insights* (William J. Perry Center for Hemispheric Defense Studies), 1, pp. 1–4.

Ellis, R. Evan (2014) *China on the Ground in Latin America. Challenges for the Chinese and Impacts on the Region*, New York: Palgrave Macmillan.

Esteban, Mario (2007) "Democratization of the People's Republic of China and Military Conflict in the Taiwan Strait," *Journal of Current Chinese Affairs-China Aktuell*, 36(6), pp. 6–31.

Fang, Tony, and Dina Chimenson (2017) "The Internationalization of Chinese Firms and Negative Media Coverage: The Case of Geely's Acquisition of Volvo Cars," *Thunderbird International Business Review*, 59(4), pp. 483–502.

Fichtner, Jan (2014) "Privateers of the Caribbean: The Hedge Funds-US-UK-Off shore Nexus," *Competition & Change*, 18(1), pp. 37–53.

Fichtner, Jan (2016) "Perpetual Decline or Persistent Dominance? Uncovering Anglo-America's True Structural Power in Global Finance," *Review of International Studies*, 43(1), pp. 3–28.

Flockhart, Trine (2006) "Complex Socialization": A Framework for the Study of State Socialization," *European Journal of International Relations*, 12(1), pp. 89–118.

Fraser, Mark (2013) "T&T, China Talk Trade, Energy," *Trinidad and Tobago Daily Express*, May 20, https://www.trinidadexpress.com/news/local/t-t-china-talk-trade-energy/article_b05fd62e-07c9-5a0c-88d5-63a81b823fec.html.

Fraser, Mark (2014a) "From Shanghai to Trinidad," *Daily Express*, September 15, https://www.trinidadexpress.com/news/local/from-shanghai-to-trinidad/article_d4507526-0182-55f7-89d1-cfde43c8bf74.html.

Fraser, Mark (2014b) "PM to Consider Removing Visas for Chinese," *Trinidad Express*, June 16, http://www.trinidadexpress.com/news/PM-to-consider-removing-visas-for-Chinese-263377741.html.

Freedom House (2017) "Trinidad and Tobago," in *Freedom in the World 2017. Populists and Autocrats: The Dual Threat to Global Democracy*, https://freedomhouse.org/report/freedom-world/2017/trinidad-and-tobago.

Freedom House (2018) "Trinidad and Tobago Profile," *Freedom in the World 2018*, https://freedomhouse.org/report/freedom-world/2018/trinidad-and-tobago.

Freeman, Carla P. (ed.) (2015) *Handbook on China and Developing Countries*, Cheltenham, UK; Northampton, MA, USA: Edward Elgar Publishing.

French, Howard W. (2014) *China's Second Continent. How a Million Migrants Are Building a New Empire in Africa*, New York: Alfred A. Knopf.

Gallagher, Kevin P. (2016) *The China Triangle. Latin America's China Boom and the Fate of the Washington Consensus*, New York: Oxford University Press.

Gallagher, Kevin P., and Roberto Porzecanski (2010) *The Dragon in the Room: China and the Future of Latin American Industrialization*, Stanford: Stanford University Press.

Gang, Ding (2015) "Win-Win Hospital Plan in US Backyard," Global Times, July 16, http://www.globaltimes.cn/content/932337.shtml.

Gao, Charlotte (2017) "China Evacuates 462 Nationals From Dominica After Hurricane Maria," *Diplomat*, September 27, https://thediplomat.com/2017/09/china-evacuates-462-nationals-from-dominica-after-hurricane-maria/.

Garnaut, John (2018) "Australia's China Reset," *Monthly* (Australia), August, https://www.themonthly.com.au/issue/2018/august/1533045600/john-garnaut/australia-s-china-reset.

Gateva, Eli (2015) *European Union Enlargement Conditionality*, Houndmills, Basingstoke, Hampshire: Palgrave Macmillan.

Girvan, Norman (2011) "Global and Regional Reconfigurations of Power: Implications for Caribbean-EU Relations," Paper presented at the Joint Caribbean-EU Strategy: Reflections and Analysis Workshop, European Centre for Development Policy Management / Institute of International Relations, UWI, April 15.

Gonzalez-Vicente, Ruben (2015) "The Limits to China's Non-Interference Foreign Policy: Pro-State Interventionism and the Rescaling of Economic Governance," *Australian Journal of International Affairs*, 69(2), pp. 205–223.

Grabbe, Heather (2006) *The EU's Transformative Power. Europeanization Through Conditionality in Central and Eastern Europe*, Basingstoke, Hampshire: Palgrave Macmillan.

Green, Cecilia A. (2012–2014) "Outbound China and the Global South. New Entrepreneurial Immigrants in the Eastern Caribbean," *Ideaz*, 10–12, pp. 24–44.

Green, Cecilia A., and Yan Liu (2017) "A "Transnational Middleman Minority" in the Eastern Caribbean? Constructing a Historical and Contemporary Framework of Analysis," *Social and Economic Studies*, 66(3–4), pp. 1–31.

Gurtov, Mel (2015) "China's Third World Odyssey: Changing Priorities, Continuities, and Many Contradictions," in Carla P. Freeman (ed.), *Handbook on China and Developing Countries*, Cheltenham, UK; Northampton, MA, USA: Edward Elgar Publishing, pp. 71–86.

Hallams, Ellen, and Benjamin Schreer (2012) "Towards a 'post-American' Alliance? NATO Burden-Sharing after Libya," *International Affairs*, 88(2), pp. 313–327.

Hamilton, Clive (2018) *Silent Invasion: China's Influence in Australia*, Melbourne: Hardie Grant Books.

Han, Ai Guo (2008) "Building a Harmonious Society and Achieving Individual Harmony," *Journal of Chinese Political Science*, 13(2), pp. 143–164.

Hao, Shinan (2015) "China's Socialization in East Asian International Society. An Assessment from the English School Perspective 1," *Quarterly Journal of Chinese Studies*, 3(4), pp. 82–104.

Haro Navejas, Francisco (2011) "China's Relations with Central America and the Caribbean States: Reshaping the Region," in Adrian H. Hearn and José Luis León-Manríquez (eds.), *China Engages Latin America: Tracing the Trajectory*, Boulder, CO: Lynne Rienner, pp. 203–219.

Haro Navejas, Francisco Javier (2013) "China in the Central American and Caribbean Zone," *Latin American Policy*, 4(1), pp. 144–156.

Harris, Richard L. (2015) "China's Relations with the Latin American and Caribbean Countries. A Peaceful Panda Bear instead of a Roaring Dragon," *Latin American Perspectives*, 42(6), pp. 153–190.

Harris, Richard L., and Armando A. Arias (2016) "China's South-South Cooperation with Latin America and the Caribbean," *Journal of Developing Societies*, 32(4), pp. 508–556.

Hassanali, Shaliza (2017) "China Railway Gets $221m Contract," *Trinidad and Tobago Guardian Online*, August 16, http://ftp.guardian.co.tt/news/2017-08-16/traffic-relief-ahead%E2%80%94nidco.

Haugen, Heidi Østbø, and Jørgen Carling (2005) "On the Edge of the Chinese Diaspora: The Surge of Baihuo Business in an African City," *Ethnic and Racial Studies*, 28(4), pp 639–662.

Hearn, Adrian H., and José Luis León-Manríquez (2011) "China and Latin America: A New Era of an Old Exchange," in Adrian H. Hearn and José Luis León-Manríquez (eds.) (2011) *China Engages Latin America: Tracing the Trajectory*, Boulder, CO: Lynne Rienner, pp. 1–20.

Henderson, Jeffrey, Richard P. Appelbaum, and Suet Ying Ho (2013) "Globalization with Chinese Characteristics: Externalization, Dynamics and Transformations," *Development and Change* 44(6), pp. 1221–1253.

Hess, Steve, and Richard Aidoo (2015) *Charting the Roots of Anti-Chinese Populism in Africa*, Cham; Heidelberg; New York; Dordrecht; London: Springer.

Hirono, Miwa, and Shogo Suzuki (2014) "Why Do We Need "myth-busting" in the Study of Sino-African Relations?," *Journal of Contemporary China, 23*(87), 443–461.

Hitchens, Peter (2008) "How China Has Created a New Slave Empire in Africa," *Daily Mail*, September 28, http://www.dailymail.co.uk/news/article-1063198/PETER-HITCHENS-How-Chinacreated-new-slave-empire-Africa.html.

Hobson, John M. (2002a) "What's at Stake in 'Bringing Historical Sociology *Back* into International Relations'? Transcending 'Chronofetishism' and 'Tempocentrism' in International Relations," in Stephen Hobden and John M. Hobson (eds.) *Historical Sociology of International Relations*, Cambridge: Cambridge University Press, pp. 3–41.

Hobson, John M. (2002b) "The Two Waves of Weberian Historical Sociology in International Relations," in Stephen Hobden and John M. Hobson (eds.) *Historical Sociology of International Relations*, Cambridge: Cambridge University Press, pp. 63–81.

Holbig, Heike, and Bruce Gilley (2010) "Reclaiming Legitimacy in China," *Politics & Policy*, 38(3), pp. 395–422.

Hongbo, Sun (2017) "China's Aid to Latin America and the Caribbean Region," in Hong Zhou and Hou Xiong (eds.) *China's Foreign Aid. 60 Years in Retrospect*, Singapore: Springer, pp. 281–324.

Honore-Gopie, Venus (2009) "Chinese Kitchen Closed," *Newsday*, October 17, 2009, http://archives.newsday.co.tt/2009/10/17/chinese-kitchen-closed/.

Hu, Shaohua (2015) "Small State Foreign Policy: The Diplomatic Recognition of Taiwan," *China: An International Journal*, 13(2), pp. 1–23.

Hughes, James, Gwendolyn Sasse, and Claire Gordon (2004) "Conditionality and Compliance in the EU's Eastward Enlargement: Regional Policy and the Reform of Sub-National Government," *Journal of Common Market Studies*, 42(3), pp. 523–551.

Hughes, James, Gwendolyn Sasse, and Claire Gordon (2005) *Europeanization and Regionalization in the EU's Enlargement to Central and Eastern Europe: The Myth of Conditionality*, Basingstoke, Hampshire: Palgrave Macmillan.

Hunte, Camille (2018) “Rowley Reveals Plan for Couva Children’s Hospital,” *Daily Express*, April 26, https://www.trinidadexpress.com/news/local/rowley-reveals-plan-for-couva-children-s-hospital/article_5edd2e04-4995-11e8-b86b-73098f0d9c6c.html.

Huynh, Tu T., Yoon Jung Park, and Anna Ying Chen (2012) “Faces of China: New Chinese Migrants in South Africa, 1980s to Present,” *African and Asian Studies* 9(3), pp. 286–306.

Ikenberry, G. John, and Charles A. Kupchan (1990) “Socialization and Hegemonic Power,” *International Organization*, 44(3), pp. 283–315.

Jamaica Observer, October 25, 2017, “Trinidad Investing Millions to Revive Aluminium Smelter Joint Venture Project,” http://www.jamaicaobserver.com/business-observer/trinidad-investing-millions-to-revive-aluminium-smelter-joint-venture-project_114909?profile=1283&template=MobileArticle.

Javeed, Asha (2017) “Shanghai Caught,” *Daily Express*, August 19, http://web.trinidadexpress.com/20170819/news/shanghai-caught.

Jenkins, Rhys (2015) “Is Chinese Competition Causing Deindustrialization in Brazil?,” *Latin American Perspectives*, 42(6), pp. 42–63.

Jepma, Catrinus J. (1991) *The Tying of Aid*, Paris: Development Centre of the OECD, http://www.oecd.org/development/pgd/29412505.pdf.

Jesse, Neal G., and John R. Dreyer (2016) *Small States in the International System. At Peace and at War*, London: Lexington Books.

Johnston, Alastair Iain (2001) “Treating International Institutions as Social Environments,” *International Studies Quarterly*, 45(4), pp. 487–515.

Kakaire, Sulaiman (2014) “Uganda: Railway Deal Winner Banned by World Bank over Graft,” *Observer* (Kampala), September, 2, https://allafrica.com/stories/201409030522.html.

Kent, Ann (2002) “China’s International Socialization: The Role of International Organizations,” *Global Governance*, 8(3), pp. 343–364.

Khan, Aleem (2017) “China Infrastructure Projects in T&T Employed 12,700 over Last Decade,” *Daily Express*, September 20, https://www.trinidadexpress.com/news/local/china-infrastructure-projects-in-t-t-employed-over-last-decade/article_5e685fd1-7812-51d0-b873-c394b17c6328.html.

Killick, Tony, with Ramani Gunatilaka and Ana Marr (1998) *Aid and the Political Economy of Policy Change*, London: Routledge.

Kirton, Raymond Mark, Marlon Anatol, and Niki Braithwaite (2010) *The Political Culture of Democracy in Trinidad & Tobago: 2010. Democracy in Action*, St. Augustine: Institute of International Relations, The University of the West Indies.

Kohona, Palitha (2018) “One Belt One Road—A Unique Opportunity for Sri Lanka,” InDepthNews, February 10, https://www.indepthnews.net/index.php/opinion/1666-one-belt-one-road-a-unique-opportunity-for-sri-lanka.

Konings, Piet (2007) “China and Africa: Building a Strategic Partnership,” *Journal of Developing Societies*, 23(3), pp. 341–367.

Kowlessar, Geisha (2018) “MoU Signed for US$104m Industrial Park,” *Trinidad & Tobago Guardian*, June 19, http://www.guardian.co.tt/business/2018-06-19/mou-signed-us104m-industrial-park.

Kurlantzick, Joshua (2008) *Charm Offensive: How China's Soft Power is Transforming the World*, New Haven: Yale University Press.

Lahtinen, Anja (2018) *China's Diplomacy and Economic Activities in Africa. Relations on the Move*, Cham, Switzerland: Palgrave Macmillan.

Lairson, Thomas D. (2018) "The Global Strategic Environment of the BRI: Deep Interdependence and Structural Power," in Wenxian Zhang, Ilan Alon, and Christoph Lattemann (eds.) *China's Belt and Road Initiative. Changing the Rules of Globalization*, Cham, Switzerland: Palgrave Macmillan, pp. 35–53.

Lam, Katy N. (2017) *Chinese State-Owned Enterprises in West Africa. Triple-Embedded Globalization*, New York: Routledge.

Latham, Andrew, and Kabir Sethi (2012) "The Transformation of War," in Craig A. Snyder (ed.) *Contemporary Security and Strategy*, Basingstoke: Macmillan Education UK, pp. 175–200.

le Pere, Garth L. (2015) "The China-Africa Connection: an Ambiguous Legacy?," in Carla P. Freeman (ed.) *Handbook on China and Developing Countries*, Cheltenham, UK; Northampton, MA, USA: Edward Elgar Publishing, pp. 359–385.

Lee, Margaret C. (2006) "The 21st Century Scramble for Africa," *Journal of Contemporary African Studies*, 24(3), pp. 303–330.

Lekorwe, Mogopodi, Anyway Chingwete, Mina Okuru, and Romaric Samson (2016) "China's Growing Presence in Africa Wins Largely Positive Popular Reviews," Afrobarometer Dispatch No. 122, October 24, http://afrobarometer.org/sites/default/files/publications/Dispatches/ab_r6_dispatchno122_perceptions_of_china_in_africa1.pdf.

Lemos, Anabela, and Daniel Ribeiro (2007) "Taking Ownership or Just Changing Owners?," in Firoze Manji and Stephen Marks (eds.) *African Perspectives on China in Africa*, Nairobi and Oxford: Fahamu, pp. 63–70.

Li, He (2005) "Rivalry between Taiwan and the PRC in Latin America," *Journal of Chinese Political Science*, 10(2), pp. 77–102.

Li, Shubo (2017a) *Mediatized China-Africa Relations. How Media Discourses Negotiate the Shifting of Global Order*, Singapore: Palgrave Macmillan.

Li, Xiaojun (2017b) "Does Conditionality Still Work? China's Development Assistance and Democracy in Africa," *Chinese Political Science Review*, 2(2), pp. 201–220.

Li, Yitan (2014) "Constructing Peace in the Taiwan Strait: a Constructivist Analysis of the Changing Dynamics of Identities and Nationalisms," *Journal of Contemporary China*, 23(85), pp. 119–142.

Lin, Chun (2006) *The Transformation of Chinese Socialism*, Durham, NC: Duke University Press.

Lin, Chun (2007) "Recasting Development in China," *Development*, 50(3), pp. 11–16.

Löfflmann, Georg (2016) "The Pivot between Containment, Engagement, and Restraint: President Obama's Conflicted Grand Strategy in Asia," *Asian Security*, 12(2), pp. 92–110.

Look Lai, Walton (2000) *The Chinese in the West Indies, 1806–1995: A Documentary History*, Kingston: Press University of the West Indies.

Loop News, August 10, 2017, "T&T, China Sign Framework Agreement for Patrol Vessel," http://www.looptt.com/content/tt-china-sign-framework-agreement-patrol-vessel.

Lowe Shinebourne, Jan (2004) *The God-Mother and Other Stories*, Leeds, UK: Peepal Tree Press.

Ma Mung, Emmanuel (2008) "Chinese Migration and China's Foreign Policy in Africa," *Journal of Chinese Overseas*, 4(1), pp. 91–109.

Maingot, Anthony P., and Wilfredo Lozano (2005) *The United States and the Caribbean: Transforming Hegemony and Sovereignty*, New York: Routledge.

Mander, Benedict (2013) "China-Trinidad and Tobago: a Closer Embrace," *Financial Times*, June 14, https://www.ft.com/content/41991098-5703-3dce-b452-877f541c73eb.

Manning, Richard (2006) "Will 'Emerging Donors' Change the Face of International Co-operation?," *Development Policy Review*, 24(4), pp. 371–385.

Massicotte, Marie-Josée (1999) "Global Governance and the Global Political Economy: Three Texts in Search of a Synthesis," *Global Governance*, 5(1), pp. 127–148.

Mattlin, Mikael, and Matti Nojonen (2011) "Conditionality in Chinese Bilateral Lending," *Bank of Finland Institute for Economies in Transition* (BOFIT) Discussion Paper No. 14, https://helda.helsinki.fi/bof/handle/123456789/8282.

Mattlin, Mikael, and Matti Nojonen (2015) "Conditionality and Path Dependence in Chinese Lending," *Journal of Contemporary China*, 24(94), pp. 701–720.

Mawdsley, Emma (2008) "Fu Manchu versus Dr Livingstone in the Dark Continent? Representing China, Africa and the West in British Broadsheet Newspapers," *Political Geography*, 27(5), pp. 509–529.

McAdams, Dan P. (2016) "The Mind of Donald Trump," *Atlantic*, June, http://www.theatlantic.com/magazine/archive/2016/06/the-mind-of-donald-trump/480771/.

McElroy, Jerome L., and Wenwen Bai (2008) "The Political Economy of China's Incursion into the Caribbean and Pacific," *Island Studies Journal*, 3(2), pp. 225–246.

McPherson, Alan (2016) *A Short History of U.S. Interventions in Latin America and the Caribbean*, Malden, MA: Wiley-Blackwell.

Mendelson Forman, Johanna, and Susana Moreira (2008) "Taiwan-China Balancing Act in Latin America," *Elcano Royal Institute*, ARI 154/2008, November 26, http://www.realinstitutoelcano.org/wps/wcm/connect/ac6f4d804f018b67b5dff53170baead1/ARI154-2008_MendelsonForman-Moreira_Taiwan_China_LatinAmerica.pdf?MOD=AJPERES&CACHEID=ac6f4d804f018b67b5dff53170baead1.

Mendes-Franco, Janine (2015a) "Trinidad & Tobago's Chinese Community Is Dog-Tired of Racial Stereotyping," *Global Voices*, July 16, https://globalvoices.org/2015/07/16/trinidad-tobagos-chinese-community-is-dog-tired-of-racial-stereotyping/.

Mendes-Franco, Janine (2015b) "Enough With the "Us Versus Them Mentality"—We Are All Trinidadian," *Global Voices*, July 17, https://nouzie.com/enough-with-the-us-versus-them-mentality-we-are-all-trinidadian/.

Menéndez, Fernando (2014) "The Toll of China's Slowdown Depends on Latin America's Policy Choices," China-US Focus, April 17, https://www.chinausfocus.com/finance-economy/the-toll-of-chinas-slowdown-depends-on-latin-americas-policy-choices/#sthash.dGLVyHUC.dpuf.

Millette, Trevor (1993) *The Chinese in Trinidad*, Port of Spain: Imprint Caribbean, https://peopleofthedragon.wordpress.com/chinese-culture-in-trinidad/religion/.

Ministry of Foreign Affairs (2004) "The Ministry of Foreign Affairs of the Republic of China Solemnly States that It Is Terminating Diplomatic Relations with the Commonwealth of Dominica as of Today," March 30, http://www.mofa.gov.tw/en/News_Content.aspx?n=0E7B91A8FBEC4A94&sms=220E98D761D34A9A&s=1B2F5C68105FF8F0.

Ministry of Foreign Affairs (2005) "In Order to Uphold Our National Interests and Dignity," January 28, http://www.mofa.gov.tw/en/News_Content.aspx?n=0E7B91A8FBEC4A94&sms=220E98D761D34A9A&s=316175F9FC278C30.

Ministry of Foreign Affairs of the People's Republic of China (2018) China and Trinidad & Tobago, http://www.fmprc.gov.cn/mfa_eng/wjb_663304/zzjg_663340/ldmzs_664952/gjlb_664956/3528_665138/.

Ministry of Foreign Affairs of the Republic of China (2016) "China's Policy Paper on Latin America and the Caribbean," November 24, http://www.fmprc.gov.cn/mfa_eng/zxxx_662805/t1418254.shtml.

Misrahi-Barak, Judith (2012) "Looking In, Looking Out: The Chinese-Caribbean Diaspora through Literature—Meiling Jin, Patricia Powell, Jan Lowe Shinebourne," *Journal of Transnational American Studies*, 4(1), pp. 1–15.

Mohan, Giles, Ben Lampert, May Tan-Mullins, and Daphne Chang (2014) *Chinese Migrants and Africa's Development. New Imperialists or Agents of Change?*, London: Zed Books.

Montoute, Annita (2013) "Caribbean-China Economic Relations: What Are the Implications?," *Caribbean Journal of International Relations & Diplomacy*, 1(1), pp. 110–126.

Mourdoukoutas, Panos (2018) "China Is Doing the Same Things to Sri Lanka that Great Britain Did to China after the Opium Wars," *Forbes*, June 28, https://www.forbes.com/sites/panosmourdoukoutas/2018/06/28/china-is-doing-the-same-things-to-sri-lanka-great-britain-did-to-china-after-the-opium-wars/#61f8dba27446.

Mullen, Jethro (2017) "Chinese Exports Fall as Beijing Braces for Trump," *CNN Money*, January 13, http://money.cnn.com/2017/01/13/news/economy/china-exports-trade-trump/.

Naím, Moisés (2007) "Rogue Aid," *Foreign Policy*, 159, March/April, pp. 95–96.

Neaves, Julien (2016) "TT Owes China Hundreds of Millions," *Trinidad and Tobago Newsday*, October 21, http://archives.newsday.co.tt/2016/10/21/tt-owes-china-hundreds-of-millions/.

Newsday, October 17, 2009, "Living Conditions Shock Minister," http://archives.newsday.co.tt/2009/10/17/living-conditions-shock-minister/.

Nyíri, Pál (2001) "Expatriating is Patriotic? The Discourse on 'New Migrants' in the People's Republic of China and Identity Construction among Recent Migrants from the PRC," *Journal of Ethnic and Migration Studies*, 27(4), pp. 635–653.

Nyíri, Pál (2011) "Chinese Entrepreneurs in Poor Countries: A Transnational 'Middleman Minority' and its Futures," *Inter-Asia Cultural Studies*, 12(1), pp. 145–153.

OECD (2001/2013) "Tied Aid Credits," Glossary of Statistical Terms, https://stats.oecd.org/glossary/detail.asp?ID=3089.

Office of the Prime Minister (2013) "Couva Children's Hospital expected to be complete by March 2015," June 1, http://www.news.gov.tt/content/couva-childrens-hospital-expected-be-complete-march-2015#.XAXESGhKi1s.

Office of the Prime Minister Republic of Trinidad and Tobago (2018) "Chinese Fact Finding Delegation to Visit Trinidad and Tobago to Explore Investment Opportunities," May 18, https://www.opm.gov.tt/chinese-fact-finding-delegation-to-visit-trinidad-and-tobago-to-explore-investment-opportunities/.

Oosterveld, Willem, Eric Wilms, and Katarina Kertysova (2018) "The Belt and Road Initiative Looks East. Political Implications of China's Economic Forays in the Caribbean and the South Pacific," *The Hague Centre for Strategic Studies*, https://hcss.nl/report/belt-and-road-initiative-looks-east.

Ouyang, Jun, and Qiong Qiu (2015) "Research on the Investment Opportunities and Risks in the Caribbean Region," *Journal of Latin American Studies* (China), 37(4), pp. 20–25 (pp. 1–8 of Yaguang Zhu's English translation available at http://jtp.cnki.net/bilingual/detail/html/LDMZ201504004).

Overbeek, Henk (2004) "Transnational Class Formation and Concepts of Control: towards a Genealogy of the Amsterdam Project in International Political Economy," *Journal of International Relations and Development*, 7(2), pp. 113–141.

Paladini, Stefania (2011) "A View from the Isthmus: China's Strategic Interests in Latin America between Taiwan and the USA," *Journal of Comparative Asian Development*, 10(1), pp. 62–89.

Panda, Ankit (2014) "Reflecting on China's Five Principles, 60 Years Later," *Diplomat*, June 26, https://thediplomat.com/2014/06/reflecting-on-chinas-five-principles-60-years-later/.

Park, Susan (2014) "Socialisation and the Liberal Order," *International Politics*, 51(3), pp. 334–349.

Pokam, Hilaire de Prince (2015) *Migration chinoise et développement au Cameroun*. Paris: L'Harmattan.

Power, Marcus, Giles Mohan, and May Tan-Mullins (2012) *China's Resource Diplomacy in Africa. Powering Development?*, Basingstoke, Hampshire: Palgrave Macmillan.

Power102fm News, February 25, 2014, "China Sending Ships to Trinidad and Tobago," http://news.power102fm.com/china-sending-ships-to-trinidad-and-tobago-16727.

President of the United States (2017) *National Strategy of the United States of America*, December 18, 2017, https://www.whitehouse.gov/wp-content/uploads/2017/12/NSS-Final-12-18-2017-0905.pdf.

Rajkumar, Fiona (2013) "The Chinese in the Caribbean during the Colonial Era," in Romain Cruse and Kevon Rhiney (eds.) *Caribbean Atlas*, http://www.caribbean-atlas.com/en/themes/waves-of-colonization-and-control-in-the-caribbean/daily-lives-of-caribbean-people-under-colonialism/the-chinese-in-the-caribbean-during-the-colonial-era.html.

Rauch, James E. (2001) "Business and Social Networks in International Trade," *Journal of Economic Literature*, 39(4), pp. 1177–1203.

Ray, Rebecca (2017) "The Panda's Pawprint: The Environmental Impact of the China-led Re-Primarization in Latin America and the Caribbean," *Ecological Economics*, 134, pp. 150–159.

Raymond, Afra (2015) "Riding the Dragon," *AfraRaymond.net*, March 19 https://afraraymond.net/2015/03/19/riding-the-dragon/.

Reilly, James (2012) "A Norm-Taker or a Norm-Maker? Chinese Aid in Southeast Asia," *Journal of Contemporary China*, 21(73), pp. 71–91.

Reuters, September 8, 2010, "Update 1-Trinidad Cancels $600 Mln Aluminum Smelter Project," *Metals News*, https://www.reuters.com/article/trinidad-aluminum-smelter-idAFN0813743920100908.

Risse, Thomas, Stephen C. Ropp, and Kathryn Sikkink (eds.) (1999) *The Power of Human Rights: International Norms and Domestic Change*, Cambridge: Cambridge University Press.

Roett, Riordan, and Guadalupe Paz (2015) "China's Expanding Ties with Latin America," in Carla P. Freeman (ed.) *Handbook on China and Developing Countries*, Cheltenham, UK; Northampton, MA, USA: Edward Elgar Publishing, pp. 496–517.

Rogers, Atiba (2016) "Broken Is the Road of Political Promises in Trinidad & Tobago," *Global Voices*, February 7, https://globalvoices.org/2016/02/07/broken-is-the-road-of-political-promises-in-trinidad-tobago/.

Rosales, Osvaldo, and Mikio Kuwayama (2012) *China and Latin America and the Caribbean*, Santiago, Chile: ECLAC.

Röschenthaler, Ute, and Antoine Socpa (2017) "The China Challenge: Cameroonians between Discontent and Popular Admiration," in Young-Chan Kim (ed.) *China and Africa. A New Paradigm of Global Business*, Cham, Switzerland: Palgrave Macmillan, pp. 155–188.

Rotberg, Robert I. (2008) "China's Quest for Resources, Opportunities and Influence in Africa," in Robert I. Rotberg (ed.) *China into Africa. Trade, Aid, and Influence*, Washington, DC: Brookings Institution Press, pp. 1–20.

Sakwa, Richard (2010) *Russia and Turkey: Rethinking Europe to Contest Outsider Status*, Russie Nei Visions, 51, Paris: Ifri.

Salama, Pierre (2017) "Brasil y China: caminos de fortalezas y desconciertos," *Problemas del Desarrollo*, 48(188), pp. 9–28.

Samaroo, Akash (2017) "China Unveils US$15Bn Mega Bridge. Engineering Marvel Could Be Answer to Domestic Travel Woes in T&T," *Trinidad and Tobago Guardian*, October 17, http://www.guardian.co.tt/news/2017-10-16/china-unveils-us15bn-mega-bridge.

Sanders, Ronald (2014) "Making Caribbean Tourism 'Chinese-ready,'" September 4, http://www.sirronaldsanders.com/viewarticle.aspx?ID=460.

Santibañes, Francisco De (2009) "An End to U.S. Hegemony? The Strategic Implications of China's Growing Presence in Latin America," *Comparative Strategy*, 28(1), pp. 17–36.

Saunders, Phillip C. (2006) "China's Global Activism: Strategy, Drivers, and Tools," *Institute for National Strategic Studies Occasional Paper No. 4.* Washington D.C.: National Defense University Press, https://apps.dtic.mil/dtic/tr/fulltext/u2/a463366.pdf.

Sautman, Barry, and Hairong Yan (2007) "Friends and Interests: China's Distinctive Links with Africa," *African Studies Review*, 50(39), pp. 75–114.

Schimmelfennig, Frank (2000) "International Socialisation in the New Europe: Rational Action in an Institutional Environment," *European Journal of International Relations*, 6(1), pp. 109–139.

Schimmelfennig, Frank, Stefan Engert, and Heiko Knobel (2006) *International Socialization in Europe: European Organizations, Political Conditionality, and Democratic Change*, Basingstoke, Hampshire: Palgrave Macmillan.

Sevastopulo, Demetri (2017) "Trump Gives Glimpse of 'Indo-Pacific' Strategy to Counter China," *Financial Times*, November 10, https://www.ft.com/content/e6d17fd6-c623-11e7-a1d2-6786f39ef675.

Shelton, Garth, and Farhana Paruk (2008) *The Forum on China-Africa Cooperation: A Strategic Opportunity*, Pretoria: Institute for Security Studies.

Shelton, Joel T. (2015) *Conditionality and the Ambitions of Governance. Social Transformation in Southeastern Europe*, Basingstoke, Hampshire: Palgrave Macmillan.

Shen, Simon (2015) "Another Angle on a New Intimacy: Chinese Perceptions of Africa and Latin America," in Carla P. Freeman (ed.) *Handbook on China and Developing Countries*, Cheltenham, UK; Northampton, MA, USA: Edward Elgar Publishing, pp. 109–132.

Shiwei, Shen (2018) "Opinion: China and Trinidad and Tobago Strengthen Ties on BRI Cooperation," *China Global Television Network*, May 16, https://news.cgtn.com/news/3d3d414d3145544e77457a6333566d54/share_p.html.

Simón, Luis, and James Rogers (2010) "The Return of European Geopolitics," *RUSI Journal*, 155(3), pp. 58–64.

Sinclair, Timothy J. (2016) "Robert W. Cox's Method of Historical Structures Redux," *Globalizations*, 13(5), pp. 510–519.

Skovgaard, Jakob (2011) "Power beyond Conditionality: European Organisations and the Hungarian Minorities in Romania and Slovakia," *Journal of International Relations and Development*, 14(4), pp. 440–468.

Sookraj, Radhica (2013) "Chinese Firm Picked for T&T Project Faces Corruption Probe," *Trinidad and Tobago Guardian*, October 6, https://www.guardian.co.tt/news/chinese-firm-picked-tt-project-faces-corruption-probe-6.2.408820.600f15629e.

Sookraj, Radhica (2018) "Couva Children's Hospital Tower Collapses," *Trinidad & Tobago Guardian Online*, January 9, http://www.tobagotoday.co.tt/news/2018-01-08/couva-children%E2%80%99s-hospital-tower-collapses.

Southerland, Dan (2017) "China Makes Inroads in Caribbean Nations Through Aid, Trade," *Radio Free Asia*, August 30, https://www.rfa.org/english/commentaries/caribbean-china-08302017165130.html.

Stahl, Anna Katharina (2018) *EU-China-Africa Trilateral Relations in a Multipolar World: Hic Sunt Dracones*, London: Palgrave Macmillan.

Stokke, Olav (1995/2006) "Aid and Political Conditionality: Core Issues and State of the Art," in Olav Stokke (ed.) *Aid and Political Conditionality*, London: Frank Cass, pp. 1–87.

Su, Yen-Pin, and Oscar-René Delgado (2017) "Is China Becoming a Hegemonic Challenge in Latin America and the Caribbean? A Political Economy Analysis of the Nicaragua Interoceanic Canal Project," *Issues & Studies: A Social Science Quarterly on China, Taiwan, and East Asian Affairs*, 53(1), pp. 1–32.

Summers, Tim (2018) "Rocking the Boat? China's 'Belt and Road' and Global Order," in Anoushiravan Ehteshami and Niv Horesh (eds.) *China's Presence in the Middle East. The Implications of the One Belt, One Road Initiative*, Abingdon, Oxon: Routledge, pp. 24–37.

Superville, Shane (2017) "Ambassador Not Alarmed by Attacks on Chinese," *Trinidad and Tobago Newsday*, September 28, http://newsday.co.tt/2017/09/28/ambassador-not-alarmed-by-attacks-on-chinese/.

Tack, Clint Chan (2007) "TT Army Status Coming," *Trinidad and Tobago Newsday*, April 25, https://archives.newsday.co.tt/2007/04/25/tt-army-status-coming-2/.

Tao, Jing (2015) "China's Socialization in the International Human Rights Regime: Why Did China Reject the Rome Statute of the International Criminal Court?," *Journal of Contemporary China*, 24(96), pp. 1–19.

Taylor, Jon R., and Carolina E. Calvillo (2010) "Crossing the River by Feeling the Stones: Grassroots Democracy with Chinese Characteristics," *Journal of Chinese Political Science*, 15(2), pp. 135–151.

Terhalle, Maximilian (2011) "Reciprocal Socialization: Rising Powers and the West," *International Studies Perspectives*, 12(4), pp. 341–361.

The Confucius Institute (2018) https://sta.uwi.edu/confucius/.

The Economist, March 10, 2012, "A Chinese Beachhead?," https://www.economist.com/node/21549971.

The Economist, January 23, 2016, "Hallucinations and Fleeting Clouds," http://www.economist.com/news/asia/21688851-responding-unwelcome-election-result-taiwan-china-has-few-good-options-mainland-and.

The Economist, March 26, 2016, "The Gambia Gambit," http://www.economist.com/news/asia/21695563-china-resumes-old-diplomatic-game-gambia-gambit.

The Economist, November 9, 2017, "Endangered," https://www.economist.com/news/leaders/21731132-presidential-tour-asia-cannot-hide-fact-america-has-turned-inward-hurting-itself.

The Economist, February 1, 2018, "China Moves into Latin America," https://www.economist.com/news/americas/21736192-asian-giant-taking-advantage-other-powers-lack-interest-region-china-moves.

The Economist, May 3, 2018, "Chinese Investment May Help Greenland Become Independent from Denmark," https://www.economist.com/news/europe/21741589-islanders-think-rare-earths-and-tourism-will-make-them-self-reliant-chinese-investment-may-help.

The Economist, October 4, 2018, "Chinese Investment, and Influence, in Europe is Growing," https://www.economist.com/briefing/2018/10/04/chinese-investment-and-influence-in-europe-is-growing.

The Economist, October 18, 2018, "America's New Attitude towards China is Changing the Countries' Relationship," https://www.economist.com/briefing/2018/10/18/americas-new-attitude-towards-china-is-changing-the-countries-relationship.

The Economist, November 8, 2018, "New Zealand Agonises about Chinese Meddling," https://www.economist.com/asia/2018/11/08/new-zealand-agonises-about-chinese-meddling.

The Guardian, October 6, 2015, "Antiguan Ex-President of UN General Assembly Faces $1m Corruption Charges," http://www.theguardian.com/world/2015/oct/06/antiguan-ex-president-un-general-assembly-faces-corruption-charges.

The State Council of the People's Republic of China (2008) "China's Policy Paper on Latin America and the Caribbean," http://www.gov.cn/english/official/2008-11/05/content_1140347.htm.

The Trinidad and Tobago Guardian, July 5, 2009, "12,212 Non-Caricom Nationals Get Work Permits," http://m.guardian.co.tt/archives/news/general/2009/07/04/foreign-invasion.

The Trinidad and Tobago Guardian, February 20, 2012, "The Saga of Udecott and Calder Hart," http://www.guardian.co.tt/business-guardian/saga-udecott-and-calder-hart-6.2.416593.b663e934c5.

The Trinidad and Tobago Guardian, August 21, 2016, "Millions Needed to Repair Napa Defects," http://www.guardian.co.tt/news/2016-08-20/millions-needed-repair-napa-defects.

The Trinidad and Tobago Guardian, March 29, 2017, "Government Still Pursuing Aluminium Downstream Options," http://www.guardian.co.tt/business/2017-03-29/government-still-pursuing-aluminium-downstream-options.

The Trinidad and Tobago Guardian, July 30, 2017, "Businessmen Warn of Second Exodus of Chinese from T&T," http://www.guardian.co.tt/news/2017-07-29/businessmen-warn-second-exodus-chinese-tt.

The World Bank (2018) "World Integrated Trade Solution," https://wits.worldbank.org/CountryProfile/en/Country/TTO/Year/2015/TradeFlow/EXPIMP/Partner/CHN/Product/all-groups.

Thunø, Mette (2018) "China's New Global Position. Changing Policies toward the Chinese Diaspora in the Twenty-First Century," in Bernard P. Wong and Tan Chee-Beng (eds.) *China's Rise and the Chinese Overseas*, Abingdon, Oxon: Routledge, pp. 184–208.

Tian, Hao (2018) "China's Conditional Aid and Its Impact in Central Asia," in Marlene Laruelle (ed.) *China's Belt and Road Initiative and Its Impact in Central Asia*, Washington, DC: George Washington University, Central Asia Program, pp. 21–33.

Tjon Sie Fat, Paul B. (2009) *Chinese New Migrants in Suriname: The Inevitability of Ethnic Performing*, AUP Dissertation Series, Amsterdam: Amsterdam University Press.

Transparency International (2017) *People and Corruption: Latin America and the Caribbean. Global Corruption Barometer*, https://www.transparency.org/whatwedo/publication/global_corruption_barometer_people_and_corruption_latin_america_and_the_car.

Transparency International (2018) *Corruption Perceptions Index 2017*, https://www.transparency.org/country/TTO.

Trinidad and Tobago Daily Express, April 10, 2018 (printed version), "The Dawn of a New Era: Prospects for China-Trinidad and Tobago Cooperation," paid advertisement.

Trinidad and Tobago Daily Express, June 20, 2018, "China to Fund Phoenix Park Industrial Estate," https://www.trinidadexpress.com/business/local/china-to-fund-phoenix-park-industrial-estate/article_31be9880-7498-11e8-aa35-134f694d9978.html.

Trinidad and Tobago Newsday, May 31, 2012, "Demolishing Las Alturas," https://archives.newsday.co.tt/2012/05/31/demolishing-las-alturas/.

Trinidad Express, November 22, 2016, "NAPA Reopens," http://web.trinidadexpress.com/20161122/features/napa-reopens.

Trinidad, Dennis D. (2013) "The Foreign Aid Philosophy of a Rising Asian Power: A Southeast Asian View," in Yasutami Shimomura and Hideo Ohashi (eds.) *A Study of China's Foreign Aid. An Asian Perspective*, Basingstoke, Hampshire: Palgrave Macmillan, pp. 19–45.

TTWhistleBlower, August 31, 2016, "$20M spent to repair NAPA," http://ttwhistleblower.com/20m-spent-to-repair-napa/.

Tudoroiu, Theodor (2011) "The Neo-Communist Regime of Present-Day China," *Journal of Chinese Political Science*, 16(4), pp. 407–429.

Tudoroiu, Theodor (2015) "The Reciprocal Constitutive Features of a Middle Eastern Partnership: the Russian-Syrian Relation," *Journal of Eurasian Studies*, 6(2), pp. 143–152.

Tudoroiu, Theodor (2017) "Taiwan in the Caribbean: a Case Study in State De-Recognition," *Asian Journal of Political Science*, 25(2), pp. 194–211.

Tudoroiu, Theodor (2018) *Brexit, President Trump, and the Changing Geopolitics of Eastern Europe,* Houndmills, Basingstoke, Hampshire: Palgrave Macmillan.

Tull, Denis M. (2008) "China in Africa: European Perceptions and Responses to the Chinese Challenge," SAIS Working Papers in African Studies, https://www.swp-berlin.org/fileadmin/contents/products/fachpublikationen/Tull_China_Africa_SAIS_WP.ks.pdf.

United Nations Office for South-South Cooperation (2017) "What Is South-South Cooperation?," http://unossc1.undp.org/sscexpo/content/ssc/about/what_is_ssc.htm.

The United Nations Office of the High Commissioner for Human Rights (2018) "Committee on the Elimination of Racial Discrimination Reviews the Report of China," Geneva, August 13, https://www.ohchr.org/EN/NewsEvents/Pages/DisplayNews.aspx?NewsID=23452&LangID=E.

UWI Campus News, October 23, 2015, "UWI Fosters Agricultural Innovation with New Park at Orange Grove," http://sta.uwi.edu/news/releases/release.asp?id=1499.

UWI Campus News, December 16, 2016, "UWI Degrees Now Accepted in China," http://sta.uwi.edu/news/releases/release.asp?id=1639.

UWI Campus News, February 7, 2018, "UWI Students Set for Historic China Initiative," http://sta.uwi.edu/news/releases/release.asp?id=21784.

Van Apeldoorn, Bastiaan (2004) "Theorizing the Transnational: A Historical Materialist Approach," *Journal of International Relations and Development*, 7(2), pp. 142–176.

Van der Pijl, Kees (1998) *Transnational Classes and International Relations*, London and New York: Routledge.

Vukovich, Daniel (2012) "The Battle for Chinese Discourse and the Rise of the Chinese New Left: Towards a Postcolonial Politics of Knowledge," in Ban Wang and Lu Jie (eds.) *China and New Left Visions: Political and Cultural Interventions*, Lanham, MD: Rowman and Littlefield, pp. 61–80.

Waithe, Melanie (2018) "China Belts TT," *Trinidad and Tobago Newsday*, June 21, https://newsday.co.tt/2018/06/21/china-belts-tt/.

Waltz, Kenneth (1979) *Theory of International Politics*, Reading, Massachusetts: Addison-Wesley.

Ward, Jared (2017) "Making Sense of China's Caribbean Policy," *China Brief*, 17(10), pp. 13–17, https://jamestown.org/program/making-sense-of-chinas-caribbean-policy/.

Webb, Yvonne (2018) "US$500m Windfall. China Harbour Promises Returns on La Brea Dry Dock Project," *Trinidad and Tobago Newsday*, September 13, https://newsday.co.tt/2018/09/13/us500m-windfall/.

Wendt, Alexander (1999/2003) *Social Theory of International Politics*, New York: Cambridge University Press.

Wenping, He (2007) "The Balancing Act of China's Africa Policy", *China Security*, 3(3), pp. 23–40.

Wiener, Antje (2004) "Contested Compliance: Interventions on the Normative Structure of World Politics," *European Journal of International Relations*, 10(2), pp. 189–234.

Wigglesworth, Robin (2013) "Caribbean in Crisis: Chequebook Diplomacy," *Financial Times,* December 17, https://www.ft.com/content/7f7b0d8e-5ea8-11e3-8621-00144feabdc0.

Wilkinson, Bert (2007) "Caribbean: Influx of Chinese Workers Irks Local Unions," *Inter Press Service News Agency*, July 27, http://www.ipsnews.net/2007/07/caribbean-influx-of-chinese-workers-irks-local-unions/.

Williams, Laurel (2018) "Govt Talks Couva Children's Hospital," *Trinidad and Tobago Newsday*, May 14, https://newsday.co.tt/2018/05/14/govt-talk-couva-childrens-hospital/.

Williamson, John (2012) "Is the 'Beijing Consensus' now Dominant?," *Asia Policy* 13, pp. 1–16.

Wissenbach, Uwe (2011) "China-Africa Relations and the European Union Ideology, Conditionality, Realpolitik and What is New in South-South Co-Operation," in Christopher M. Dent (ed.) (2011) *China and Africa Development Relations*, Abingdon, Oxon, and New York: Routledge, pp. 21–41.

Wong, Edward (2013) "Cost of Environmental Damage in China Growing Rapidly Amid Industrialization," *New York Times*, March 29, https://www.nytimes.com/2013/03/30/world/asia/cost-of-environmental-degradation-in-china-is-growing.html.

Wong, Yong (2016) "Offensive for Defensive: The Belt and Road Initiative and China's New Grand Strategy," *The Pacific Review*, 29(3), pp. 455–463.

World Economic Forum (2017) *The Global Competitiveness Report 2017–2018*, Geneva, http://www3.weforum.org/docs/GCR2017-2018/05FullReport/TheGlobalCompetitivenessReport2017%E2%80%932018.pdf.

Xinhua News Agency (2006) "China Publishes 'Harmonious Society' Resolution," October 19, http://www.china.org.cn/english/2006/Oct/184810.htm.

Xuefeng, Sun, Matti Nojonen, Mikael Mattlin, and Matt Ferchen (2012) "Conditionality in China's Aid Model," January 10, *Carnegie Endowment for International Peace*, Beijing, http://carnegieendowment.org/2012/01/10/conditionality-in-chi-na-s-aid-model-event-4024.

Yap, O. Fiona, and Spencer Henson (2016) "Introduction: Can Africa Manage the Power of the Chinese Dragon?," in Spencer Henson and O. Fiona Yap (eds.) *The Power of the Chinese Dragon. Implications for African Development and Economic Growth*, Basingstoke, Hampshire: Palgrave Macmillan.

Yue, Zhang (2018) "Belt, Road Will Assist in Country's Development," *China Daily*, May 15, http://usa.chinadaily.com.cn/a/201805/15/WS5afa124da3103f6866ee851c.html.

Zhang, Qingmin (2015) "China's Relations with Developing Countries: Patterns, Principles, Characteristics, and Future Challenges," in Carla P. Freeman (ed.) *Handbook on China and Developing Countries*, Cheltenham, UK; Northampton, MA, USA: Edward Elgar Publishing, pp. 51–70.

Zhao, Suisheng (2014) "A Neo-Colonialist Predator or Development Partner? China's Engagement and Rebalance in Africa," *Journal of Contemporary China*, 23(90), pp. 1033–1052.

Zhou, Hong (2017) "Preface," in Hong Zhou and Hou Xiong (eds.) *China's Foreign Aid. 60 Years in Retrospect*, Singapore: Springer, pp. v–xiii.

Zimelis, Andris (2011) "Conditionality and the EU-ACP Partnership: A Misguided Approach to Development?," *Australian Journal of Political Science*, 46(3), pp. 389–406.

Ziso, Edson (2018) *A Post State-Centric Analysis of China-Africa Relations. Internationalisation of Chinese Capital and State-Society Relations in Ethiopia*, Cham, Switzerland: Palgrave Macmillan.

Zoellick, Robert (2017) "The Conflict at the Heart of Trump's Foreign Policy: Opinion," *Financial Times*, August 23, p. 9.

Index

About the Authors

Theodor Tudoroiu earned his Ph.D. from the Université de Montréal. He is a senior lecturer and head of the International Relations unit of the Department of Political Science of the University of the West Indies, St. Augustine Campus (Trinidad and Tobago). His publications include *The Revolutionary Totalitarian Personality* (2016) and *Brexit, President Trump, and the Changing Geopolitics of Eastern Europe* (2018).

Amanda R. Ramlogan is a doctoral student at the Institute of International Relations of the University of the West Indies, St. Augustine campus, who works toward the completion of a doctoral dissertation on the China-Trinidad and Tobago relationship. She is also a part-time lecturer and a research assistant at the Department of Political Science of the same university.

www.ingramcontent.com/pod-product-compliance
Ingram Content Group UK Ltd.
Pitfield, Milton Keynes, MK11 3LW, UK
UKHW041630031026
15587UKWH00001B/192

9 781793 603227